OUT OF SIGHT

OUT OF SIGHT

THE LONG AND DISTURBING STORY OF CORPORATIONS OUTSOURCING CATASTROPHE

ERIK LOOMIS

THE NEW PRESS

NEW YORK
LONDON

For Katie

Requests for permission to reproduce selections from this book should be mailed to: Permissions Department, The New Press, 120 Wall Street, 31st floor, New York, NY 10005.

Published in the United States by The New Press, New York, 2015
Distributed by Perseus Distribution

LIBRARY OF CONGRESS CATALOGING-IN-PUBLICATION DATA

Loomis, Erik.
  Out of sight : the long and disturbing story of corporations outsourcing catastrophe / Erik Loomis.
    pages cm
  Includes bibliographical references and index.
    ISBN 978-1-62097-008-9 (hardback) -- ISBN 978-1-62097-077-5 (e-book) 1. Contracting out--Moral and ethical aspects--United States. 2. Manufactures--Contracting out--United States. 3. Industrial relations--United States. 4. Labor--United States. 5. Labor--Developing countries. 6. Industrial safety--Developing countries. 7. Employee rights--Developing countries. I. Title.
  HD2368.U6L66 2015
  338.6--dc23

                             2014039758

The New Press publishes books that promote and enrich public discussion and under-standing of the issues vital to our democracy and to a more equitable world. These books are made possible by the enthusiasm of our readers; the support of a committed group of donors, large and small; the collaboration of our many partners in the independent media and the not-for-profit sector; booksellers, who often hand-sell New Press books; librarians; and above all by our authors.

www.thenewpress.com

Composition by Bookbright Media
This book was set in Minion Pro and Gotham

Printed in the United States of America

10 9 8 7 6 5 4 3 2 1

CONTENTS

ACKNOWLEDGMENTS

There are so many people to thank when writing any book. I want to express my appreciation for my editor Jed Bickman and the rest of the staff at The New Press for their great help and support in putting together this project. They have been nothing but professional throughout this process, and it's an honor to be published by a press that has distributed so many seminal books that have created positive social change.

This book synthesizes a tremendous amount of literature, both scholarly and journalistic. I hold everyone whose work I cited in this book in great esteem. Thank you for your hard work and dedication to your craft of gathering the information we need to build a more just society.

I would very much like to thank my colleagues in the history department at the University of Rhode Island for their support as well: Timothy George, Robert Widell, Bridget Buxton, Alan Verskin, Rosie Pegueros, Rae Ferguson, Miriam Reumann, James Ward, Eve Sterne, Rod Mather, Joelle Rollo-Koster, Michael Honhart, and Marie Schwartz. It is rare for a historian to have the opportunity to bridge the past and present in such a public forum, and I have received nothing but support from my colleagues in this endeavor.

A very special thanks goes to my colleagues at the blog *Lawyers, Guns, & Money* for allowing me to work out these ideas in our collective public forum: Robert Farley, Scott Lemieux, David Watkins, Paul Campos, David Brockington, Bethany Spencer, David Noon, Steven Attewell, and Scott Eric Kaufman. I also thank LGM's commenting community for its support of my good ideas and its pushback against my bad ideas. In an era where the nastiness of anonymous Internet commenting threatens the entire enterprise of online communities, LGM has proven an exception.

My dissertation adviser and longtime writing mentor Virginia Scharff also deserves a great deal of credit for this project. Her work on my writing over many years gave me the tools to articulate the thoughts in this project.

I have also received a tremendous amount of support over the past several years from the Internet's labor and left-leaning communities, including journalists, labor organizers, and historians. This has included encouragement for my writing, the opening of venues for my work, and support in hard times. There are really too many people to thank, but I want specifically to mention Sarah Jaffe for her constant advocacy for my work and her excellent editing of many articles of mine she commissioned; Mike Elk for welcoming me into the labor journalist community; and Brett Banditelli for his knowledge, Class War Kitteh, and labor history tours of Pennsylvania. Ryan Edgington provided insightful comments on a draft of chapter four that were extremely helpful.

A debt I cannot repay is that I owe Lindsay Beyerstein, who began the process that led to this book.

My family has always been incredibly supportive of all my endeavors. Many thanks and much love to my brother, Daryl Loomis; my sister and brother-in-law, Kris and Carlie DiOrio; and my in-laws Bill and Cassie McIntyre, Kevin and Claire McIntyre, Sean and Megan McIntyre, Bill McIntyre, and Siobhan and Mike Bubel and all their children. Most of these people were exposed to cranky author syndrome for the first time and took it in good humor.

As for my parents, their support and pride in me could not be matched by anyone in the world. Ray and Linda Loomis always sacrificed to make sure I had what I needed to go from the timber mill town of Springfield, Oregon, to the halls of academia. Better parents would be hard to imagine.

Finally and as always, my wife, Kathleen McIntyre, has given me more love and devotion than I can possibly deserve.

INTRODUCTION:
THE SCOURGE OF CAPITAL
MOBILITY

> Now capital has wings . . . capital can deal with twenty
> labor markets at once and pick and choose among them.
> Labor is fixed in one place. So power has shifted.
>
> —*Robert Johnson, New York financier, circa 1993*[1]

On the morning of March 25, 1911, around five hundred workers started another day at the Triangle Shirtwaist Company
in New York City, as they did six days a week. Mostly young Jewish
and Italian immigrant women, the workers could not have guessed
that many of them would die that afternoon. Max Blanck and Isaac
Harris owned the factory, making shirtwaists—a popular garment
for women of the era—on the eighth, ninth, and tenth floors of
the Asch Building, just off Washington Square Park in Greenwich
Village. Like other apparel manufacturers, Blanck and Harris did
not market clothing. Instead, they took orders from designers and
department stores under contracts that allowed sellers maximum
flexibility in a rapidly changing fashion world without responsibility for the workers. So long as Blanck and Harris made the clothes
for the agreed cost, the stores asked no questions.

Clothing sweatshops could burst in flame at any time. Bosses
crammed workers into tiny spaces and piled flammable cloth

around them. The factories were hot and the air filled with fibers. Blanck and Harris had ordered the fire exits locked so that workers' bags could undergo inspection for stolen cloth before they left. At about 4:40 p.m., just before the workers were to depart into the sunny afternoon, a fire started on the eighth floor, probably from a cigarette or match dropped in a scrap bin. When the fire started, workers on the eighth floor called up to the tenth to alert the bosses. Almost all workers from the eighth and tenth floors escaped. However, the ninth floor had no working telephone, and no one got the word to flee. By the time workers realized that smoke was rising from the floor below it was too late. Some workers escaped on the elevator before it became too hot to operate. Others got out via a fire escape, but it collapsed under the weight of the fleeing women. The fire department's ladders were useless, since they reached only the sixth floor. More than one hundred young women were stuck on the ninth floor and faced the grim choice of burning to death or jumping. Many workers jumped, landing on the street below with a sickening thud. Others were burned beyond recognition. One hundred forty-six workers died that day. The Triangle Fire was the deadliest factory disaster in American history.[2]

We think we remember Triangle today for the unique horror of its massive death count. But in fact we remember it because it spawned national outrage that led to long-term change in workplace safety. The fire itself was not an aberration for the time. Millions of American workers in the early twentieth century risked their lives daily by going to work. Coal miners died by the thousands from mine explosions and cave-ins. The Cherry Mine fire in Illinois in 1909 killed 259 workers. The Darr Mine explosion in Pennsylvania in 1907 killed 239. Meatpackers perished from electrocutions, meat hooks knocking them in the head, and tuberculosis. Falling trees crushed loggers, and timber mill workers lost limbs and lives after getting caught in saws and machines. Just a few months before the Triangle Fire, on November 26, 1910, a textile factory in Newark, New Jersey, caught fire and killed twenty-six workers. Each incident made newspaper headlines, but none of these disasters spawned national outrage or long-term change. Today, we have almost forgotten all of these earlier incidents.[3]

What made Triangle stand out from all the other disasters of the time was its visibility. As the tragedy unfolded, a crowd watched from Washington Square Park—a fashionable area of New York City. Among the witnesses was Frances Perkins. At the time, Perkins was a thirty-year-old recent graduate of Columbia University and secretary of the National Consumers League, an organization of largely wealthy female reformers led by Florence Kelley, demanding manufacturers produce products in safe factories and without employing child labor. Before coming to New York, she volunteered for five years at Hull House in Chicago, where Jane Addams and other settlement house workers provided a space for social reform and community services to the immigrant poor. Deciding on social work as her career, Perkins had moved to New York to obtain a master's degree.

Seeing smoke, Perkins rushed to the scene. More than fifty years later, she remembered, "Every one of them was killed, everybody who jumped was killed. It was a horrifying spectacle. We had our dose of it that night and felt as though we had been part of it all. The next day people, as they heard about it in all parts of the city, they began to mull around and gather and talk."[4] Seeing these deaths reinforced Perkins's anger over the terrible working conditions of American factories that led to the Triangle disaster. She helped create the New York Factory Investigating Commission in June 1911, which had the power to document and regulate working conditions throughout New York. Within a year of its founding, the commission drew up eight bills that became law, including one that mandated automatic sprinklers and another that forced factories to register with the state for regular inspections. Perkins became one of the nation's most powerful advocates for working Americans. She served as the nation's first female cabinet secretary when President Franklin Delano Roosevelt named her secretary of labor in 1933. During her twelve years in the cabinet, she oversaw the implementation of the National Labor Relations Act and the Fair Labor Standards Act, leading to the greatest expansion of unionization in American history.[5]

Before the Triangle Shirtwaist workers died that Saturday afternoon, New York textile workers had done all they could to make their struggles and dangerous working conditions known to the general public. In 1909, they walked off the job, led by a young Jewish immigrant worker named Clara Lemlich. In what became known as the Uprising of the 20,000, they struck for safer working conditions, shorter hours, and higher pay. One of the major targets of the strike was the Triangle factory. The employers hired prostitutes to pick fights with them in the streets, and police arrested and beat the workers. Lemlich suffered broken ribs from a police truncheon. Their struggle won the workers sympathy from wealthy female reformers interested in the plight of women workers, including Frances Perkins and Anne Morgan, daughter of the capitalist J.P. Morgan. The strike achieved limited gains, but poverty forced the strikers back to work after eleven weeks, without having won the safety improvements that would have prevented the Triangle Fire.[6]

Nothing spurred meaningful reform until wealthy and powerful New Yorkers saw workers die. Before the fire, they could easily walk past the Asch Building and be ignorant of what went on inside. They could read about coal mine fires in Illinois, but the deaths of poor people in distant places did not spur them to action. But when Perkins and others saw for themselves the people who made the clothes die fiery deaths, they felt moral outrage. Thus began a process by which American factories slowly became safer places to work during the twentieth century.

Fifty-eight years later, in 1969, public outrage over corporate behavior again revolved around disturbing images that flashed before Americans' eyes. Two events that year changed Americans' views on how industry should treat the environment. First, on January 28, the largest oil spill to that point in American history took place off the coast of Santa Barbara, California, when a well blew out on an oil platform owned by Union Oil. Up to one hundred thousand barrels spilled. People watching their evening news saw sea lions and birds covered in oil, dead fish and marine wildlife, and a paradise spoiled.

The oil industry had long played a controversial role in Southern California. As the state's beaches became a national attraction in the early twentieth century, tourists and developers protested the oil industry's presence in that beautiful part of the country. Beachgoers in the 1920s found themselves between the picturesque Pacific and a sea of oil derricks on land. Local residents, led by oil workers' unions, demanded the industry maintain the character of their towns and beaches. The oil workers' unions held beach cleanups, advocated for drilling limits, and wanted their towns free of the filth of oil pollution, even though they depended on oil for their livelihoods. By the 1960s, much of the production had moved offshore, but oil derricks and refineries remained a major feature of the Southern California landscape.[7]

When the spill took place, the people of Santa Barbara and Southern California responded quickly. An organization named Get Oil Out! (GOO) quickly developed. Led by Santa Barbara resident Bud Bottoms, GOO urged people to cut back on driving and boycott gas stations that received fuel from Union Oil. It lobbied to ban all oil drilling off the California coast and succeeded in enacting new regulations when drilling did resume. Thomas Storke, editor of the *Santa Barbara News-Press* wrote, "Never in my long lifetime have I ever seen such an aroused populace at the grassroots level. This oil pollution has done something I have never seen before in Santa Barbara—it has united citizens of all political persuasions in a truly nonpartisan cause." Union Oil suffered greater repercussions for this environmental disaster than any corporation in U.S. history to that time. Company president Fred Hartley couldn't understand, saying, "I am amazed at the publicity for a loss of a few birds." The spill made people around the nation realize the importance of preserving the landscapes they loved. In the two years after the oil spill, national membership in the Sierra Club doubled. California banned new leases for drilling on offshore state lands, although existing leases continued to operate. Today, companies do still drill in California, but the visual impact is much lower than a half century ago.[8]

Just a few months after the Santa Barbara oil spill, on June 22, 1969, in Cleveland, Ohio, the Cuyahoga River caught fire near where it enters Lake Erie. Industries had dumped pollution in the river ever since John D. Rockefeller, the wealthiest person in American history, founded his Standard Oil monopoly in Cleveland in 1870. A century later, factories owned by enormous industrial concerns, including steel mills, chemical plants, and meat-rendering companies, lined this foul, polluted river. The industrial jobs that had built Cleveland into an important manufacturing center had already begun to leave, but corporations such as Republic Steel and Sherwin-Williams paint employed tens of thousands of Clevelanders. In Cleveland's century-long industrial history, there had been almost no laws regulating the pollutants factory owners dumped into the rivers and air. Most Americans saw pollution as a sign of progress and learned to live with it. But by the late 1960s, the United States had changed. The outrage expressed over the Santa Barbara oil spill came with demands: that industries show responsibility for the environments where people lived, played, and worked.

At the same time, the civil rights movement spawned calls for justice of all kinds around the country. In 1967, Cleveland elected Carl Stokes, the first black mayor of a major American city. But when he took office, the city was in bad shape, and whites had already begun to flee to the suburbs, decimating the city's tax base. City governments had neglected the sewer system for decades and it was breaking down. Just before the fire, a sewer break had dumped 25 million gallons of raw sewage into the Cuyahoga. Even without the fire, Cleveland was already in a lot of trouble by 1969.[9]

The Cuyahoga had caught fire at least nine times prior to 1969, but no one had much cared, except for some locals concerned that the fires would destroy bridges. The 1969 fire caused very little damage and initially received scant news coverage. But in August an anonymous reporter at *Time* magazine picked up on the story. Calling such pollution "The Price of Optimism," the reporter described the Cuyahoga as "chocolate-brown, oily, bubbling with subsurface gases, it oozes rather than flows."[10] The fire was relatively brief; firefighters put it out before news photographers could get there. So the *Time* reporter chose to use a file photo of a Cuyahoga fire from 1952. This photo was unforgettable for people who saw it, most of whom assumed it was of the 1969 fire. Soon, the fire became the icon not only of Cleveland's environmental crisis, but of the whole nation's dysfunctional relationship with nature. In 1970, *National Geographic* ran a long story on the United States' ecological crisis that included a large foldout photograph of the polluted Cuyahoga, and in 1972 the songwriter Randy Newman had a hit song about the fire called "Burn On."[11]

Mayor Stokes called the fire a "terrible reflection on our city" and blamed the state of Ohio, saying the city had no control over what industry dumped into the water. The fire also gave Clevelanders an image to start conversations about the city's decline. Congressman Louis Stokes, brother of the mayor, told Congress that the "rape of the Cuyahoga River has not only made it useless for any purpose other than a dumping ground for sewage and industrial waste, but also has had a deleterious effect upon the ecology of the one of the Great Lakes."[12] Even before the fire, the mayor had tried to clean up his long-polluted city. Stokes had appointed Ben Stefanski Jr., a young lawyer, as director of Cleveland's public utilities. Stefanski and Stokes began to create an urban environmentalism for Cleveland. Stokes took up Stefanski's idea of making Lake Erie swimmable again by placing weighted curtains in the lake to create pockets of sanitary water. Stokes and Stefanski pushed for a major renovation of the city's sewer systems to prevent future leaks. People started returning to their beaches. Slowly, Cleveland began turning its environmental problems around, making the city's waterways safe again for recreation.[13]

By 1969, Americans were increasingly rejecting the idea that economic progress should come at the cost of their health, their water, and their air. The Cuyahoga fire, the Santa Barbara oil spill, smog choking Los Angeles and Denver, and pollution fouling local rivers seemed unacceptable for the planet's wealthiest nation. The same issue of *Time* that chronicled the Cleveland fire also included an article about the "remarkable bill" called the National Environmental Policy Act (NEPA), guided through Congress by

Senator Henry "Scoop" Jackson.[14] NEPA, arguably the most important environmental law in American history, committed the federal government to protecting the environment through a wide array of new regulations. Popular support for this bill skyrocketed after the Cuyahoga fire and Santa Barbara spill. Other legislation followed over the next few years, including the Endangered Species Act and stronger Clean Air and Clean Water Acts. On April 22, 1970, 20 million Americans came out to protest environmental degradation on the first Earth Day. Workers' demands for safe workplace environments were partially met by the Federal Coal Mine Health and Safety Act of 1969 and the Occupational Safety and Health Act of 1970. Soon new regulations against leaded gasoline, asbestos, and other toxic materials began protecting people from unnecessary environmental risks. Within a decade, American environments became much safer, national health improved, and quality of life jumped significantly.[15]

The experience of seeing charred bodies in New York, burning rivers in Cleveland, and oil on California beaches had spurred Americans to demand action. They fought for some level of corporate and government responsibility for human health, workplace safety, and clean air and water. Frances Perkins, Carl Stokes, Clara Lemlich, and ordinary people watching television at home forced corporations to acquiesce to regulations that improved people's lives at the time and continue to make our lives better today.

Americans today rarely experience workplace disasters, burning rivers, or fatal smog. There are two reasons for this. First, the regulations that Americans demanded in the sixties and seventies have had tremendously positive results. Workplaces became safer and waterways cleaner. Americans live healthier and safer lives than their parents and grandparents.

The second reason is far more alarming: corporations moved their operations across the globe to escape these very regulations. They could have become responsible citizens and made their products in ways that gave workers dignified lives and kept both consumers and ecosystems safe, but instead they chose to move their operations and re-create the old toxic and unsafe environments. Rather than protecting their American workers from breathing in fibers, cloth manufacturers moved to Latin America and Southeast Asia, where workers today get sick from the same conditions that were common in the United States a century ago. Heavy industries moved overseas instead of investing in clean factories in the United States. New industries such as technology and computing have built factories in poor nations in order to take advantage of lax environmental- and workplace-regulation enforcement. Companies justify this with language about "competitiveness in a global marketplace," which only obscures the enormous profits they make by investing so little in their workers. If wages rise too high or workers try to unionize or nations begin to enforce environmental regulations, the companies happily pack up their factories to another country more willing to do their bidding.

On April 24, 2013, the Rana Plaza textile factory collapsed in Savar, Bangladesh, killing 1,134 workers and injuring another 2,500. The day before the collapse, workers saw cracks in the building. Foremen told employees to go to work or lose a month's precious pay. Sohel Rana, a well-connected Bangladeshi businessman with many friends in the nation's parliament, owned the building. It was not designed to hold the weight of its top four floors or to accommodate the constant vibration of sewing machines. Bangladesh has building codes and safety standards, but the apparel manufacturers control the political system, so enforcement is nonexistent unless outside pressure for accountability develops. Political corruption runs amok. Even before the Rana collapse, terrible working conditions and unsafe factory buildings had already cost workers their lives in many other instances.[16]

None of this concerned the twenty-seven multinational corporations that signed production contracts with Rana, including Benetton, popular Canadian brand Joe Fresh, and the British apparel giant Primark. Walmart claimed to have no contracts with the factory but was listed as a buyer by one of the companies operating at Rana Plaza. Clothing made for J.C. Penney was produced there, though the company says it did not know of it.[17] As at Triangle, none of these companies directly employ the apparel workers who make their products, nor do any of the Western apparel companies contracting clothing in Bangladesh. Instead, they contract with Bangladeshi managers who employ workers to make clothing. Each of these companies could have employed their own workers and built their own factories to stitch clothing. They could have demanded more and better inspections of the factories with whom they contract. But they do not, because they care only about one thing: low costs. Indeed, they fund the system that incentivizes the Bangladeshi factory owners to profit from cutting corners. The details are not of their concern, so long as they can stay out of sight of consumers that might hold them accountable if they knew the conditions in which their clothing was produced.[18]

As at Triangle, the survivors of Rana Plaza find themselves traumatized. A woman named Shima worked on the fifth floor of the factory and miraculously survived. Now she wakes up screaming at night, remembering her dead friends and suffering nightmares of being buried alive or dying.[19] Another woman, Reshma Begum, was trapped in the rubble for seventeen days and said upon her rescue, "I never dreamed I'd see the daylight again."[20] Rehana Khatun lost both of her legs in the collapse. Just twenty years old, she worked at Rana to save money for her marriage. She has given up on that dream and just hopes to learn to walk again with prosthetic legs.[21]

Western reporters brought Shima, Begum, and Khatun's stories to a suddenly interested Western readership. The collapse drew attention to how our clothing is produced. We saw that the apparel industry had learned to hide production far away from American consumers in order to lower prices, increase profits, and insulate corporations from responsibility for the conditions of the factories. The difference between Rana Plaza and Triangle, Santa Barbara, and Cleveland is only one of location. Like their counterparts a century ago, Bangladeshi workers have attempted to organize to improve their conditions, and militant labor unions have even burned their own factories in frustration.[22] But unlike the Uprising of the 20,000, these Bangladeshi workers live far away from the people who buy the clothing they make. In the earlier era, middle-class reformers and workers could unite in New York City and demand changes to building codes, fire safety, and the conditions of work. Frances Perkins could see the Triangle Fire, but no Walmart shoppers saw the Rana Plaza collapse.

Americans, not knowing clothing workers and unable to locate Bangladesh on a map, maintain only a vague awareness of conditions inside the factories. The collapse has had a negligible effect on the bottom lines of the apparel corporations. To make sure nothing comes of the collapse, leading American retailers such as Walmart, Gap, and J.C. Penney have created fake safety codes with no enforcement mechanism that allow them to tell consumers that they have taken steps, even if those steps are meaningless. Production remains hidden from consumers. Distance matters.

Corporate mobility—supported by state and federal governments through trade agreements, free trade zones, and labor law exceptions—has outsourced industrial risk to the world's poor, separating the costs of industrial production from consumers and undermining labor rights and environmental protections in the United States and around the world. To quote labor geographer Andrew Herod, corporations engage in "geographical subterfuge" by trying to "hide in far away and isolated communities various parts of the production process, especially those in which workers are particularly exploited or exposed to noxious chemicals."[23] Union-free workplaces, poverty-level wages, and unregulated pollution all lead to maximum shareholder profit at the cost of working-class dignity and health. This book shows that when corporations have the ability to move production sites around the world, it undermines the American middle class while intensively exploiting the world's poor. No one's job is safe and no one can organize for a better job when companies can move so easily. Busted labor unions, pollution, unsafe workplaces, and economic instability result when multinational corporations hold us all hostage to their whims. The corporate exploitation of labor and the planet are intertwined parts of an economic system that seeks to create profit without concern for long-term consequences, working-class dignity, or environmental sustainability. To the company, the quarterly profit statement means more than a sustainable ecosystem or a worker with ten fingers.

This book tells the story behind this crisis of globalized capitalism. It takes us forward from the Industrial Revolution's beginnings to the present and shows specific historical roots of modern problems, while also highlighting the people and groups who have stood up to corporate misbehavior. It shows when and why corporations chose to move production overseas. The book also suggests alternative paths corporate leaders could have taken to shape an economy that generates reasonable profit while providing dignified middle-class lives for workers and sustainably uses the resources on this precious and endangered planet. But they didn't take those paths. Instead, corporations chose to re-create their habitual way of operating, paying little attention to worker safety and health, avoiding responsibility to workers who get sick on the job, and dumping their factory wastes into the rivers and air, forcing additional suffering on the global poor.

Triangle fires still happen in Bangladesh. Santa Barbara oil spills repeat themselves in Nigeria. Chinese rivers are polluted like the Cuyahoga. In 1991, Lawrence Summers, then chief economist of the World Bank, wrote a memo saying, "I've always thought that under-populated countries in Africa are vastly UNDER-polluted, their air quality is probably vastly inefficiently low compared to Los Angeles or Mexico City." He urged the World Bank to facilitate the transfer of toxic waste to "under-polluted" Africa. People around the world lambasted Summers, but it did not stop his rise to the highest echelons of power, becoming a close economic adviser to Presidents Bill Clinton and Barack Obama.[24] Sadly, outsourcing risk has become a bipartisan project. Politicians like to talk about creating American jobs, but the actual policies supported by Beltway elites—whether politicians, lobbyists, or pundits—instead promote U.S. investment overseas in the name of "free trade" and "economic competitiveness."

Globalization has transformed the United States alongside Mexico, India, Bangladesh, and nearly every nation in the world. We know that globalization has led to the transfer of industrial jobs outside the United States. Cities like Cleveland, Detroit, and Flint have struggled to recover after corporations fled, seeking cheap labor and lax environmental regulations. Working people in America have seen wage stagnation, long-term unemployment, and a declining standard of living over the past forty years. This book adds to this story by focusing on the effects of globalization on undermining environmental and labor activism in the United States and the result this has had on domestic politics.

Economist Joseph Stiglitz has defined globalization as the "closer integration of the countries and peoples of the world which has been brought about by the enormous reduction of costs of transportation and communication, and the breaking down of artificial barriers to the flows of goods, services, capital, knowledge, and (to a lesser extent) people across borders."[25] Globalization is the spread of ideas, culture, political systems, food, animals, plants, and disease. Beginning in the thirteenth and fourteenth centuries, trading networks connected East Asia, India, the east coast of Africa, the Middle East, and Europe, and globalization started the centuries-long transformation of the world, leading to the European conquest of the Americas and the genocide of indigenous peoples, the expansion of the world's food sources, the depletion of wildlife, and the movement of capital and jobs around the world.[26]

Of course, globalization itself is neither bad nor good. I like having access to Vietnamese food, and many Vietnamese like eating American fast food. But the system's promoters ignore or explain away the tremendous injustices caused by globalization today, especially the exploitation of the world's poor through both corporate and government policies that throw them off their land and out of their towns and villages and force them to make a living in the modern corporate economy as low-wage workers. Modern globalization creates great profit for shareholders but has undermined stable employment and middle-class lifestyles for American workers while forcing the world's poor to work in polluted, deadly workplaces.

Thanks to the outsourcing of our industrial work, the American public rarely experiences industrial risk anymore. We have lost knowledge about industrialization's realities. Clothing just appears on the store shelves as if by magic, and meat comes nicely packaged and removed from the brutality of its production. It makes it easy for us to give no thought to how these products arrived at our fingertips, who suffered to make them, and how faraway ecosystems have been transformed. This has changed American politics. Without the visceral reminders of industrialization's impact on nature, polls have shown consistently decreasing support for environmental issues even as climate change becomes an international crisis. International polls consistently show fewer Americans think climate change is a major problem than any other nationality.[27] Too many of us have forgotten why the environmental movement is so important. A 1978 poll asked people a series of questions about whether federal workplace and environmental regulation were worth higher costs of consumer goods. Sixty-nine percent of respondents said that federal regulations adding to the cost of consumer goods was worth it versus only 18 percent who disagreed.[28] They supported higher costs to protect the environment by 42 percent to 19 percent. Recent polls have shown a significant decline in environmental support. In 2000, a Gallup poll still showed Americans supporting environmental protection over economic growth by a 70 to 23 margin. In 2013, the same question saw economic growth favored by a 48 to 43 margin.[29]

Notably, recently intensified industrial fossil fuel production in North America is the one arena where Americans are seeing a spike in both dangerous work and environmentalist resistance, particularly to the proposed Keystone XL pipeline, which would send dirty oil from the Canadian tar sands through the American Midwest to Texas. When we see problems, citizens can react. But we mostly stopped seeing these problems when corporations responded to environmentalism by moving jobs overseas in the 1970s, making Americans afraid of the economic costs of environmental regulations. With a decline in working-class support, many environmental organizations shifted focus in the 1980s from the cities and the air and water shared by us all to wilderness protection for places most working people never visit. Saving Oregon's last old-growth trees had great value, but for the loggers needing to cut those trees to feed their families, environmentalism began to seem like a threat. Groups like the Sierra Club, the National Wildlife Federation, and the National Resources Defense Council often prioritized campaigns on the Amazon rain forest or for wilderness protection over how pollution affected communities of color or the need to create jobs sustainable for both the planet and the livelihoods of working Americans. These strategies worked to raise money from wealthy donors for big green organizations but did nothing to convince working-class Americans that environmentalism meant something to them. Earth Day transformed from a challenge to capitalism in 1970 to a day to go pick up some litter on the riverbank, often with corporate sponsorship, in the early twenty-first century.

In part because of their reputation for representing the interests of rich greens rather than everyday Americans, environmental groups have found tepid public support for their initiatives in recent years, including the cap-and-trade bill to fight climate change that they put so much energy into in the aftermath of President Obama's election. When in 2014 the Environmental Protection Agency issued new regulations limiting coal emissions from power plants, Republicans and even Democrats in coal-producing states again called it part of Obama's "war on coal." In fact, a majority of Americans do support limiting emissions, in theory, but only as a low priority for most.[30] In a time of economic instability, environmental protections seem like a luxury, especially when the vision of nature in the American mind has shifted from the chemicals flowing into the nearby river to the Amazon rain forests or polar bears in Alaska. Too many Americans view climate change—not only the greatest environmental threat ever faced by human beings but also one caused entirely by the same industrial system that outsources production today—as an issue without impact on their lives or even as a leftist conspiracy.

Globalization created a race to the bottom through corporate incentives to move production to the cheapest possible location. This has had cascading effects on organized labor. The greatest period for American working-class empowerment was between the

1930s, when the federal government forced corporations to collectively bargain with labor unions, and the 1970s, when corporations began moving abroad. In the 1930s and 1940s, the Congress of Industrial Organizations (CIO) took advantage of the government's new stance during President Franklin Roosevelt's New Deal, organizing the giant industrial unions of the twentieth century such as the United Automobile Workers and Steel Workers Organizing Committee (later the United Steelworkers of America). Not only did these unions provide the strongest organized voice for American workers in history, they also made unions a central part of American life. Americans knew why unions were necessary, how they gave workers a voice on the job, and how they helped improve people's lives. Strong labor unions ensured the growth of the middle class, with rising incomes, better health and unemployment insurance, and, eventually, safer workplaces.

Moving industrial production has busted unions, which has allowed the nation to forget these lessons. Today, only 11 percent of workers are union members, and over half of all union members reside in just six states. In the majority of the nation, organized labor is nearly dead, especially in the private sector, where less than 7 percent of workers have a union.[31] Corporate propaganda about unions destroying jobs, crushing the freedom of the individual to work, and stealing members' dues for corruption dominates public knowledge about labor unions. For example, not only Republicans but also too many Democrats attack teachers' unions for standing in the way of "education reform." These attacks are part of a strategy to privatize K–12 education and turn a public service into a profit-generating enterprise.[32] The same 1978 poll in which respondents said greater environmental protections were worth higher costs also showed that 52 percent of people approved of higher costs to protect worker health and safety while only 12 percent opposed them. Today, government underfunding of the Occupational Safety and Health Administration (OSHA) means that factories rarely, if ever, receive even a minimal safety inspection. The fertilizer plant explosion that killed fifteen people in West, Texas, in April 2013 took place in a factory that had last received an OSHA inspection in 1985, when it received a $30 fine for violations. Today, there are so few OSHA inspectors that it would take 129 years to inspect every American workplace once.[33] The decline of unions means that American workers have become less safe and less healthy at work even while the most dangerous jobs have been outsourced to nations that suppress union organizing to make those jobs safer.

The constant threat of our jobs disappearing, of our employers moving to Mexico or Thailand or even to a nonunion factory in another state, throws our lives into chaos. It becomes harder to justify buying a home or to plan a long-term future. Saving for our children's college tuition seems an impossible dream. We are told we will switch careers three times in our lives. We are encouraged to move around the country to find work. Many Americans have answered that call, causing populations in Texas and North Carolina to explode while Rhode Island and Pennsylvania stagnate. Globalization's promoters promised Americans that an information economy with a flexible workforce would replace industrialization and create a bright twenty-first century for an innovative and dynamic country and its entrepreneurial citizens. That has not happened. Instead, the new economy has concentrated profits in the offshore bank accounts of the 1 percent while forcing ever-greater debt burdens on Americans who face dire chances of finding well-paid and stable employment. The dismantling of the nation's industrial infrastructure has condemned parts of the United States to long-term poverty.

It's a neat circle for corporations. Moving operations to nonunion states and nations undermines organized labor's effectiveness and increases corporate profits. Increased corporate power and decreased union power in Washington means business exerts more and more control over politicians. Those politicians then ally with corporations to finish the job and kill organized labor through a thousand cuts, including not confirming members to the National Labor Relations Board, subcontracting jobs to create multiple employers in the same workplace, defunding OSHA and occupational safety programs, and pushing right-to-work legislation in formerly strong union states. This last goal is the most pernicious. The term *right-to-work* is a corporate-created euphemism for giving workers the option to opt out of their organization while forcing the union to defend them on the job and bargain their wages and hours for free. These free riders effectively undermine unions by taking away their dues money, thus limiting their ability to fight for workers' rights through organizing and lobbying and in the political arena. With each lost union job, organized labor loses more of its ability to resist complete corporate domination over our lives. Corporations know this, which is why the U.S. Chamber of Commerce, the Koch brothers, Art Pope, and other antiunion extremists have pushed their Republican Party allies so hard to finish the job against unions.

Corporations have always wanted a union-free workplace. They had it in the late nineteenth century, lost it briefly, and today have it again on a global scale. The inheritors of the Triangle Shirtwaist Company's utter disregard for human life canvass the world seeking cheap, female, and underage labor to exploit. Looking to avoid the unions that garment workers in New York demanded in 1909—and continue to demand wherever they go—the textile industry began moving to states like North Carolina and Tennessee in the 1920s, Mexico in the 1960s, and Southeast Asia by the 1980s. In November 2012, a fire killed 112 people in a Dhaka, Bangladesh, clothing factory—an inescapable echo of Triangle made even louder by the April 2013 Rana Plaza factory collapse.

The death of so many workers brought unwanted attention to the details of the clothing-outsourcing system. The global apparel system is explicitly designed to shield clothing corporations from responsibility for the deaths. In the aftermath of Bangladesh, American businesses said they had no responsibility for what happened. Because companies contract with suppliers for their clothing rather than make it with their own employees, they can claim they have no accountability. They tried to blame it on Sohel Rana and corruption within Bangladesh. Rana and his cronies are culpable, but this obscures the role the apparel companies play in creating the dangerous working conditions. As they did in 1911, companies outsource the work to subcontractors, awarding the work to the factory that can do it the cheapest. When price is the only factor that counts, the costs get pushed down onto workers in the form of low wages and unsafe factories. In other words, nothing has changed in the apparel industry over the past hundred years except the location of its factories.

Workers do not have to die on the job. People do not have to be poisoned in their homes by factories. We can have consumer products made with reasonable standards of environmental and workplace safety at prices not much higher than we currently pay. Politicians and corporate leaders tell us a story about the inevitability of the current economic model. It's the invisible hand of the market, they say. They create stories that tell us labor unions made American workers uncompetitive, so they had no choice but to ship jobs to Mexico and Taiwan. American environmental regulations gave foreign corporations marketplace advantages, so what choice did American companies have but to migrate?

This is all false. The current system of economic and environmental exploitation abroad and the decline of the middle class at home is the result of a choice made by corporate leaders to profit at the expense of working people around the world. Exposing their behavior and showing the long history of this system has the potential to shine a light on what they have tried to cover up for a century. Capitalism is made up of individuals. That means there are alternative choices that corporate leaders can make. Americans have made those alternative choices in the past. The free market is not a natural force. It is not gravity. Calling "market decisions" natural law is a mythology created to hide the very real choices made by corporate leaders and politicians. We can reconcile capitalism and dignified employment, profit and environmental stability. But this can happen only when we unpeel the layers of myths around corporate behavior and organize in our home nations to empower workers around the globe.

How do we work toward these solutions? How do we fight for stable jobs in this country while supporting the struggles of the poor around the world? It's a big task! But I close this book with suggestions for citizens to fight for justice, for organizations to craft meaningful alliances to create international pressure on business and governments, and for governments to intervene in the market in ways that address these problems both in the United States and overseas.

Ultimately, this means holding corporations legally accountable for their actions overseas. If a corporation wants the tax benefits and political clout it gets in the United States, it must hold to a minimum of American workplace safety and environmental regulations wherever it builds or contracts with a factory. These standards must be strong, and international inspectors must enforce them. American corporations have decoupled capital mobility from legal accountability. Today, they move their capital wherever in the world they desire, but laws remain tied to national borders. This creates a race to the bottom, with states and nations offering to look the other way on their legal standards in order to attract corporate investment. American corporations give lip service to national law and nonbinding agreements but flee at the first hint of legal liability or enforcement. Many industries also seek to separate themselves from responsibility by subcontracting work to dozens of factories, allowing them to claim ignorance when workers die or rivers get polluted and making concerted action against corporations much harder.

Supporters of corporate migration and capital mobility inevitably say that critics of globalization want to condemn Bangladeshi workers to unemployment and even greater poverty by holding sweatshops to such high standards that they would have to close. That is ridiculous. People in Bangladesh do need to make money. They need jobs. They deserve a living wage, and paying them one would cost corporations far less than the American minimum wage. But those workers also need safety and a clean environment. We cannot roll the world back to the 1960s, when most American-consumed products were made in the United States. Buy American campaigns or longing for protectionism will not bring the jobs back. They will, however, create divides between domestic and foreign workers—by encouraging rhetoric about Bangladeshi or Mexican workers "stealing our jobs"—rather than build solidarity among workers exploited by corporations worldwide.

I suggest strategies that we in the world's wealthy nations can take to ensure workplace and environmental justice for people around the world. I focus on the United States because I am a historian of American labor and environmental movements, but most of these points have relevance for readers in Canada, Australia, Europe, Japan, South Korea, and other wealthy nations. First, we as activists, consumers, and citizens must learn about capital mobility and articulate and demand the changes we want to see. We need to pay attention to these issues within our union locals and environmental groups; on our Reddit pages, Facebook feeds, and Twitter accounts; and in any other ways we communicate about the world with our neighbors, friends, families, and co-workers. We need to support the plethora of activist organizations that fight for global justice. We can take to the streets and protest corporations who violate international health and safety standards. All of us can build a movement that shifts the conversation around global trade, just as Occupy Wall Street did for economic inequality.

These issues must become a political priority for us as voters and activists. We must emphasize global labor and environmental justice in the political arena, rewarding politicians who support labor and environmental protections and fighting politicians who do not. I also outline in the last chapter how to target these issues within the political system around a grassroots movement for social, environmental, and economic justice. We have to take over the government and make it work for everyday people instead of corporations. All social movements in American history have required government action to codify their successes, and without significant government action we are not going to make conditions better for workers in Bangladeshi factories. Corporate self-monitoring is nearly worthless because it leaves the fox in charge of the henhouse and does not give workers power to demand change. Consumer-based campaigns are important but can go only so far.

Ultimately, we need to create the legal and judicial framework for enforceable international workplace safety and environmental standards. We have to take away incentives for capital mobility that outsource dangerous work, pollution, and illness to the world's

poor. Corporations simply should not be able to move their operations in order to escape workplace health and safety standards or
emissions requirements. I discuss successful attempts to create international standards in the past and how we can emulate those
successes today. We must work toward international legal and
regulatory frameworks that would make corporations legally and
financially responsible for their own behavior. This would force
corporations to abide by standards of workplace safety and environmental quality regardless of where they place their factories,
leading the working class of the world toward a more just and sustainable society. There might be good reasons to move operations
to different countries—proximity to natural resources or markets,
for instance—but corporations should not be allowed to increase
profits by dumping pollution onto poor people or re-creating the
unsafe workplaces that Americans largely eliminated decades ago.
We need to empower UN agencies such as the International Labour Organization with meaningful inspection and enforcement
authority, grant workers in developing countries the right and ability to sue their employers in the countries of corporate origin when
workplace and environmental regulations are violated, and disal-
low corporations to flee legal responsibility through subcontracting. None of this will be easy; globalized corporate capitalism is an
entrenched system. But working people have won real gains in the
past and can do so again.

Taken as a whole, these goals, challenging yet sensible and
achievable, provide us our best hope for creating a just, equitable
world where people can live and work in dignity, where ecosystems
remain healthy and whole, and where corporate interests are bal-
anced with the interests of the working class and the planet. This is
the society for which we should fight.

1

STANDING UP TO
CORPORATE DOMINATION:
A BRIEF HISTORY

Americans live in a society where media portray corporate leaders as heroes. The race to be the richest man in the world is now an unofficial competition detailed by *Forbes* and reported on TV, websites, and Twitter. The twenty-four-hour news cycle always makes plenty of time for stock market reports and stories of how business can solve all our national problems. Capitalists are the "job creators," or so we hear. Congress passes tax cuts to businesses and the rich to create jobs, although the cuts lack stipulations that the wealthy don't use that money to buy new yachts. Wealth alone creates policy expertise. For our problems with public education, politicians turn to for-profit schools as a solution. Bill Gates can help solve health crises while Mark Zuckerberg helps design public school reform plans for Newark, New Jersey. What these people know about health policy or public school education can be put in a thimble, but it doesn't matter in the United States, because they are rich. Wealth is something to aspire to. Being the next John D. Rockefeller, Henry Ford, Donald Trump, or Mark Zuckerberg—that's the dream of many. People watch films like Oliver Stone's *Wall Street* or Martin Scorsese's *The Wolf of Wall Street* and perceive their corporate executives as models, even if they are meant as critiques of Wall Street excess. Greed is good indeed.

Americans' national myth is that we are all individuals who can succeed if we pull ourselves up by our bootstraps. We can all become Andrew Carnegie, rising from nothing to magisterial wealth. The flip side of the myth is that if you do not become a success, it's your fault. Never mind that you do not have the advantages of rich white men in American society, that you are African American, a woman, transgender, or lack running water or Internet in your house. Those are just excuses in our supposed Horatio Alger paradise. If you can't find a job, you are the lazy one, the person who drinks, who has sex outside of marriage, who is on welfare, who is a loser. National mythology ignores structural inequality in favor of cheap narratives of individual responsibility.

Corporations and their lackeys in politics have pushed this line of thinking for 150 years. Andrew Carnegie said, "People who are unable to motivate themselves must be content with mediocrity." John D. Rockefeller expressed similar sentiments: "God gave me my money. I believe the power to make money is a gift from God." When you believe your money is a gift from God, that probably means you think God has blessed you because of the values and ethics that separate you from others. You become the worthy rich while the 99 percent are poor because they are lazy, drunkards, shiftless.

But just because this myth has great power today doesn't mean that Americans have always accepted it. We have always challenged and rejected it, fighting against inequality and for a just society. Those who have fought it have come in all stripes. Some wanted to overthrow capitalism, others reform it. Some were unemployed workers demanding jobs. Radical labor such as the Industrial Workers of the World (IWW) wanted a socialist or syndicalist society and worker control over the shop floor, while more conservative unions such as many of those affiliated with the American Federation of Labor (AFL) wanted worker power to force concessions from the capitalists on wages, hours, and working conditions. Farmers revolted against the exploitation they faced from railroads and bankers. Miners wanted protections from dying on the job. Early twentieth-century middle-class reformers found the conditions workers lived in disturbing, unfair, and a threat to social stability, lobbying for the end of child labor, restriction on the hours of women workers, garbage collection, workers' compensation laws, and a host of other reforms. Wealthy reformers such as Theodore Roosevelt believed the nation needed to protect its trees from rapacious timber corporations and thus created the U.S. Forest Service. Reformers and radicals both rallied for the most popular economic justice movement of the early twentieth century: the federal income tax, which became the Sixteenth Amendment to the Constitution in 1913. What all of these people wanted was for corporations to take at least some responsibility for their behavior.

Eventually, after great struggle, the American working class forced corporations to treat them like people. Between the 1930s and the 1970s, protesting workers and a federal government increasingly sympathetic to their plight (and scared about what would happen if they did not finally help the poor) moved to clamp down on the corporate greed that had created such suffering. The government mandated the eight-hour day, the minimum wage, Social Security, workplace safety regulations, pollution restrictions, unemployment insurance, Medicare, Head Start, and much more. The catastrophes of capitalist America became rarer. After World War II, the nation's workers saw a huge increase in their standard of living, as the working class became the middle class thanks to union contracts, an expanding economy, and progressive taxation that created the modern welfare state. With disposable income and vacation time, Americans wanted to preserve their natural spaces from corporate despoilment, and the modern environmental movement developed in the 1960s, saving ecosystems from degradation and animals from extinction. Americans in the 1960s believed they could have good jobs and clean environments. They believed catastrophe could be avoided entirely.

That seems like eons ago. Today, we are losing ground on every issue American workers fought for during the twentieth century. At the core of this problem is capital mobility. Moving jobs overseas allowed corporations to undercut the gains made by the American people. Throwing off the controls that limited catastrophe allowed corporations to return to the days of dominating the national and world economy without restraint. Within the United States, unionization rates are the lowest in a century. The environmental movement's political power has declined precipitously in the past thirty years, and with the failure of the cap-and-trade bill in 2009, greens are struggling with how to revive their power in Washington. The nation does next to nothing to fight climate change. Student debt hamstrings an entire generation of young people. The dream of home ownership is dead for millions. Corporations now rule our politics in ways they have not in a century. The Supreme Court has given corporations and the wealthy enormous power over our elections. The Koch brothers, Sheldon Adelson, and other right-wing plutocrats spend millions in every election attacking Democrats and rigging the political game in their favor. When Republicans win state elections, they gerrymander legislative districts to keep themselves in power and pass laws to reduce the voting power of people of color. Their friends in the Supreme Court then rule the key clause of the Voting Rights Act unconstitutional, allowing further voting suppression of people of color. Extreme gerrymandering has ensured that a conservative minority controls the House of Representatives and many state legislatures, repealing progressive legislation there. The catastrophes of capitalism have returned, not in the United States, but exported to India, Bangladesh, Honduras, and Guatemala while Americans lack any stable work. Will our children inherit a better nation than we did? Unfortunately, I am skeptical.

This chapter provides a brief history of the battle between American corporations and working people over whether the economy should serve the many or the few. Corporations have always sought to exploit their employees and the people who live near their plants. They are never partners with the working class. *Never*. Corporations exist for one reason: profit. If you don't help shareholders make money, you have no value. Corporations have done an excellent job of fooling Americans into believing they are responsible members of our society. For instance, petroleum companies such as ExxonMobil, Chevron, and BP produce "greenwashing" advertisements that disseminate a message of them as environmentally accountable organizations when in fact they do more than anyone to transform the climate and block environmental reform on the state, national, and international levels. Corporate leaders demonstrate their immorality by moving all the jobs away and then seeking to repeal the entire realm of twentieth-century regulations that created the good life for the American people. Understanding the history of corporate misbehavior and citizen activism is necessary to recover what we have lost.

English workers in the eighteenth century were the first to experience the world-changing impact of the Industrial Revolution. At its most fundamental level, an industrial economy processes the raw materials of the natural world into finished products through the use of human, water, and fossil fuel energy. This has cascading effects on both workers and the planet. In nineteenth-century England, workers struck over dangerous mines and dank mills. Charles Dickens portrayed these dark, horrid places in his novels, bringing international attention to the intense poverty created by capitalism. Events such as the 1819 Peterloo massacre of striking Manchester textile workers meant British labor would first feel the iron fist of a military force serving industrialists. This incident took place after an economic collapse led the working poor to demand political and economic reforms to British society. Centered among the cotton weavers of Lancashire, sixty thousand to eighty thousand workers gathered in a field near Manchester in protest. A frightened British upper class sent in the army. A cavalry charge led to eleven to fifteen dead, and the upper class clamped down on all reform efforts. This is far from the last time the wealthy would respond to working-class revolt with violence.[1]

The Industrial Revolution came to the United States in 1793, when Samuel Slater opened a textile factory in Pawtucket, Rhode Island. Americans feared the nation's nice little towns would become domestic versions of the nightmarish English industrial cities. Industrialists created Lowell, Massachusetts, in 1822 as an experimental factory town that would foster morally upright workers while spurring intensive production of textiles. Lowell employers recruited young farm women from around New England to come work in the factories, have a bit of an adventure, and live in a respectable fashion. The "mill girls" lived in dormitories under the watchful eyes of older women and attended talks by Ralph Waldo Emerson, Henry Wadsworth Longfellow, and other early nineteenth-century intellectuals. Workers produced their own magazines, took classes, and, in the eyes of the factory owners, prepared themselves for marriage while producing profit for their employer.

Almost immediately, American apparel operators sought to hire women because they viewed them as easily controlled labor with dexterous fingers. This process of gendering work, or defining work as naturally belonging to men or women, had the effect of making textile work low paid, because women's work was poorly valued in American society. The struggles for decent working conditions and for women's rights became intertwined. The mill girls liked the working conditions far less than the book salons and camaraderie. They labored fourteen-hour days, from 5:00 a.m. to 7:00 p.m. The factories roasted in the summer with windows that brought in maximum sunlight and heat to make it easier to work the fabric. These were young farm women used to work, so they had no problem with the strenuous nature of the labor, but they did not like being locked up in that factory tending those machines minute after minute, day after day, month after month. Historians have dated the beginning of the American working class's romanticization of the environment to these early textile factory workers who began believing nature was something to escape into rather than tame. As more factories opened around New England, other employers hired women at lower rates, without the supervised housing and Emerson lectures. The Lowell operators felt threatened by their competition. In 1834, the owners announced a 15 percent wage reduction to compete with this lower-paid labor. The Lowell mill girls went on strike, and they struck again in 1836 over another wage cut.[2]

Cutting down the wages was not their only grievance, nor the only cause of this strike. Hitherto the corporations had paid twenty-five cents a week toward the board of each operative, and now it was their purpose to have the girls pay the sum; and this, in addition to the cut in the wages, would make a difference of at least one dollar a week. It was estimated that as many as twelve or fifteen hundred girls turned out and walked in procession through the streets. They had neither flags nor music, but sang songs, a favorite (but rather inappropriate) one being a parody on "I won't be a nun."

> *"Oh isn't it a pity, such a pretty girl as I—*
> *Should be sent to the factory to pine away and die?*
> *Oh! I cannot be a slave*
> *I will not be a slave,*
> *For I'm so fond of liberty*
> *That I cannot be a slave."*[3]

Employers sought to replace these empowered and therefore rebellious young women with a new group of workers. Over 1.6 million Irish immigrated to the United States between 1840 and 1860. The New England factory owners happily gave these immigrants work—at the wages, hours, and working conditions determined by the employers. Soon apparel factories became a place of first employment for recent immigrants who needed to contribute to their meager family income. When the Irish moved out of the industry, Italians and Jews took their place. Poor, desperate, and easily exploitable, they became the ideal labor force for textile mill owners. These were hard, brutal jobs, and the vile conditions of English factory towns indeed did appear in the United States.[4]

These factories needed cotton for their spinning wheels, so the other side of the textile economy was the Southern plantations where slave labor grew that cotton. Northern factory owners benefited directly from the exploitation of enslaved African and African American labor. In the South, slave owners drove their human property to the point of death in order to grow as much cotton as possible. Maximizing profit and dehumanizing the slaves went hand in hand. Malnutrition, overcrowded and dilapidated housing, insufficient clothing that did not keep slaves warm, forced reproduction through sexually assaulting female slaves: all of this meant profit. Slaves fought back in any number of ways, from breaking

tools and stealing food to running away and murdering their masters. Slave rebellions were rare, but Nat Turner's Rebellion in 1831
killed sixty white Virginians, and Southerners constantly feared
their slaves slaughtering them in the night. Still, Northern textile
mills led to a rapidly expanding slave system that fueled westward
expansion into Mississippi, Louisiana, and Texas in search of more
sources of cotton. Southern elites dedicated their society to the production of this key crop for American economic growth. The early
capitalist system relied on both slave and free (but exploited) labor
for the textile mills, a system with increasing tension in the 1850s
that eventually led to the South seceding from the Union.[5]

When the Civil War broke out, the Confederacy fought to defend its institution of slave labor, but Northerners held a range of
opinions on slavery. Some were strongly opposed to the institution; others had no sympathy for the slaves. Witnessing the horrors of slavery while in the South turned many Northern soldiers
into abolitionists. Most Union soldiers were from small towns and
farms. They traveled little and may never have even seen an African
American, not to mention never having visited the slave states.
Seeing slavery firsthand, with its whippings, beatings, and degra-
dations, mortified the soldiers. Even if they had opposed Abraham
Lincoln in 1860, many wrote home to their anti-Lincoln families
about slavery, and their support pushed him over the top in a tough
reelection fight in 1864.[6]

The Civil War ended slavery in 1865, but it did not end the reliance on black labor for harvesting cotton for the textile mills. After
a brief period of federal occupation that ensured some rights for
the 4 million freed slaves, by the mid-1870s the white South began
retaking control over their former slaves and instituted a system of
sharecropping combined with segregation and organized violence
that ensured African Americans remained cheap and exploitable
labor. Sharecropping replaced slavery, but economic exploitation
and Jim Crow were far from the land-ownership and political
freedom African Americans demanded during Reconstruction. It
would take a century for the federal government to again care about
advancing the African American freedom agenda, and even then,

the civil rights movement never successfully rallied for a long-term federal commitment to economic justice.[7]

Winning the Civil War meant the Union needed unprecedented supplies, including guns, uniforms, bullets, food, and medicine. To fill this void, industrialists arose in new fields. John D. Rockefeller, soon to be the wealthiest man in American history, got his start in the oil business during the war, eventually creating the powerful Standard Oil monopoly. Financiers like Jay Gould and J.P. Morgan became new power players in the American economy, causing fear among people because of the control these very few men had over the nation's finances. The nation entered the Gilded Age, a period in American history marked by extreme income inequality, labor exploitation, and unsafe work. While the Republican Party was founded on limiting slavery, it also held industrial growth as key to national expansion. Most of these capitalists were Republicans, and they opposed slavery but also cared little about the conditions of workers. They used social Darwinism to justify their wealth, arguing that society reflected the survival of the fittest and their success proved their worthiness. They looked down on the nation's workers as undeserving drunkards from foreign lands who should feel grateful to have a job thanks to capitalists' beneficence.[8]

At best, they were like Andrew Carnegie, building libraries so that people could study in their off hours. Of course, when workers labored fourteen-hour days for little money, realistic education was impossible, but it made Carnegie feel as if he were doing something to assuage his guilt. Carnegie had plenty of that. In 1892, Carnegie and his chief lieutenant, Henry Clay Frick, decided to destroy the union that had successfully organized their Homestead steel mill just outside Pittsburgh. A unionized workplace was rare at the end of the nineteenth century, but the Amalgamated Association of Iron and Steel Workers won a surprising victory in 1889. This outraged and embarrassed Carnegie and Frick. With the union contract coming up in 1892, Carnegie decided to sail to his native Scotland and let Frick crush the union, avoiding direct implication in the matter himself. Frick offered an insulting contract, calling for a 22 percent wage decrease. When the workers struck, Frick called in the Pinkertons, a widely loathed private army of strikebreakers, to use violence against the union. As the Pinkertons tried to disembark from their boat on the shore of the Monongahela River, the workers met them with gunfire. Three Pinkertons and nine strikers died. The Pinkertons retreated, but the workers could not hold out against hunger, and the strike collapsed four months after it had started. The Homestead mill remained union-free for the next forty years. Carnegie openly expressed his guilt over his actions late in his life, but a few libraries could not make up for these crimes.[9]

In order to acquire the natural resources to power the booming Gilded Age economy, the nation drove Native Americans in the West onto reservations. The wars of conquest against the Native Americans would be largely completed by 1880, though the project of genocide would continue for nearly another century through Indian schools, the suppression of native languages, and forced elimination of traditional ways of life. With Native Americans off the land, capitalists could bring logs from Oregon, silver from Nevada, copper from Montana, and beef from Texas into the national marketplace. The government gave millions of acres of western land to railroad companies to build the transportation infrastructure needed to get those raw materials back east, subsidizing these corporate investments.[10]

Horrifying working conditions developed throughout the American West. When Chinese railroad workers, dying by the thousands building the Transcontinental Railroad over the Sierra Nevada, went on strike over the dangerous conditions of blasting tunnels through the mountains, the Central Pacific Railroad busted the strike by refusing to feed them. Isolated and starving, they had little choice but to work. Later, when workers fled back toward San Francisco, Central Pacific sent cowboys to round them up like animals. This was not quite slave labor, but it certainly was not free either. Mines collapsed throughout the West, trapping workers inside and killing them by the dozens. The whirring saws of the Northwest forests and timber mills took a horrible toll on workers. Thousands died over the decades.[11]

The terrible death toll of the unregulated economy became increasingly obvious to Americans during the late nineteenth century. Mining companies ran the Appalachian coal country like a medieval fiefdom, controlling every aspect of their workers' lives and murdering union organizers who challenged that authority. In 1907 alone, 3,242 people are known to have died in coal mining accidents.[12] Chopping away at coal in tiny underground spaces, miners inhaled coal dust, leading to pneumoconiosis, commonly known as black lung disease. The miners called it "miner's asthma" and knew why they were sick. But the coal companies denied any connection between work and illness. Coal company doctors even said coal mining was healthy and that the coal dust protected workers from the far greater hazard of tuberculosis. Despite scientific evidence clearly showing the connections between coal mining and lung disease, the coal industry successfully resisted any meaningful reforms to help workers until 1969. Even today the coal companies fight it. In 2013, a report by the Center for Public Integrity exposed how coal companies had used Dr. Paul Wheeler of Johns Hopkins University to deny thousands of miners black lung benefits. Wheeler served as an expert on at least 1,500 cases since 2000, never once finding coal workers' pneumoconiosis, the most severe form of black lung, in a worker, even though more than a hundred of these examined workers later died of the syndrome.[13] The situation in coal repeated itself over and over throughout the Gilded Age—in mining, logging, and meatpacking, in paint shops, watch factories, and textile mills. Corporations had an almost unlimited ability to poison and destroy their workers' bodies with no repercussions.[14]

Underlying all of this was massive business and political corruption. Gilded Age corporations enforced their will through friendly courts and politicians, often buying favors. Political scandals routinely rocked the nation as politicians looked to cash in on their corporate connections, even implicating Ulysses S. Grant's vice president Schuyler Colfax and future president James Garfield. Companies lied, cheated, and bribed their way to riches. They created massive railroad bubbles that sent the economy spiraling into depression when they busted in 1873 and 1893. In this pro-corporate atmosphere, courts routinely ruled against injured workers when they sued their employers for damages, saying they took on the risk of work when they agreed to the job. When people complained that industry polluted rivers, destroyed fish runs, and ruined their property, courts ruled that these were acceptable sacrifices in the name of progress. Corporations could pollute the air and water without the slightest concern or responsibility for the people affected. Companies used the federal and state governments as police forces against unions. Judges ruled labor legislation unconstitutional and interpreted antitrust laws designed to regulate business, such as the Sherman Antitrust Act, against unions while ignoring them for corporate actions. The Sherman Act, passed in 1890, intended to crack down on the monopolistic trusts of the Gilded Age that undermined consumer choice. The courts largely ignored the letter of the law. But because the law prohibited "restraint of commerce" across state lines, the courts did use the law to issue injunctions against labor unions whose strikes restricted trade by workers refusing to produce. In 1894, courts used this law against the Pullman Palace Car Company strikers, leading to the arrest and imprisonment of Eugene V. Debs and other labor leaders. Debs became a socialist while serving time in prison after his arrest.[15]

Plutocrats could also buy elections. Copper king William Clark directly bought a Montana Senate seat in 1899 by paying off state legislators with $140,000. A Senate resolution to declare his election void because of the fraud led to him vacating the seat in 1900, but in 1901 the state legislature sent him back to Washington, where he served one term. Clark later said, "I never bought a man who wasn't for sale." Actions like this led to the Seventeenth Amendment to the Constitution in 1913, mandating the direct election of senators. Today, many in the Tea Party want to repeal the amendment so that once again corporations can subvert democracy and rule with cronies.[16]

Workers in the late nineteenth century looked for answers to why rapacious capitalism had seemingly come out of nowhere to dominate their lives. In 1877, this discontent boiled over into the first large-scale working-class rebellion in American history. In Martinsburg, West Virginia, railroad workers walked off the job after their employer forced them to take their second pay cut in a year. The strike almost immediately spread to railroad workers from St. Louis to Chicago to Philadelphia. The Great Railroad Strike of 1877 brought the nation's transportation network to a halt. Thomas Alexander Scott, president of the Pennsylvania Railroad, said that strikers should receive a "rifle diet for a few days and see how they like that kind of bread." His hopes were answered in Pittsburgh on July 21 when militiamen fired on strikers, killing twenty. President Rutherford B. Hayes ordered the U.S. Army to crush the strike. Dozens more workers died. This set a precedent that the government would intervene with the police or military on the side of corporations. It happened again and again. President Grover Cleveland sent the military to break the Pullman Strike in Chicago in 1894 when workers walked off the job in protest of the company town lowering wages by 25 percent while keeping rental rates the same. In 1913, coal miners in southern Colorado working in mines owned by John D. Rockefeller Jr. went on strike for the eight-hour day, the right to choose their own homes and doctors, a pay raise, and the enforcement of existing state mine safety laws. In response, they were kicked out of the company town and forced to pitch tents. Then, on April 20, 1914, the Colorado National Guard and thugs from the Colorado Fuel and Iron Company decided to eliminate the tent town. After a day of killing strike leaders and burning the town, at least nineteen people had died, most of them women and children suffocated by the fire while hiding in a cellar built to escape the bullets.[17]

Despite this brutality, workers throughout the nation maintained the struggle for dignity, respect, and life. Through the Knights of Labor in the 1880s, the nation's first large labor union, hundreds of thousands of American workers demanded the eight-hour day. The government suppressed the movement's growing radicalism after a bomb went off in Chicago's Haymarket Square in 1886, killing seven policemen and leading to the execution of four Chicago-area anarchists without solid evidence of their culpability in the bombing. The Knights crumbled soon after, but the eight-hour demand remained a powerful dream for American workers.

Unemployment movements began in New York and Ohio. A riot occurred in Tompkins Square in New York City in 1874 when police became scared of a growing movement of the unemployed who wanted a meeting with the mayor of New York. In 1893, a railroad speculation bubble, caused by the unregulated capitalism of the Gilded Age, burst. The ensuing Panic of 1893 threw millions of Americans out of work. In response, a sand quarry owner named Jacob Coxey launched a march from Ohio to Washington, D.C., in 1894 to demand work. Coxey's Army scared the capitalists in Washington, who ordered the group's encampment destroyed. Coxey was arrested on charges of walking on the grass of the Capitol and imprisoned for twenty days.

The American Federation of Labor (AFL) was a longer-lasting movement. Formed in 1886, the AFL was led by Samuel Gompers, an immigrant cigar maker, and focused on craft work. Gompers and most of the unions making up the federation had the relatively conservative aims of improving wages and hours while ignoring larger political questions. The AFL showed little to no interest in organizing women, the new industrial workplaces, African Americans, children, and most immigrants. Because of this, its impact as a social force was severely limited. But for the workers it represented, AFL unions created real power on the job.[18]

After 1880, immigrants from southern and eastern Europe flooded into the United States to fill the millions of jobs spurred by American industrialization. In 1907 alone, 1.29 million immigrants entered the United States, 81 percent from southern and eastern Europe. Many brought socialist and anarchist ideas that began influencing workers' responses to capitalism. In 1892, after the Homestead Strike, Russian immigrant and anarchist Alexander Berkman attempted to assassinate steel magnate Henry Clay Frick. In 1901, anarchist Leon Czolgosz succeeded in killing President William McKinley at the Pan-American Exposition in Buffalo, New York. These actions scared corporate leaders, but not enough for them to do anything substantial to alleviate the conditions that caused such reactions. Instead, they called for vigorous policing of radicals. In 1905, the Industrial Workers of the World formed with the goal of organizing all American workers regardless of color, sex, or creed. Famous strikes in the textile mills of Paterson, New Jersey, and Lawrence, Massachusetts, and the farms, mines, and forests of the West followed. Organizers such as Joe Hill, Frank Little, Elizabeth Gurley Flynn, and Big Bill Haywood became American labor legends through their sacrifices for the IWW cause.[19]

In the South and Great Plains, the Farmers' Alliance, developed in the 1880s by farmers angry about how Gilded Age capitalism kept them in poverty, demanded economic fairness, political reform, and protection from avaricious railroads. They wanted federal regulation of utilities and transportation, currency policy that allowed everyday people to pay off their debts, income taxes, and the direct election of senators. Soon to become known as the Populists, they began running candidates for statewide office and then the presidency in 1892. Eventually co-opted by the Democratic Party in 1896, many Populist goals became law by World War I, even though the farmers remained poor. At the same time, middle-class Americans began to worry about the impact of unchecked capitalism on the nation. They believed in the capitalist system that had made their lives comfortable, but they also worried about the extreme poverty, class conflict, and income inequality of the late nineteenth century. This group, soon to be known as Progressives, sought to tame the excesses of Gilded Age capitalism, using voluntarism and some government action to fight corruption, end child labor, limit the hours of labor for women, pass workers' compensation legislation, and enact other reforms intended to smooth out the worst injustices of the period. Even before the Triangle Fire, female reformers such as Jane Addams and Florence Kelley, working out of urban settlement houses, were pressing for child labor laws and a limitation on the working hours of women. The eight-hour day gained additional support. Photographers such as Lewis Hine and writers such as Jacob Riis brought the conditions of America's poor to the attention of the middle and upper classes through their powerful documentary arts.[20]

Other Progressives became concerned about the corporate despoilment of American nature. Would the nation continue to grow if America did not protect its timber, wildlife, and clean water? This worried a new generation of young elites such as Theodore Roosevelt, who saw an expanding young nation flexing its muscles threatened by the very corporations profiting off of its bountiful resources. Decades of timber companies despoiling forests in states such as Maine, Michigan, and Alabama led to Roosevelt's creation of the U.S. Forest Service in 1905 before the trees of Washington and Oregon disappeared, too. Agencies like the Forest Service served as an important precedent for the government taking control over the nation's natural resources from corporations who would pillage them and leave residents to deal with the aftermath.[21]

The Progressives continued gaining momentum on their reforms throughout the 1910s, but when the United States entered World War I in 1917, corporations and the government used it as an excuse to crack down on the militants challenging corporate domination over American life. The federal government passed the Espionage Act (1917) and Sedition Act (1918), both severe crackdowns on civil liberties that made criticizing the war effort a crime. Despite a complete lack of evidence, the IWW was tied to pro-kaiser sentiment. Among many Americans, anti-immigrant feelings ran amok and many Wobblies were immigrants. In Bisbee, Arizona, copper mine companies rounded up suspected IWW members, loaded them on train cars, and dropped them in the desert near the New Mexico border, using the fear of German sympathy as an excuse to clear their town of radicals. In the Northwest, the U.S. Army had to create a logging division because the terrible working conditions of the timber camps caused so many strikes that the military could not acquire the Sitka spruce it needed for airplane construction. The army reformed the timber camps and reorganized labor under its auspices. In doing so, it banned active IWW members from working, effectively destroying the union in the forests. The Red Scare continued after the war. Starting in 1919, 556 radicals were rounded up and deported as part of the Palmer Raids, a widespread expulsion of immigrant radicals the government feared would launch a violent revolution.

One of the exported radicals was Emma Goldman, a longtime

anarchist, birth control advocate, and lover of Alexander Berkman, the man who had attempted to assassinate Henry Clay Frick in 1892. Arrested for encouraging Americans to resist the draft, Goldman was deported to the Soviet Union, which she soon left and moved to Toronto. Meanwhile, Big Bill Haywood, the one-eyed miner who started his career organizing the Colorado miners and was leader of the IWW from its beginning in 1905, fled to the newly founded Soviet Union to escape prison time for urging a strike during the war. Haywood would die in exile. The nation declared an abrupt end to the reforms of the 1910s, and workers would have to wait another generation before achieving significant power in the workplace.[22]

The antiradical feelings expressed during the war would continue during the 1920s. The Immigration Act of 1924 ended most immigration from eastern and southern Europe for the next four decades. Yet southwestern farmers, dependent on exploiting Mexican labor to pick crops, carved out exceptions to the law allowing Mexican migration and creating a tradition of exempting agricultural labor from labor law, a tradition that contributes to poor conditions and low wages for farmworkers to the present day. The nation's employers went on the offensive against the labor movement, busting both radical and AFL unions and creating company unions that granted workers a few amenities but no power. Corporate profits built on unsound credit and a lack of government regulation allowed shady financial practices to rule the 1920s. The top 1 percent of income earners made more money than the bottom 42 percent combined. The nation's love affair with its new rich obscured deepening poverty on its farms and in its cities.[23]

The bubble burst in the fall of 1929 with the Great Depression. By the winter of 1933, unemployment reached 25 percent. Millions more worked short hours and were underemployed and poor. President Herbert Hoover showed little sympathy, instead calling on Americans to organize relief groups in their local communities. But communities were completely overwhelmed by the scale of the problem, and Hoover, who feared the effects of welfare on people's work ethic, did far too little to use government to help. When

World War I veterans marched on Washington, D.C., in 1932 to demand that a $1,000 bonus promised to be paid in 1945 be issued immediately, not only did Hoover refuse, he sent the army under Douglas MacArthur and George Patton to burn the Bonus Army protesters' camp. Americans became disgusted with the government's callousness toward poverty. Membership in the Communist Party grew, while people such as Father Charles Coughlin, a right-wing Catholic priest with a popular radio show, offered a proto-fascist challenge to democracy. People around the world turned to communism and fascism as potential solutions, and the rise of the Nazi Party in Germany led to concerns that such movements could overtake democratic countries around Europe and maybe even the United States.[24]

Anger over Hoover's weak response to the Great Depression led to the election of Franklin Roosevelt in 1932 and a shift in American politics away from the Republican Party that would last a half century. Roosevelt's New Deal, a series of programs intended to stimulate the economy through short-term employment programs and new regulations designed to prevent similar crises in the future, reoriented the purpose of government toward leveling the playing field between workers and corporations. Regulations on banking, government employment programs, Social Security, and a national minimum wage combined to give working Americans hope for the future. Federal programs like the Works Progress Administration, Civilian Conservation Corps, and Public Works Administration not only put Americans to work and alleviated poverty but also built the infrastructure that created a powerful United States after World War II. Americans today still benefit from the roads, schools, post offices, and hiking trials constructed by New Deal workers.[25]

In 1934, encouraged by early New Deal legislation that seemed favorable to unions, workers around the country struck in protest of the low wages they were receiving for their hard work. Teamsters in Minneapolis, longshoremen in San Francisco, autoworkers in Toledo, and textile workers in New England and the South walked out in one of the largest strike waves in the nation's history. The National Labor Relations Act of 1935 codified a new regime in labor relations, creating the National Labor Relations Board and forcing embittered employers to recognize unions. The Fair Labor Standards Act of 1938 created the federal minimum wage and mandated overtime pay after a forty-hour workweek.[26]

In 1935, United Mine Workers of America president John L. Lewis created the Committee for Industrial Organization within the American Federation of Labor in order to organize all workers in a factory into a single union. The AFL had traditionally opposed this kind of organizing, preferring that workers organize around skill rather than industry. This meant there were millions of Americans who wanted to be in unions but were unable to join them. The CIO stepped in, breaking away from the AFL in 1936 after Lewis punched the anti-industrial unionist United Brotherhood of Carpenters president Big Bill Hutcheson in the face during the AFL national convention. Now called the Congress of Industrial Organizations, the CIO quickly moved to organize the big industrial factories of the Northeast and Midwest. Autoworkers in Flint, Michigan, sat down on the job in their General Motors plant to demand union recognition. GM wanted to use the National Guard to evict the strikers, but workers had elected Frank Murphy governor of Michigan and the pro-union future Supreme Court justice refused, instead sending troops in to protect the strikers from GM strikebreakers. The landslide victory for the United Auto Workers (UAW) led to a wave of industrial organizing and the growth of the CIO across the nation's industrial belt. Total union membership in the United States surged from fewer than 4 million to more than 10 million workers during the 1930s. By 1945, the CIO had 6 million members, led by the UAW and United Steelworkers of America.[27]

American workers did much with that new voice. During World War II, corporations hoped to crush unions again, as they had during World War I, but the unions fought to maintain their hard-won gains. Although they issued a no-strike pledge during the war, unions sought to increase wages so that workers could partake in the huge wartime profits. Workers were champing at the bit to strike because they wanted a bigger piece of the growing economic pie. The Roosevelt administration instituted wage and price controls, but short wildcat strikes sprang up throughout the war. The government told workers to wait until the end of the war, but after more than a decade of depression and war workers were tired of sacrificing.[28]

Reconstructing the free world after World War II also led to the creation of new international financial institutions that would later create tremendous incentives for unrestricted free trade and the export of work around the world. In 1944, at a conference in Bretton Woods, New Hampshire, the United States and its allies created the International Monetary Fund (IMF). The IMF pegged international currency to the U.S. dollar, making the U.S. economy the backbone of the international economy after the war. They also founded the World Bank, creating an international lending institution that would receive money only if it played by the rules of U.S. and western European bankers and politicians. This would eventually severely undercut development options for the nations of the developing world, opening them up to American corporate exploitation. Finally, in 1947, the General Agreement on Tariffs and Trade (GATT) was created to reduce tariffs and trade barriers around the world, creating an integrated global economy open to U.S. products and investment. Together, these institutions vastly increased the wealth and power of American corporations. At first, this did not come at a negative cost to most U.S. labor, and it even had support from labor leaders, but as growing global integration opened up poor nations for American investment in new factories without tariffs as products crossed the U.S. border, the effects would become cataclysmic for American workers.[29]

At the end of the war, workers' pent-up desire for higher wages blew up in the 1946 strike wave. Four and a half million Americans went on strike that year, the largest labor stoppage in American history. A general strike of one hundred thousand workers in Oakland, California, sparked by workers' anger at low wages and police cooperation with employers to suppress labor shut down the city for two days. Workers throughout the country received major wage increases that year. But this new militancy scared conservatives as they connected it with the growing political power of Soviet communism, even if few of the people on strike had any interest in the Communist Party. The Taft-Hartley Act of 1947, passed by Congress over President Harry S. Truman's veto, showed the power of antilabor conservatism in American politics. Taft-Hartley outlawed many of labor's most successful tactics, such as secondary strikes and wildcat strikes, while forcing union leaders to take a pledge that they did not belong to the Communist Party. Organized labor has never recovered from the blow and has never even come close to raising enough support in Congress to defeat or even modify the odious law. Shedding its radical past, the CIO expelled its communist-led unions from the federation, and radicals within other unions were fired as well.[30]

Yet despite this, organized labor's power in the workplace continued to grow into the 1950s. Union contracts turned traditional low-paying industrial jobs into increasingly well-compensated positions. Workers could buy houses. The GI Bill allowed veterans to receive higher education. Benefits and pensions became a normal part of a working person's expectations. Gains for African American workers lagged because of racism within government, companies, and unions that wanted to keep jobs reserved for whites. But they also managed to make significant economic gains as they fought their way into the industrial workforce. Women entered the workforce in record numbers, and while gender discrimination was a major problem in all tiers of employment, women expressed their own demands from their employers and from their unions. In 1945, the Airline Stewardesses Association started a decades-long fight by flight attendants resisting the age and weight discrimination they faced on the job. Corporations tried to repel all of these gains. In 1959, the steel companies attempted to retake control over the shop floor and weaken the unions, but the United Steelworkers of America went on strike and won, despite the Eisenhower administration invoking Taft-Hartley against the union. For both unions and corporations, 1959 was a far cry from 1929. Unions thought the bad old days would never return. So did corporate leaders, who longed to take power away from the hated unions.[31]

Companies were shocked at this sudden turn in their fortunes.

They hated the existence of unions, but it would take decades before they would be able to develop a strategy to re-create the union-free workplaces of the Gilded Age. After World War II, business groups such as the National Association of Manufacturers created bitter propaganda against labor unions and the New Deal, claiming they undermined American values and were turning the United States socialist. Corporations developed business curricula for public schools, reached out to evangelical Protestant churches, started children's programs for their workers, and taught workers that taxes were bad, all in order to create allegiance between workers and employers and reclaim corporations' role as not just economic leaders of America but political and moral leaders as well.[32]

Capital mobility slowly became central to the new antiunion strategy. This began with textile companies in the late nineteenth century, but it did not really become a central tenet of corporate strategy until the 1960s. Shuttering unionized workplaces and re-opening them in nonunion states and countries would eventually become the corporate trump card over all challenges to their control. Workers continued fighting for justice wherever corporations exploited them, but those fights were undermined by the very real fear of their jobs going away. Retaking control of the workplace through geographical subterfuge not only helped crush the unions, but in doing so weakened the voices of everyday people in American political life, starting a downward spiral for the American middle class and creating a new global Gilded Age, a phenomenon deepening in the world today.

As early as the 1880s, textile companies looking to avoid strikes in the Northeast started setting up shop in the South. Larger industrial firms expanded upon this in the 1930s. Immediately after workers at a General Motors plant in Flint, Michigan, won their 1937 sit-in to establish the United Auto Workers as their union, GM started moving production out of that plant to Buffalo, New York, in order to undermine the company's reliance on activist workers. As the historian Jefferson Cowie has shown, the Radio Corporation of America (RCA) began to move its operations from Camden, New Jersey, to Bloomington, Indiana, after workers successfully organized unions at its factory in the Garden State in the 1930s. When Indiana workers did the same, RCA repeated the process twice more over the next forty years, moving first to Tennessee and then to Mexico. But moving operations to the South was just the tip of the iceberg for corporate America. After 1960, this strategy would grow rapidly, helped by faster communication and transportation technologies that would revolutionize employment around the world.[33]

The actions of General Motors, RCA, and other corporations that made early moves to avoid unions sounded an alarm to the CIO, which realized it had to organize the South in order to survive and prosper; otherwise, industries would simply move operations there. In 1946, the CIO placed a huge investment in organizing southern factories in what became known as Operation Dixie. Companies played up racial divides in their southern factories to discourage union organizing, and the largely northeastern-based CIO organizers lacked a fluid understanding of organizing in the South. The CIO's strategy to downplay racial equality in order to attract white workers alienated the black workers excited about unionization while also not actually attracting many whites. Operation Dixie was an abject failure, and the CIO's fears of increasing numbers of companies looking to the South for cheaper labor soon came true. The rise of anticommunism led to the passage of the Taft-Hartley Act and the expulsion of the communists from organized labor. With these events, the CIO soon ended its militant phase. In 1955, it would rejoin with the American Federation of Labor, a sensible move since by then it differed little from that older federation. The era of workers' unions directly challenging corporate control over the nation had ended.[34]

The failure of Operation Dixie does not mean all southern workers were hostile to unions. In 1934, textile workers across the East Coast went on strike, including in the South, which by then produced 70 percent of American textiles. Southern mill workers wanted a reduction of their fifty-five- to sixty-hour workweek and an end to the notorious "speedup," which made workers labor ever faster in order to expand profits without employers hiring more workers. While the strike was defeated, it first alarmed clothing companies to the potential for unionization in their previously nonunion plants. Despite Operation Dixie's ultimate failure, many workers enthusiastically supported the CIO. In the 1970s, the textile plants again experienced a union drive. Most famously, Crystal Lee Sutton, a worker at a J.P. Stevens textile mill in Roanoke Rapids, North Carolina, began organizing her fellow workers who had tired of the plant's poor working conditions. Her boss fired Sutton, but before she left she wrote the word UNION on a large placard, stood on a table, and held it out proudly before walking out the door. As she did so, her fellow workers, who wanted a union but feared losing their jobs, shut down their machines one by one. Sutton's bravery helped the successful organizing campaign of her plant into the Amalgamated Clothing and Textile Workers Union in 1974. A fictional version of Sutton's life reached the big screen in the 1979 film *Norma Rae* starring Sally Field.[35]

But the textile companies were planning to relocate out of the South to cheaper labor even before pesky women started organizing unions. In the early twentieth century, a few textile manufacturers experimented with producing goods in Puerto Rico and fought to keep U.S. labor laws from applying to the colony. Even when the laws did apply, the American government did little to enforce them. The federal minimum wage did not apply to Puerto Rico until 1975, and Puerto Rican officials used its cheap labor to appeal to New England textile manufacturers.[36]

But the real beginning of modern corporate outsourcing was the creation of the Border Industrialization Program by Mexico in 1965, which encouraged American companies to move south of the U.S.-Mexico border to take advantage of low wages. For twenty years prior, Mexico had sent labor north to the United States through the Bracero Program, under which Mexican workers would sign contracts with American employers and then return home when the contracts expired. The braceros were highly exploited and suffered overcrowded housing, dangerously hot fields without shade or proper water, and stolen wages. Mexico finally canceled the program in 1964, in part because of these abuses.

The Border Industrialization Program, designed with advice from American corporations interested in moving abroad, intended to keep Mexican labor south of the border and lure U.S. corporations to it. Corporate investment in overseas factories received support from both Democrats and Republicans, including President Lyndon Johnson.[37]

The Border Industrialization Program started an enormous growth in the number of nations attracting American work that continues today. Between 1982 and 1988 alone, the number of maquiladoras, industrial plants constructed just on the Mexican side of the U.S.-Mexico border for export production, jumped from 500 to 1,500, and the number of workers increased from 150,000 to 360,000. Asian and Latin American nations began creating free trade zones where foreign companies could invest in new factories without having to pay tariffs for the export market. For example, Mexico taxed U.S. exports from maquiladoras only 3.5 percent versus around 10 percent from other parts of the nation. Taking advantage of such low costs, American steel companies laid off 40 percent of their workers between 1979 and 1984 while the United Auto Workers lost half its members between 1970 and 1985. The incentives to move became ever greater. As late as the 1990s, there were tens of thousands of jobs in textile plants in the American South. But these were the last remnants of a once-robust manufacturing base. Beginning in 1995, for instance, Fruit of the Loom closed a series of Alabama mills and moved production to Mexico, Central America, and the Caribbean, a process that continued through 2009, when two last factories closed, laying off 270 workers.[38]

Labor responded with "Buy American" campaigns that made short-term sense for beleaguered and scared workers but created divisions across borders and made solidarity with the aspiring working classes of foreign nations impossible, accompanied as these campaigns were by American rhetoric about Mexican, Japanese, or Chinese workers "stealing our jobs." For UAW members, it seemed like a good idea to destroy a Toyota with sledgehammers. Unfortunately, as historian Dana Frank has delineated, corporations, politicians, and even union executives constructed an

illusion that only two choices were possible—globalization or protectionism. In fact, there was and is much room in the economy for
good jobs at home and American corporate investment overseas,
but business leaders were able to use this false dilemma to paint
unions as backward organizations restricting the economy and
making a future of all industrial labor exported overseas seem inevitable. In any case, for union leadership, hostility toward foreign
competition was easier than reaching out to Asian workers or organizing Japanese-owned auto plants in the United States, which first
opened in the early 1980s as a response to pressure from American
politicians about auto imports.[39]

By the 1970s and 1980s, companies began becoming more aggressive in repealing the gains of the working class. Led by free
market economist Milton Friedman, scholars worked with corporations and business-friendly politicians to undermine unions,
the welfare state, and decent lives for working people in the United
States and around the world. Conservative politicians such as
Ronald Reagan in the United States and Margaret Thatcher in
Great Britain embraced this new economic orthodoxy. Both im-
plemented corporate-friendly policies and busted powerful unions
in the 1980s. In the United States in 1981, the attack on unions
went national. That year, the Professional Air Traffic Controllers
Organization (PATCO) went on strike, shutting down the nation's
air system. They had legitimate beefs. They were overworked and
underpaid and were angry at the government for their poor treatment. In fact, the union's relationship with the Carter administration was so bad that PATCO was one of the only unions to endorse
Ronald Reagan in 1980. But when the air traffic controllers went
on strike, Reagan chose to fire them all. Despite the great danger—
never realized—that the use of untrained replacements would lead
to airplane crashes, Reagan's move was politically popular and
foreshadowed national approval for a new aggressive antilabor
stance. The following years would see a stark rise in corporate attacks on their unions. In 1983, the Phelps Dodge mining company
in Arizona completely eliminated its unions. The state of Arizona
created a state private detective association to assist Phelps Dodge

in its antiunion activities. Despite a heroic and desperate attempt to hold on, the United Steelworkers of America and the other smaller unions in the mines were crushed.[40]

Deregulation became the order of the day, both in the United States and in developing nations. Governments withdrew from their commitments to the poor, and corporations took over basic services. For instance, hundreds of American cities privatized their water, and today cities and states are slowly privatizing public schools to crush teachers' unions. Corporations used the language of freedom—*free markets* and *free trade*—to describe actions that took freedom away from people around the world. The International Monetary Fund and the World Bank demanded that poor nations slash funding and privatize social services in order to receive needed loans. The economic and social upheaval this caused opened up the developing world to corporate exploitation as there were few labor or environmental stipulations in nations now desperate for work and investment.[41]

By the 1990s, the prophets of globalization were in complete control of the world economy. Questioning globalization, promoting unions, or demanding corporate accountability to the world's citizens became unfashionable among elite opinion makers and politicians. Former World Trade Organization director general Renato Ruggiero said fighting globalization was "tantamount to trying to stop the rotation of the earth," while Bill Clinton stated that globalization was "not a policy choice, it's a fact."[42] When American union members did indeed question globalization, not wanting to lose their jobs, they were called old-fashioned and out of touch. When environmentalists protested the lack of meaningful protections in the treaties that enabled globalization, they were seen as irrelevant.

Capital mobility's seemingly unstoppable momentum reached its peak with the enactment of the North American Free Trade Agreement (NAFTA) in 1994. NAFTA eliminated tariffs on most products passing between the United States, Mexico, and Canada, creating the largest free trade bloc in the world. Tariff elimination would incentivize American and Canadian investment in factories sited in Mexico, allowing corporations to avoid the high wages and union contracts of their home nations. Organized labor fought hard against NAFTA, seeing it as the job killer it would prove to be, while environmentalists worried that it would outsource American corporate pollution to Mexico. Some environmental groups such as the National Audubon Society decided in the end to support NAFTA to gain leverage on environmental issues with the Clinton administration, while others, such as Friends of the Earth, the Sierra Club, and Greenpeace, staunchly opposed the treaty. Despite all this opposition, President Clinton decided to make NAFTA a centerpiece of his new moderate, pro-business Democratic Party. He paid lip service to workers' and environmentalists' complaints but showed no interest in mandating enforceable labor and environmental standards in the final agreement. Clinton said, "NAFTA means jobs. American jobs, and good-paying American jobs. If I didn't believe that, I wouldn't support this agreement." Maybe Clinton did believe this, but it never came true. The passage of NAFTA allowed the flight of American manufacturing to enter its peak phase. Between 1994 and 2010, American trade deficits with Mexico were $97.2 billion, displacing 682,900 jobs. Of those, about 80 percent were U.S. manufacturing jobs. Since the passage of NAFTA, the United States has lost 5 million manufacturing jobs.[43]

Almost immediately after the passage of NAFTA, employers began to use their ability to pack up and move to Mexico as a direct threat against unions. A 1996 report by labor scholar Kate Bronfenbrenner showed that it was widespread for companies to use capital mobility as an intimidation tactic against unionization attempts. In a survey of workers in over 600 organizing or first contract campaigns between 1993 and 1995, Bronfenbrenner found that 62 percent of bosses in mobile industries, such as manufacturing, threatened to close the factory if workers voted for the union and 15 percent actually did shut down and move, triple the rate of the late 1980s. In 19 percent of union election campaigns, bosses actually threatened to move to Mexico as an intimidation tactic, taping maps of North America with arrows pointing to Mexico or sticking Mexican address labels on machines. Bronfenbrenner concluded, "NAFTA has created a climate that has emboldened employers to more aggressively threaten to close, or actually close their plants to avoid unionization."[44]

Aggressive corporate mobility shocked organized labor. Unions were caught off guard. Labor's radical organizing tradition had been a distant memory as early as the 1970s. Unions found themselves completely unable to offer a strategy of resistance. In 1997, General Motors announced a plan to increase its workforce in Mexico from 300,000 to 607,000 workers. When the UAW went on strike, GM agreed to "slow the erosion" of jobs and the parties came to an agreement after fifty-four days. The next week, the company announced plans to send more jobs to Mexico. American workers have suffered such defeats again and again over the past forty years. Twenty-four percent of corporate executives in a 1992 survey admitted they would use NAFTA to drive down wages in their American workplaces. American unions had no effective response to this newfound aggression.[45]

Union membership plummeted as members of the industrial unions that made up the heart of the American labor movement found their jobs exported to Mexico, Taiwan, and China. In 1950, 36 percent of nonagricultural workers in the United States were union members. This fell to 12.5 percent in 2005 and 11.3 percent in 2013. Even that number obscures the collapse of unions because in 1950 there were no organized public sector workers, a group that today makes up a growing percentage of organized labor. Only 6.7 percent of private sector workers were union members in 2013.[46] As unions become weaker and lose the financial base to hire organizers or influence legislation in Washington, they have less ability to fight off additional attacks on wages and working conditions. With each crushed union local, corporations have more political power in Washington and more control to shape the lives of American workers without opposition. In 2006, the Ford Motor Company announced a $14 billion investment in opening new factories in Mexico while closing fourteen plants in the United States and slashing thirty thousand mostly unionized jobs. The UAW could do nothing.[47]

A Ford plant with UAW representation defined mid-twentieth-century American work, even if not all American workers won such excellent union contracts. Walmart defines twenty-first-century American work. The supply chain economy has replaced the industrial economy. Taking its cue from the century of apparel industry exploitation that led to the Triangle Fire and Rana Plaza collapse, Walmart has a business model predicated on outsourcing products to the cheapest possible production points. It requires suppliers to fulfill large orders at low prices, and it takes no responsibility for the conditions in which those products are made. This silence on the working conditions of global supply chains not-so-subtly encourages the exploitation of workers as the only way to fill those contracts. Within its stores, Walmart pays low wages, offers few benefits, and is vociferously antiunion. There are no unionized Walmart stores in the United States, despite significant worker discontent and constant interest by the United Food and Commercial Workers International Union in organizing the stores. Walmart thrives in a nation and a world lacking stable, well-paid work. Industries ranging from automobiles to electronics have been built on Walmart's model. Supply chain management is a growing major at many colleges and universities as higher education adjusts to a new world of a business model based upon a global sourcing of products predicated on low prices and the necessity of cheap labor.[48]

Most other American employers have followed Walmart's path of depressing the lives of American workers. The temp worker industry has allowed employers to outsource the risk of new employees to contractors at low cost to themselves, sometimes classifying workers as "temporary" even if they have worked in the same place for a decade.[49] The pensions and health care plans without large co-pays of the late twentieth century are things of the past. And if workers in the United States complain about the conditions of their work, the work itself can be outsourced, either directly through corporate mobility or through the supply chains that allow companies to outsource production around the world through contractors, the system in place in Sohel Rana's collapsed Bangladeshi factory. Service workers in American call centers often work twelve-hour days with few benefits; if they complain, their companies will move the call centers to India or the Philippines, where workers make a quarter of American workers' wages. This phenomenon has increasingly spread to the middle class as well, with computing, legal work, and medicine increasingly outsourced to India and other nations with large English-speaking populations. The future of the middle class is increasingly precarious because of this phenomenon.[50]

We now have a society in which corporate heads and elite share-holders own the vast majority of the world's wealth. In 2013, the United States reached levels of income inequality not seen since 1928, the year before the Great Depression. Companies do not need to treat workers poorly to make money; the high corporate profits of the heavily unionized postwar American economy demonstrate this fact. But the harsher the working conditions and the more companies can avoid responsibility for the catastrophes they cause, the more money can go into the pockets of the rich. Consumers pay high prices for Apple products because of the look, the functional-ity, and the cultural cachet of the machines. Because of this, Apple is a tremendously profitable company. Many Americans looked upon Steve Jobs as a hero before his death. But he made the explicit decision to run his company on the cheapest labor possible. Apple outsourced its production to Foxconn Technology, a Chinese com-pany at whose factories conditions became so bad that the company had to install suicide nets so that workers would stop throwing themselves to their deaths from the tops of the buildings. Without overtime, workers at Foxconn make less than $2,000 a year, not even enough for food according to angry workers. This means an eleven-hour day in order to make the minimum income for food and shelter. Meanwhile, a new Apple laptop sells for $2,000. Those isolated acts of suicide have begun melding into a more concen-trated demand for change. Foxconn workers have gone on strike re-peatedly in recent years. Apple could easily order that more money be paid to the workers making its products or open a new factory that treated workers with respect. Instead, it continues to reap soar-ing profits from degraded workers.[51]

Cambodian apparel workers make the national minimum wage of $80 per month to make clothing for Levi's, Puma, Adidas, Columbia, Gap, and other apparel companies. Even in impoverished Cambodia this is nowhere close to a living wage. Cambodian prime minister Hun Sen, who has ruled the nation since 1985, has allied himself closely with apparel companies. Protests against low wages and political corruption at the end of 2013 and continuing through 2014 have led to the greatest challenge to Hun Sen's rule. Workers are demanding a doubling of the minimum wage, which would allow them to live dignified lives. In January 2014, the Cambodian police killed five protesters, and at least twenty-three others have disappeared. The Garment Manufacturers Association in Cambodia lauded the crackdown, and union leaders fled the capital of Phnom Penh. With the exception of mild rebuke from a few European companies, the apparel industry has remained silent.[52]

In the late 1990s, the antisweatshop and free trade movements made important links with the labor, human rights, and environmental movements to begin standing up against the neoliberal free trade regime rapidly transforming the world and concentrating resources in the hands of the global 1 percent. In November 1999, activists from around the nation and world met in Seattle to protest the meeting of the World Trade Organization, one of the key international financial institutions pressing the expansion of free trade without democratic accountability to citizens. The excitement over the coming protests was palpable among activist communities. "Teamsters and Turtles" was the order the day, as unions, environmentalists, and other groups put aside differences to unite for justice and solidarity with one another's causes. The common enemy of neoliberal globalization had great power to unite.

However, the protest did not go as planned. A few black-bloc anarchists derailed the protests by breaking windows and committing other low-level crimes. This gave the nervous police force of the city of Seattle an excuse to crack down on all the protesters. The lack of democracy in neoliberal decision making became all too obvious to activists on the streets of Seattle as tear gas and truncheons trumped nonviolence and peaceful protest. But perhaps most notable was the inability of the mass movement that came together in Seattle to hold together for further protest. With police forces restricting protesters at future world economic meetings to "free speech zones" that were really more like fenced-off segregated areas, the ability to use space to disrupt meetings disappeared. Divisions among the movements sprang back up, and as each interest group returned to fighting its own battles the spirit of solidarity faded. Finally, the terrorist attacks of September 11, 2001, and the American invasion of Iraq turned the attention of the activist community away from economic justice and toward fighting American militarism and imperialism. While the transition of activists to protesting the war in Iraq was righteous and justified, the relatively short attention span of activist communities also holds important lessons about the limitations of calling upon a mass movement to rally for change and just how more permanent progressive transformations have taken place in U.S. history, a topic this book will revisit in greater detail in its final chapter.

Americans are finally starting to protest the economic inequality and environmental costs of this new Gilded Age. The brief but spectacular run of Occupy Wall Street spread across the United States and placed debt and economic inequality back in the nation's attention. Occupy lacked a consistent critique of corporate behavior and concrete demands it could build on outside of the public plazas where it grew and eventually stagnated. Both of these problems helped contribute to its decline, but Occupy Wall Street demonstrated the anger many Americans feel—and not only those with the time and ability to protest on the street—about a nation with a declining middle class. Workers at McDonald's, Walmart, and other outposts of the service industry have participated in protests for wage increases, helping to spark new political momentum to raise state and national minimum wages. In 2014, Seattle voters elected avowed socialist Kshama Sawant to the city council, a sign of growing interest in stronger challenges to capitalism. That city passed a $15-an-hour minimum wage in May 2014. Even President Obama is now pressing for a national $10.10-an-hour minimum wage, still too low for people to make a respectable living but a significant improvement over the current atrocious $7.25 an hour. Ideally, a national minimum wage of at least $15 an hour tied to inflation would help solve income inequality. This is a cause for which we should fight.

Globalization destroyed the security of the American working class without giving workers in other places around the world the chance to create middle-class lifestyles for themselves. To quote sociologists Frances Fox Piven and Richard Cloward, "Globalization . . . seems to puncture the century-old belief in worker power. If workers once seemed to have economic power over employers because they could withdraw their labor, now they have to worry about the virtually boundless army of workers across the globe ready to replace them."[53] Instead, we have a global elite class in New York, London, Dubai, and Beijing taking advantage of the vast masses of the world's poor and creating huge global income inequality. When people in one place organize to improve their wages and lives, the companies move on again, looking for yet another nation to exploit. For two centuries, corporations have sought to keep workers in poverty while workers have fought to live dignified lives. Just when workers succeeded in the United States, corporations discovered capital mobility and global supply chains, making it nearly impossible for workers anywhere to win major victories and establishing a global Gilded Age. Corporations have moved their catastrophes around the world with increasing impunity. This is how corporations operate in the twenty-first century, and this is the behavior that we must tame.

2

WORKPLACE CATASTROPHES

In 1973, members of the Oil, Chemical, and Atomic Workers International Union (OCAW) went on strike against Shell Oil after the company refused to sign a contract with strong safety and health provisions. The union's legislative director, Tony Mazzocchi, emphasized the connections between working conditions and environmental protection. The same chemicals that polluted the air and water also exposed workers to toxins and threatened their health. Mazzocchi said, "Environmental concern is spreading; the problem cannot be dealt with unless we start with the workplace. A degraded work environment ultimately affects the general environment."[1] Mazzocchi fought for vigorous workplace safety programs in union contracts, empowered union members to become activists for workplace health, and built bridges between the labor and environmental movements.

Within a week of the strike's beginning, eleven of the nation's largest environmental organizations, including the Natural Resources Defense Council, the Izaak Walton League of America, and Friends of the Earth, endorsed the strike. In a press release, they stated, "We support the efforts of the OCAW in demanding a better environment, not just for its own workers, but for all Americans." Environmental groups encouraged their members to return their Shell credit cards, walk on OCAW picket lines, and think of toxic waste as something that affected both workers and themselves. The OCAW did not win the strike, as Shell held out and the union's strike fund became depleted to the point that it had to settle without the vigorous safety and health protections. But the alliance between labor and environmentalists grew and helped lead to environmental and workplace legislation including the Toxic Substances Control Act of 1976, a revised Clean Air Act in 1977, and the creation of Superfund, a program that mandated the cleanup of toxic sites, in 1980.[2]

Unions give workers power on the job. From the beginning of industrial America, workers have united to fight for dignified labor. That might mean better wages, it might mean shorter hours, or it might mean the ability to speak out about the conditions of your job without getting fired. In the case of the OCAW in 1973, it was to protect themselves from a dangerous workplace environment. More than a century of dangerous work and pollution had convinced workers and citizens to demand responsible corporate policies that treated workers and the planet with dignity. The labor and environmental movements that arose would create great change in the United States. So long as corporations mostly maintained their factories in a particular place, those movements could be effective because affected peoples organized to prevent additional catastrophes from harming their communities.

But most corporations hate unions. They loathe their very existence. The idea that workers can have a say in the conditions of labor is an affront to people who see themselves as "makers," providing jobs for the rest of us. There is the occasional rare exception that sees good relationship with unions as a reasonable price of doing business, but they are so unusual as to be famous for their generosity toward workers. So workers dictating safe work outrages corporate leaders, who have always sought to keep themselves from being held responsible when workers get sick or die on the job. It was that way for the paint workers suffering lead poisoning in the nineteenth century and the blast furnace workers in steel mills in the early twentieth century. Such it is today for Foxconn workers in China producing computers for Apple. Outsourcing work allows companies to escape the unions and the workplace regulations that made American labor safe and created the middle class. In doing so, corporations have imperiled the future of the 99 percent.

It did not take long after Samuel Slater opened the first modern factory in the United States in 1793 for industrial work to become dangerous. As the economy grew in the nineteenth century, protections for workers were an expense industrialists would not justify. In 1837, a train engineer named Nicholas Farwell fell off his train because of unsafe conditions, losing his hand. He sued for damages. With modern corporations just developing, it was unclear what would come of it. Five years later, in the case of *Farwell v. Boston and Worcester Railroad Corporation*, the Massachusetts Supreme Court decided that the railroad company had no liability because the worker agreed to take on the risk when he took the job. This doctrine of workplace risk meant corporations had no responsibility to their employees. "Worker Beware" became the reality every second at work. For decades, courts consistently backed up employers, ruling that if a worker did not want to accept the risk, that worker could get a job somewhere else.[3]

But there was nowhere else for the vast majority of workers to go in a society with no economic safety net except to other dangerous jobs or into unemployment. So workers became sick and died or perished in workplace accidents. Perhaps no industry was as notorious for indifference to worker safety as coal mining. Underground coal mining created a dangerous environment. Flooded mines forced workers to toil in standing water. Hazardous gases filled the cramped spaces, and miners inhaled stale, bad air with low oxygen content. They relied on animals to warn them when the gases turned deadly. Explosions were frequent, and carbon monoxide seeping through mines felled workers after the blasts. Coal dust coated miners' lungs and gave them what is today known as pneumoconiosis, or black lung disease.

All of these problems made for short, danger-filled lives. In 1907, 239 miners in Pennsylvania's Darr Mine died after a gas explosion. In 1909, the Cherry Mine in Illinois caught fire because the railroad that owned it would not fix an electrical outage. Workers had to use torches and the hay used to feed work animals caught fire. Two hundred fifty-nine miners died. Despite the fatalities, the company had broken no laws.[4] More common was a single miner dying in an accident or the slow, debilitating spread of black lung driving miners into their graves. That slow violence against workers' lives received no public attention.

While the most famous accidents were in the coal industry, workers died in nearly every job. To give just one example, in the 1920s gasoline workers suffered lead poisoning from the tetraethyl lead used to solve a fuel problem that limited automobile engines' effectiveness. General Motors and other companies could have fixed the problem with ethanol but instead chose lead because of GM's close relationship with DuPont, which made the lead additive. Dozens of workers perished soon after its adoption by the gasoline companies, and a media frenzy developed around the safety of tetraethyl lead. But in 1926, the Coolidge administration, ally of the auto and chemical companies, ruled that the product was safe and it remained on the market. Lead gasoline was finally outlawed in 1996, which led to a 75 percent decline in the mean blood-lead level in the American population.[5]

As the tetraethyl lead story suggests, the state and corporations often allied to place profit over safety. But the epidemic of lead poisoning in American workers also led to reformers investigating the impact of industrial production on workers' lives. Gasoline was only one of many lead-based products that needlessly exposed workers to danger; paint was particularly dangerous. And then there were those who worked in the lead factories themselves. Lead workers suffered from memory loss, blindness, constipation, paralysis, and many other health problems. In 1900, fourteen of sixty workers at a Tacoma, Washington, lead smeltery were hospitalized for lead poisoning.[6] Employers blamed workers, saying that if the employees washed their hands and cleaned their fingernails, they would not get sick. Owners took absolutely no responsibility, again assuming that workers chose to engage that risk upon taking the job. Such industrial diseases were common in many jobs. For example, matchworkers suffered exposure to white phosphorous, resulting in "phossy jaw," an abscessed jawbone that would glow greenish white, forcing the removal of the jaw in order to save the person from brain damage and organ failure that could lead to death.[7]

Reformers such as Alice Hamilton, a pioneer of workplace safety studies, engaged in groundbreaking research that helped prove that employers placed workers in harm's way. Industry fought Hamilton's work on lead poisoning and other hazards of the job, but the early stages of occupational medicine and public campaigns about the horrific and preventable diseases afflicting American workers made a difference. Reformers found a substitute for white phosphorus and matchworkers' lives improved. Agencies such as the U.S. Public Health Service started identifying the protection of workers as a legitimate role of government. Congress expanded the powers of the Public Health Service in 1912, a victory for the same Progressives outraged over the Triangle Fire. Once again, when consumers and reformers became aware of dangerous workplace environments, they acted. The Public Health Service investigated workplaces, authored studies, and held conferences on the nation's poisonous workplaces.[8]

Early twentieth-century judges also began rejecting the hazardous risk doctrine of *Farwell*, beginning to find for workers in lawsuits against employers over workplace injuries. This scared companies far more than the reformers did. To protect themselves from lawsuits, some corporate leaders pushed for states to set up workers' compensation systems that would limit corporate liability. In 1911, Wisconsin became the first state with workers' compensation, and most other states followed within a decade. While these programs set an important precedent of state involvement in workplace safety, the laws were intended to protect corporations more than workers, and the compensation usually did not come close to matching the wages lost. The American Federation of Labor opposed workers' compensation laws in their early years because it thought they were a bad deal for workers. Moreover, in the early decades, these laws did not apply to workers who got sick on the job from their exposure to the polluted environment created by industry. For the worker who breathed in dust in the mines or who was exposed to lead, workers' compensation did nothing.[9]

The problems with the workers' compensation system soon became apparent. In the late 1910s, wristwatches that glowed in the dark became popular. But the watches had a hideous cost, because it was radium that made the watches glow. Residents who lived near watch factories complained the radium dust emitted turned their laundry yellow when they hung it to dry. The young women hired to paint the watches in New Jersey, Connecticut, and Illinois factories had fun with the radium. They painted the watches using a paintbrush held in their mouth. One painted it on her teeth before a date so she would have a smile that glowed in the dark. Family members commented on the workers themselves giving off a faint glow. They soon developed bone cancers in the jaw from ingesting the radium. Doctors took out the teeth and then the lower jaws of the ill in a vain attempt to save them. After working in the radium factories, Amelia Maggia died in 1922; Helen Quinlan's death followed in June 1923; and Irene Randolph passed away in July 1923. Survivors suffered debilitating bone diseases. Yet the workers struggled to win any kind of compensation. The companies settled out of court with some of them, but either the victims died before seeing any of the money or it did little more than cover their enormous medical costs. Only in Illinois did the workers and the labor movement win the fight against business to get these workers covered by workers' compensation.[10]

The "radium girls," as the press called them, suffered an extreme fate, but the dangers of the workplace were all too real for millions of women. Most public health professionals were focused on the dangers of male occupations like lead work, but work without inherent dangers such as using lead or radium became dangerous because of the extreme exploitation. That's especially true in the apparel industry, which developed what historians call "merchant capitalism" during the nineteenth century. In this system, which has come back in the global supply chains of the twenty-first-century economy, traders and financiers have more control over the labor market than manufacturers. Rather than own their factories, clothing companies contract with manufacturers to make clothing to order. A contractor's profit is generated from reduced labor costs.[11]

Perhaps nowhere is this history of worker struggle and capital mobility starker than in the clothing industry. Apparel should not be a dangerous trade. Coal mines or steel furnaces have inherent risks that a textile factory does not. Yet the modern face of industrial work is a Bangladeshi woman laboring in a dangerous garment factory. The apparel industry's indifference to human and workers' rights has created many of the world's worst industrial disasters of the past century. The garment industry has long sought to employ women in its factories, taking advantage of gender inequality for a lower-paid and less empowered workforce. At Triangle and at Rana Plaza, women made up majorities of the dead. Outsourcing workplace catastrophe has become a way to exploit women; workers' rights are also women's rights, and the fight for safe workspaces is a fight for a feminist world.

By the late nineteenth century, thousands of tiny sweatshops opened in the homes of New York City's Lower East Side to make clothing for department stores. Department stores sent orders to contractors and had no interest in what happened next, so long as the product was made on time and for the right price. These contractors then subcontracted the work to families to make in their homes. An 1893 study estimated that one-half of American clothing was made in home sweatshops.[12] After 1900, factory-style sweatshops employing young women began replacing home work. Many of these were on the upper floors of New York buildings, only slightly hidden from people's everyday view. Work was seasonal and could mean no work for a long time and then up to seventy hours a week for $3 to $10 during peak seasons. The women frequently became sick due to chemical exposure. Substandard dyes poisoned women's skin and the fibers from the cloth entered their eyes and other orifices, causing significant irritation and discomfort.[13]

But these women fought back. Many of them, especially Jewish immigrants who brought socialist ideas with them from Europe, had a sharply defined idea of their rights. They formed unions, including the International Ladies' Garment Workers' Union

(ILGWU) and the Amalgamated Clothing Workers of America (ACWA). In 1909, Clara Lemlich led the Uprising of the 20,000. The strike began the important connections between female reformers and women workers that would transform the industry and the history of women's work in the United States during the early twentieth century.

The connections between workers and female reformers during the Uprising of the 20,000 and the aftermath of the Triangle Fire increased the broader interest in the catastrophes of apparel workers' lives. In 1912, reformers and workers allied to pass a new law in Massachusetts that reduced women's workweeks to a maximum of fifty-four hours. The workers thought they would receive the same wages despite reduced hours. When employers reduced their wages, textile workers in Lawrence, Massachusetts, went on strike. Industrial Workers of the World organizers and speakers came to Lawrence to rally the workers. Police killed a striker and then framed two strike leaders for her murder. A member of the Lawrence school board planted bombs around town so that people would blame the strikers. With violence rising and parents struggling to feed their children, the IWW advertised in the *New York Call*, a socialist newspaper, asking New Yorkers to allow the children of the striking workers into their homes. Within twenty-four hours, 119 Lawrence children were in New York homes, becoming traveling witnesses of the strike. More trains followed. Reformers began donating money. In response, on February 24, Lawrence police savagely beat the women as they tried to put their children on the trains. This received national press coverage and outraged many wealthy women, including Helen Herron Taft, wife of President William Howard Taft. With such bad publicity, the companies finally gave in, agreeing to provide pay increases and better working conditions.[14]

The textile companies also began to see the immigrant women of the Northeast as too politically active and effective at winning victories. Apparel companies pioneered geographical subterfuge to escape unions. Textile mills were relatively inexpensive to build, whether for spinning cloth or stitching clothing. Beginning in the

1880s, textile investors found cheaper labor in the South, particularly in mountainous towns with large populations of poor whites, few economic opportunities, limited formal education, and no immigrants bringing radical political ideas from Europe. Far away from the attention of the middle class, the South became the new home of American textiles by the 1920s, as the memory of Triangle and Lawrence helped create legal reforms in northern factories.

The companies sought to replicate the impoverishing and dangerous conditions of their northeastern factories in the South. The Dwight Manufacturing Company opened a factory in Alabama in 1895 to escape strikes at its Massachusetts mills, but only after it convinced Alabama to repeal its 1887 child labor law.[15] Again, employers sought out female employees and child labor for low wages, with women outnumbering men in North Carolina textile mills two to one. New England mill towns went into a long-term economic decline as capital fled to the South. By 1930, southern textile plants produced more than twice the output of the northern factory towns. The women suffered from byssinosis, or brown lung, which is caused from breathing in the cotton dust from the factories and blocks the lungs' airways. Workers were not eligible for workers' compensation for the illness until 1969.[16] In 1934, mill workers in New England and the South united in a national strike that began over owners speeding up production, forcing workers to handle more looms and increasing the chance of injury. The strike failed in the South because of the lack of organized unions to provide financial support and the open hostility of the state governments— precisely the situation the textile industry had hoped for when they invested there.[17]

The heavy industries that drove much of the American economy had yet to discover the benefits of capital mobility, but while successful union organizing beginning in the New Deal led to safety committees on worksites, by the 1960s a lot of work remained quite dangerous. The steel mills of Gary, Indiana, had some of the strongest United Steelworkers of America locals in the country, but these plants remained hot, loud, and sometimes deadly. Workers tied themselves to one another with rope to find their way around mills thick with smoke and particulate matter. The most dangerous work often remained the lowest paid, and it was most likely to be relegated to African Americans. In 1935, thirty-seven black steelworkers sued the United States Steel Corporation because of the diseases they contracted from smoke inhalation on the job. Throughout the 1950s, steelworkers engaged in many unauthorized short-term strikes to protest their exposure to smoke and fumes.[18]

The stable work, booming economy, and union contracts of the postwar period led workers to demand changes to their working environment by the 1960s. With workers of color routinely burdened with the greatest chances for catastrophe, the civil rights movements of the era included demands for justice in the workplace. The United Farm Workers (UFW) made the fights to protect themselves from pesticides in the fields, for access to water, and for bathrooms central themes in the campaigns that led to the first union contracts in California agriculture, in 1967. The UFW allied with the Environmental Defense Fund to fight pesticides, especially the exposure of workers to DDT, which was legal for use in the United States until 1972. In the fields at least, labor rights became civil rights.[19]

These efforts led to greater public awareness about the unnecessary dangers of American work and the passing of the Occupational Safety and Health Act in 1970. The creation of the Occupational Safety and Health Administration (OSHA) the following year was the greatest victory in the history of American workplace safety. OSHA opened its doors in 1971 and began crafting new workplace regulations, investigating illnesses, and developing rules for corporations to follow. Not all unions embraced OSHA at first, but the most reformist unions—whose agenda included broad struggles for social democracy—such as the International Association of Machinists and Aerospace Workers, the International Woodworkers of America, and, most famously, the Oil, Chemical, and Atomic Workers International Union (OCAW), led by Tony Mazzocchi, all vigorously supported the new regulatory body. As the OCAW found out during the Shell strike and the UFW discovered during the grape boycott, when consumers around the nation became outraged over the pesticide poisoning, heat exposure, and lack of water farmworkers suffered on the job, embracing a vigorous environmental agenda on the job could win important allies.[20]

Sometimes it took a revolution within unions to stop catastrophe. United Mine Workers of America (UMWA) rank-and-file members revolted over union leadership's inaction on black lung. The UMWA had done an incalculable amount for its members over the decades, but by the late 1960s it was headed by the autocratic Tony Boyle, who valued his relationships with employers over the health of his members. When Boyle failed to act on complaints about the coughing and choking deaths of miners, workers took matters into their own hands. Black lung associations formed in local union halls around Appalachia, placing direct pressure on UMWA leadership, politicians, and employers to act. UMWA members occupied the West Virginia statehouse in direct defiance of Boyle. This led to President Richard Nixon reluctantly signing the Federal Coal Mine Health and Safety Act in 1969, although only after his threatened veto of a black lung compensation program brought another strike to the mines. The law provided the first comprehensive government plan in American history to protect workers from environmental hazards on the job.[21]

Part of labor's reticence to embrace OSHA came from the fact that by 1970 capital mobility had become a threat to their jobs. The United Paperworkers' International Union refused to fight against asbestos in a Johns Manville paper mill it represented. Workers knew that asbestos was dangerous, but they feared the factory would move if they united with environmentalists to clean up the factory. Like the paperworkers' union, other unions concluded that pressing employers to provide healthy working environments could lead to factories moving abroad, mass layoffs, and community instability.[22] Steelworkers in Gary, Indiana, who had struck in the 1950s to protect themselves from smoke now feared that enforcing OSHA regulations and pollution standards would cause their aging and inefficient plant to close.[23] Companies took advantage of these fears. Westinghouse warned workers at its Bloomington, Indiana, plant that it would have to leave town if workers spoke out about polychlorinated biphenyl (PCB) exposure when environmentalists and city residents sought to make the company clean up its waste in the 1980s.[24]

Even if they did not plan to close factories, companies found threatening to do so a great way to fight reforms. In 1974, workers in a BFGoodrich factory in Louisville, Kentucky, had unusually high rates of liver cancer because of vinyl chloride exposure from making PVC. The petrochemical companies that made PVC, such as Shell, Dow Chemical, and Goodrich, claimed better workplace standards would drive up the price, imperiling the economy. General Motors stated that protecting workers from vinyl chloride would lead to 450,000 GM workers getting laid off. In fact, when the Environmental Protection Agency (EPA) did raise the standards, not a single plant closed and the companies admitted they could pay for the improvements. Union and EPA studies in the 1980s showed that most American factories that closed because of workplace protections were at obsolete facilities usually already on the chopping block.[25]

But while environmental regulation might not directly force factories to move, corporations did begin moving to avoid workplace safety regulations. Back in 1969, the General Telephone and Electronics Corporation (GTE) moved its electronic components manufacturing plant from the Silicon Valley to Albuquerque, New Mexico, because of the "good business climate." With few unions, New Mexico was the kind of state where many companies moved during the 1960s and 1970s. GTE hired a predominantly female and Latina labor force for the repetitive tasks of assembling transformers. It also wantonly exposed workers to solvents, acids, and other toxic chemicals. The women suffered from skin conditions, memory loss, mental illness, hallucinations, and cancer. Workers repeatedly struck beginning in 1978, and by 1988 over 250 workers had filed suit against GTE for their illnesses. GTE's response was to escape once more, moving the factory to Ciudad Juárez, Mexico, in 1983, re-creating there the same poisonous workplace but outside the American regulatory framework.[26]

Capital mobility became a central part of a larger corporate plan to take back control of American society after decades of labor advances. In 1971, corporate lawyer and soon-to-be Supreme Court justice Lewis Powell issued a memo to Eugene Sydnor, chairman of the U.S. Chamber of Commerce education committee. In the memo, which he titled "Attack of American Free Enterprise System," Powell urged the business community to organize against the regulations they increasingly faced. In doing so, he became an inspiration to corporate leaders to turn the tide on the regulatory state and the labor advances that had defined it since the beginning of the New Deal. Powell's memo spurred business to organize to undermine unions and environmental policies through aggressive antiunionism, lobbying, and legislative attacks. The Koch brothers, Art Pope, Sheldon Adelson, and other billionaire funders of today's conservative causes are the inheritors of Powell's ideas, as is the Chamber of Commerce, which has done so much over the past decade to undermine progressive gains.[27]

Following the Powell Memo, corporations organized to fight an OSHA that would truly protect American workers. Because Nixon never wanted to create OSHA, it was not until 1977 that the agency had full backing from the president. President Jimmy Carter's head of OSHA, Eula Bingham, brought energy to the agency and looked to develop new health standards for a variety of chemicals. But with strong corporate resistance, many of Bingham's efforts were frustrated. Then, in 1981, Ronald Reagan became president and never again would OSHA pose a real threat to business. Reagan named Thorne Auchter, a Florida construction contractor, as OSHA director. Auchter opposed OSHA's existence and sought to undermine it by reducing regulations and making it more "business friendly." Reagan and Auchter gutted the OSHA budget in 1982 and reversed a regulation that allowed construction workers to view their own medical records for information on their toxic exposure. OSHA funding stagnated after this. In 1980, OSHA employed 2,950 inspectors. By 2006, that number had dropped to 2,092, despite the near doubling of the size of the workforce. There are around 2,200 inspectors today, 1 for every 59,000 workers. In 1977, Jimmy Carter budgeted $101 million for OSHA. In 2012, Barack Obama's proposed budget was $95 million.[28] The explosion at the West Fertilizer plant in Texas on April 17, 2013, that killed fifteen people demonstrated the agency's very real limitations. There are so few OSHA inspectors that it would take 129 years to inspect every workplace in the country at current staffing levels. In 2006, the average OSHA fine for solid waste violations was $840, an amount that will deter no polluter.[29]

Even with these limitations, OSHA created enormous changes that helped workers. In 1970, 18 of every 100,000 workers died on the job in the United States. By 2006, that number had declined to about 4 per 100,000. Occupational injury and illness rates fell by 40 percent over that period.[30] On the other hand, some of that drop originates from the dangerous work being moved abroad in order to avoid these regulations. When companies move overseas, they avoid the snooping eyes of American reformers and regulators. In U.S. history, workers, writers, and government regulators exposed and then created reforms concerning thousands of different types of work. Moving that work abroad basically forced reformers to start the process all over again.

Today, American citizens simply cannot know the working conditions of the factories that make the products they buy. We cannot know how the chemicals, tools, and technologies in these workplaces affect workers. Some brave workers publicize their conditions, and investigative institutions such as Human Rights Watch expose some of the worst violations, but there is an enormous knowledge gap. This is hugely beneficial for corporations who want to keep us ignorant of their activities. We know about extreme incidents such as the Rana Plaza collapse that capture the world's attention, however briefly, or when workers get so fed up with the conditions that they strike long enough and loud enough to get the Western world's attention. But the day-to-day disasters that maim or kill a single worker or the accumulation of lead in workers' bodies—those go almost completely unreported.

Much of that has taken place in the apparel industry, which has replicated Triangle-era conditions in sweatshops around the world. That it continues targeting women for this exploitative work is hardly surprising, as garment manufacturers did this in New England and the South in the twentieth century. Women need and want to work. For women in the developing world, work can be empowering, providing extra income, independence, or a way to escape an abusive relationship. Theoretically, American companies could provide this empowerment if they paid women a decent wage and employed them in clean factories that did not collapse or catch fire. But as geographer Melissa Wright has noted, employers see these women as "disposable," workers to wring every ounce of profit from and then throw their "worthless" bodies out like garbage. This attitude pervades the entire garment industry. It is hardly surprising then that many women choose the sex trade over the garment industry in nations like Cambodia. The pay is much better.[31]

Some of the first industries to migrate to Mexico en masse after the Border Industrialization Program started were electronics and textiles—relatively low-skill and low-overhead industries find moving to flee regulations highly profitable. By 1994, 2,065 Mexican factories specifically opened using maquiladora legislation employed 579,519 people, nearly all in jobs migrated from the United States.[32] Mexico was only the tip of the iceberg, and by the 1990s the geography of production extended into Central America and through Southeast Asia. This made American companies tremendous amounts of money. In 1993, the cost of labor in Malaysia was 10 percent of that in the United States, and in China it was only 3 percent.[33]

In 1970, about one thousand women engaged in textile manufacturing in Malaysia. A decade later, eighty thousand women worked in textile, food processing, and electronics factories.[34] A 1983 study of maquiladora workers in Ciudad Juárez, Mexico, showed an overwhelming young, single, female workforce. Eighty-five percent of the maquiladora workers were female. Electronics workers averaged only twenty years of age.[35] American companies and Mexican maquiladora owners chose women for their supposed physical advantages, but really they chose them because they were paid less and were supposedly easy to control. One Juárez electronics plant manager, referring to women as "patient" and "highly productive," said, "In all cultures," women "have the greater manual dexterity. . . . This is why we prefer to use female workers in our plants."[36] This low-wage labor did not lead to improved income equality for women workers. In Mexico in 1980, women made 80 percent of men's wages. Twelve years later, that had fallen to 57 percent.[37] With women seen as disposable, plant managers do nothing to protect them from unsafe working conditions. The women soldering in electronics plants routinely burn their hands. The bad light of the factories causes their sight to diminish, while the acids and solvents workers use poison their bodies.[38]

Women make up the vast majority of the workforce, but men make up the supervisors. Sexual harassment is endemic. A 2006 report by Mexican labor and feminist organizations detailed massive sexual harassment in maquiladoras. Labor authorities ignore or downplay this harassment, not wanting to anger the corporations who could move again at a moment's notice. A Human Rights Watch survey from 2002 found widespread unreported sexual harassment and intimidation at Guatemalan maquiladoras, where women made up 80 percent of the eighty thousand workers. Forty-six percent of these factory workers had experienced mistreatment from their boss, and 5 percent had been subjected to sexual advances. Analysts consider these numbers underestimates, arguing that many women naturalize sexual harassment and refuse to report it or admit that it is happening to them.[39]

Employers also discriminate against pregnant women. This has a long history: RCA fired pregnant electronics workers in its Bloomington, Indiana, plant in the 1940s.[40] Preemployment pregnancy examinations are common today, as contractors do not want to give pregnant workers paid leave. Kimberly Estrada, a worker at a Dong Bang Fashions factory in Chimaltenango, reported that she had to undergo a gynecological exam by a company doctor at the factory before she could work. If workers became pregnant while employed, their bosses would not give them time off to go to the doctor nor the maternity leave mandated by the Guatemalan labor code. Women have miscarried at work, unable to get the medical treatment they needed to save their babies.[41]

Human rights groups in the United States and Mexico filed a complaint in 1997 over what they called "state-tolerated sex discrimination against prospective and actual female workers in the maquiladora sector along the U.S.-Mexico border," focusing on pregnancy testing and discrimination against pregnant workers. This pressure led to American companies announcing the end of pregnancy testing in the maquiladoras and Mexico issuing new directives to labor officials to stop it. Members of Congress introduced legislation to make pregnancy testing in American-owned factories illegal, suggesting that in fact American politicians could do much more to regulate the conditions of work overseas than they usually claim. But the textile companies found Mexican wages too high anyway, and they simply moved the jobs to Central America and Southeast Asia, forcing the struggle to start anew.[42]

Low wages, sexual harassment, and poor working conditions continue to plague women in the garment industry. Today, women in Bangladesh toil in apparel factories for the national minimum wage of $37 a month. In one factory, women were forced to work one hundred hours a week during peak production periods, and supervisors punched and slapped them. The victims included pregnant women, and at least one miscarried because of the treatment. Other pregnant women were forced to quit or denied their legally mandated maternity leave. Women in Cambodia and Indonesia fare little better, making $75 a month in the former and as low as $80 a month in the latter. In all these countries, women are fighting back through labor unions. In Indonesia, Nike had to pay 4,500 workers a $1 million settlement after having not paid them for more than six hundred thousand hours of overtime over a two-year period—a decision that came only after Indonesia's labor federation pressed a lawsuit.[43]

Unfortunately, the U.S. government contributes to these problems through its purchasing practices. The U.S. Marine Corps contracts its shirt production with DK Knitwear in Bangladesh. A 2010 report showed that one-third of DK workers were children, mostly young girls, and that the plant had no fire alarms despite previous fires in the facility. Women at Zongtex Garment Manufacturing in Cambodia soiled themselves at machines making clothes for the U.S. Army and Air Force. The Transportation Security Administration (TSA) signed a contract with a Mexican company in February 2013; the same company had previously treated uniforms with chemicals that caused rashes in TSA agents. Yet Republicans attacked TSA for paying too much to the Mexican workers. Like the rest of the apparel industry, the government relies on subcontractors, pays no attention to the working conditions in plants, and pushes for the cheapest price regardless of the social cost.[44]

These clothing factories often expose workers to dangers that we can barely comprehend. Distressed jeans can sell for well over $100. But how do they become distressed? Chinese workers manually sandblast the jeans. The fine silica dust of the sand used to treat distressed jeans is particularly dangerous. Silicosis has a long history in industrial labor. It was an epidemic for early twentieth-century American tunnel workers and those who worked in factories with fine rock particles in the air. Workers lost lung capacity and died, most notoriously up to one thousand African Americans who blasted the Hawk's Nest Tunnel near Gauley Bridge, West Virginia, in 1930 without even masks to protect them. Regulations in the United States cut down on the silicosis epidemic, but overseas employers re-create the deadly conditions of a century ago. Outsourced garment factories have had a problem with silicosis for a long time. Since Turkey outlawed manually sandblasting jeans in 2009, companies such as Levi Strauss & Co. and Lee have claimed they have or will stop the practice. But as sick Chinese workers will tell you, it still happens, and they pay the price. A worker in a Guangdong factory said there was so much sand and dust in the air that he could not see the exit door. The suppliers do not provide workers with basic protections such as eyewear, face masks, and gloves. There is no good reason for workers to contract silicosis today: its occurrence is only because of a system that combines profit-seeking Western companies with corrupt or indifferent governments in poor countries. Once again, because the jeans companies have outsourced production, they claim no responsibility for the problem.[45]

Around one-third of textile workers in India suffer from respiratory diseases contracted at work. When you buy a piece of clothing that is "wrinkle free" or "stain resistant," that is probably because formaldehyde is embedded in the fabric. Who put that formaldehyde there, inhaling the poison? Guatemalan activist Flor De María Salguero says of these factories, "There are some fourteen year old workers that work over ten hours a day. . . . There have been many accidents and injuries in the factories too—they use toxic chemicals that have burned some workers and are responsible for health problems and illnesses like cancer."[46]

Even if contractors want to treat their workers well, they often have little power to do so because cost is the only concern of the multinational corporations that place the contracts. When political scientist Mark Anner visited an apparel factory in El Salvador, he met a woman who had a contract to manufacture dresses for Kmart. The company forced her to limit costs to $1 per dress. When El Salvador raised the minimum wage, she could not pay the workers for the dress price. She asked Kmart to allow her a bit of leeway to pay the workers. The company refused, so she had no choice but to force workers to increase their daily productivity. In this arrangement, the American companies hold almost all the power. They could make life better for workers. They choose not to do so.[47]

While the textile industry has received the most public attention for the outsourcing of terrible working conditions, it is hardly alone in this process. Conditions in electronics factories are no better. American, Japanese, and European companies have exported dangerous working environments to overseas plants. Hu Fengchao spray-painted DVD cases at a Panasonic plant in Dalian, China. He was exposed to toxic chemicals such as benzene, toluene, and xylene. He fell ill soon after starting work, but his employers told him to keep working. Finally, at the age of twenty-eight, Hu was diagnosed with aplastic anemia. His platelet count was so low that he risked death from a hemorrhage. Panasonic could have insisted upon basic protections such as masks for workers. Instead, Hu received no protection during his three years in the factory.[48]

Tanning leather was never a pleasant job. Early American cities tried to banish it to the edge of town due to its noxious smells. Then, tanning largely used wood and contributed to deforestation in nineteenth-century New York and New England. Today, chemicals have replaced wood. Bangladesh is a modern center of tanning, exporting leather to the United States and Europe and using chemicals manufactured in rich nations and exported for poor workers to use without protection. Machines break, crushing workers' arms. The workers are exposed to chromium, formaldehyde, axocolorants, and other chemicals. A worker named Poribar quit the tanneries after four stomach operations necessitated by breathing in gases including sulfur dioxide and hydrogen sulfide. He told Human Rights Watch, "When the hides are raw there are many acids, lime, and sodium on them. When I touched them with my hands, my hands are affected. If there's a small cut, it will become much worse. The owner didn't give us any gloves. The same with masks—we were never given them. If we'd been given them we would use them." The World Health Organization estimates that 90 percent of Bangladeshi tanning workers die before the age of fifty. Neither the chemical companies nor companies buying the Bangladeshi leather takes any responsibility for these conditions.[49]

The working conditions of outsourced labor finally came to the world's attention on May 10, 1993, when the Kader toy factory near Bangkok, Thailand, caught fire, killing 188 workers and severely injuring more than 500. The largest workplace disaster in Thai history, the Kader fire should have demonstrated to the world the very real costs of outsourcing unsafe working conditions to the world's poorest countries. But very little changed after this horrifying tragedy. The factory manufactured toys, mostly stuffed animals and plastic dolls, for Hasbro, Tyco, Toys"R"Us, Mattel, and other toy companies that had closed their American factories. Most of the three thousand Kader workers were young women, some using fake IDs to get around age restrictions on labor. Thai law provided minimum wage only for full-time workers. Thus Kader and other manufacturers rarely employed people as full-time laborers. Compulsory overtime frequently kept workers until midnight, or even 5:00 a.m. if a deadline approached. Workers had their pay docked if they did not meet production quotas. On the fourth floor of Kader, eight hundred workers toiled. On that floor were eight toilets.

The fire alarm did not work and the fire spread rapidly in a factory full of finished plastic products. Bosses ordered the downstairs fire exits locked in order to maintain more control over workers. Fleeing back upstairs, the workers flooded the upper fire exits, causing them to collapse under all the weight. Workers began jumping from the upper stories to escape the flames. Said one survivor, "I didn't know what to do. Finally I had no other choice but to join others and jump out the window. I saw many of my friends lying dead on the ground beside me. I injured my legs but I came out alive." Said another, "In desperation, I went back and forth looking down below. The smoke was so thick and I picked the best place to jump in a pile of boxes. My sister jumped too. She died."

If this sounds much like the procession of events at Triangle, with young women dying in a burning sweatshop because of lax safety regulations and a system of widespread exploited labor, commenters at the time noted the same thing as well. In Thailand the main building collapsed from the heat of the fire. The building was constructed with uninsulated steel girders that collapsed after fifteen minutes of intense heat. Shoddy design combined with employer malfeasance and a lack of basic safety standards to allow an easily preventable disaster. Prime Minister Chuan Leekpai traveled to the factory site on the night of the tragedy and pledged greater fire safety for Thai workers. But not one executive or manager received even a day in jail. The management was fined $12,000 for building code violations. The toy companies, of course, took no responsibility.[50]

American corporations made no meaningful reforms after the Kader fire. Today, temperatures inside Asian toy factories routinely reach 100 degrees Fahrenheit. In the 2000s, the toy industry again received attention in the United States when Chinese-made toys used lead paint. American parents were outraged. But this was strictly a consumer reaction; we seemed to care only about the health of our own children. What impact did these lead toys have on the workers? Largely, we do not know. This system results from Mattel and Fisher-Price simply not caring how their toys are produced so long as they come in under cost. Safety last.[51]

What is happening in toys is happening in many industries. Cadmium batteries, used for toys, phones, power tools, and other machines, used to be made in the United States. But cadmium's toxicity comes at a harsh cost. After a Cold Spring, New York, battery factory closed in 1979, it became one of the nation's most expensive Superfund sites, costing $130 million to remediate. Rather than develop responsible waste disposal, battery production simply moved to China. There, the battery workers suffer from headaches, nausea, and kidney damage from cadmium exposure. Mattel and Toys"R"Us outsourced the risk of the batteries to Chinese workers while American parents did not have to think twice about the impact of the toys upon their children.[52]

There is more public knowledge about apparel factories than other overseas factories because workers and American activists made connections to publicize the horrible conditions. The discovery of sweatshop workers, including children, making apparel for Nike, Kathie Lee Gifford, and other high-profile clients in the 1990s brought these conditions to the nation's attention. American students organized to ensure their schools sourced their apparel ethically. The antisweatshop movement led by groups such as United Students Against Sweatshops (USAS) exposed conditions in apparel factories from Indonesia to Guatemala. Created in 1998 out of smaller groups of students fighting on their campus for sweat-free clothing, USAS became a national leader for American consumers seeking knowledge and action about the clothing they wore.

USAS worked with the Union of Needletrades, Industrial and Textile Employees (UNITE), the successor of the older textile workers' union. Together, they formed the Worker Rights Consortium (WRC), which helps students influence their school administrations to purchase university clothing from fair trade factories. The WRC remains an important fighter for ethically made apparel today. In 2001, USAS pressure convinced Nike to intervene in a Puebla, Mexico, factory where workers making university apparel had gone on strike against their Korean bosses. Conditions improved and Nike, as well as Reebok, committed to staying with the now unionized factory rather than contract out to a new, nonunion facility.[53]

But the concerns of American activists strayed from sweatshop labor in the aftermath of 9/11 and the Iraq War. When USAS activity languished, companies returned to their exploitative ways. Today, we have widespread exploitation in nations such as Haiti, where the contractors Gap, Walmart, and Target use to make clothing have engaged in widespread wage theft. Haiti has a monitoring program operated by the International Labour Organization and International Finance Corporation. They reported that every one of the nation's twenty-four garment factories engages in widespread wage theft. Garment workers in Port-au-Prince are paid 32 percent less than the Haitian minimum wage. American companies know this and do nothing. The Worker Rights Consortium has recommended apparel corporations tell contractors they will accept higher costs in return for fair wages and the repayment of stolen wages. Leaving for even lower wages, it argues, "would only add to the irresponsibility they have demonstrated by turning a blind eye to these violations thus far." Of course, if the apparel companies can find a nation engaging in even more widespread wage theft than Haiti, they will move there.[54]

But it is not just American consumers coming to the rescue of helpless workers. The workers lead their own fights. In the 1990s, Yesenia Bonilla became a leader in the fight to unionize her Honduran maquiladora. Kimi, a Korean-owned factory producing goods for American export, was a tough place to work. The dust inside the factory gave Bonilla and her co-workers bronchitis. Managers intimidated her and her fellow union leaders, but she persevered. This fight came to the attention of American labor, and UNITE and the AFL-CIO worked with Honduran unions to force Kimi to recognize a union. The sweatshop movement around the world celebrated a major victory.[55]

In May 2000, Kimi simply closed shop and opened a new plant in Guatemala. Before this, the unions placed pressure on Gap, a major contractor with Kimi, to get it to rehire union workers it had fired. Kimi refused. The apparel industry says it cannot control its contractors, but the companies deny their own culpability in this system. First, Gap could mandate labor standards in its contracts and hold contractors accountable. Second, Gap could operate its own factories. Doing so would make it an outlier in the apparel industry, but the idea of employing people to make your own products is hardly revolutionary. Right now, Kimi's ability to tell Gap "no" in fact reinforces Gap's ability to take no responsibility for its own products. Short of the extremely unlikely event of Gap taking stronger actions to ensure safe labor practices, the next option has to be international labor standards. Without them, Honduran garment worker unions are unlikely to succeed, since the company will just cross the border into Guatemala or El Salvador. Workers can fight, international labor can become involved, citizen groups around the world can work to force decent conditions. But the corporations hold all the power because they can simply move operations for any reason.[56]

However, resistance can occur when public knowledge of the conditions in these factories embarrasses the corporations. In the aftermath to the Rana Plaza collapse, international outrage has created some positive change. European companies created the Accord on Fire and Building Safety in Bangladesh. This covers only issues of building safety and does not address the many other problems with outsourced factories. But it does mark an advance in monitoring in that it requires monitors to be experts in building safety and gives labor groups an equal voice in choosing the inspectors. It also creates health and safety committees in the factories, a huge advance in giving workers some voice. Most important, it provides legally binding mechanisms to ensure that companies invest in factory safety.[57] But American companies, more emboldened in dismissing the concerns of labor than European companies, who must deal with stronger left-wing social movements, have refused to join. Gap's chief executive Glenn Murphy has rejected the accord. "In the United States, there's maybe a bigger legal risk than there is in Europe," said Murphy. "If we were to sign onto something that had unlimited legal liability and risk, I think our shareholders should care about that."[58] In other words, any agreement that would actually hold companies responsible in any meaningful way cannot be considered. Instead, Gap has joined the rival Alliance for Bangladesh Worker Safety, which is nothing more than an industry group claiming an interest in improving conditions but without workers' voices, independent monitors, or enforcement mechanisms.

The story of textiles is to a great extent the story of dozens of industries where work has been moved overseas. Catastrophes at work occur in many ways. The famous ones, the ones we will remember a century from now, are the horrible events that kill a hundred or more workers. Triangle is shorthand for the horrors of the Gilded Age. Rana Plaza will serve the same function for twenty-first-century globalized labor. But there is also the slow, day-to-day violence against workers that never makes the headlines. This is the real killer: the disease, poverty, malnourishment, and hopelessness.

Corporations never want consumers to hear about the conditions of outsourced work, but their aim is to maintain entrenched poverty for the current workforce. None of this is necessary. The companies of wealthy nations could profit without dooming workers to black lung, silicosis, or factory fires. But that might slightly diminish the quarterly profit report or take a few cents away from shareholder dividends. It is those things that determine corporate decision making today, not basic human and labor rights for those doing the hard work. A globalized economy could exist that brings some jobs to the world's poor nations while ensuring safe work exists no matter where corporations are sited. But that is anathema to corporate leaders. Unfortunately, so is respecting the planet, and it is to that issue we now turn.

3

OUTSOURCING POLLUTION

In late October 1948, an inversion—a weather condition where warmer air traps a pocket of colder air below, leading to air stagnation, sometimes for days—settled in the valley that is home to Donora, Pennsylvania. This steel- and zinc-producing town southeast of Pittsburgh was subject to inversions, creating dense fog. These fogs mixed with pollutants from the U.S. Steel smokestacks that belched pollution into the atmosphere. The company had long poisoned the area. Nearly all vegetation within a half mile of the company's Donora Zinc Works was already dead. On October 27, air pollution and weather patterns became a deadly combination. Thick, yellowish smog hung over the town as people breathed in poisonous gases such as nitrogen dioxide, sulfuric acid, and fluorine. The smoke lasted until November 2. Despite heroic efforts by local fire and police forces as well as the town's eight doctors, who worked night and day, twenty people in Donora died and another seven thousand became sick. Nearly eight hundred pets also died.[1]

On the night of December 2, 1984, a Union Carbide pesticide plant in Bhopal, India, sprang a gas leak. That night and into the morning, between 200,000 and 500,000 residents were exposed to 93,000 pounds of methyl isocyanate gas and other chemicals. The gas killed people in their sleep. Those who did not die instantly struggled to survive; unable to breathe, they choked, gasped for air, and vomited as overwhelmed doctors tried to keep them alive. Medical student Moira Sutcliffe was in Bhopal the night of the leak. She remembered, "The dead and dying arrived by the truckload, others came by rickshaw or were carried by relatives." We don't know how many people died. The company's official release said 2,259. The local government said 3,787. Others put the total at up to 16,000, including those who died later from the illnesses they contracted after exposure. By death toll, the Bhopal disaster was probably the largest industrial disaster in history.

Workers had long complained about the poor conditions inside the plant. They had been exposed to toxic chemicals time and time again, with some receiving severe chemical burns that required long-term hospitalization. By 1983, Union Carbide had fourteen plants in India, making chemicals, batteries, pesticides, and other dangerous and highly polluting products. At its Bhopal plant, it produced a pesticide named Sevin. A brand name for carbaryl, Sevin is the third most popular insecticide in the United States, and it is used by home gardeners, agribusiness, and foresters. Carbaryl contains methyl isocyanate, an extremely toxic substance. What is poisonous to insects is often poisonous to humans in large doses. Union Carbide could have easily prevented this leak. But it shut off some of its safety systems in order to save money, sacrificing safety for profit. Operating manuals were in English, but most workers read only Hindi. Local officials worried about processing these chemicals in a big city like Bhopal, but Union Carbide executives overrode their concerns because they wanted to centralize production at that facility and sell the insecticide to other Asian nations.[2]

After the disaster, Union Carbide sought to escape all responsibility. Without evidence, it claimed that someone must have sabotaged the plant. When an Indian court ordered the company to pay $270 million in damages, Union Carbide continued appealing the decision, allowing it to delay payments. By 2001, no more than half of survivors' compensation cases had been processed. Dodging responsibility certainly did nothing for the people of Bhopal, who suffered long-term respiratory problems and lung disease. The factory closed in 1986. Union Carbide, later purchased by Dow Chemical, has taken no responsibility for remediation of the factory site, while 91 percent of people living in a resettlement colony near the factory site use water contaminated by its legacy.

Meanwhile, when a Union Carbide plant in West Virginia that also produced Sevin released a toxic plume of aldicarb oxime and methylene chloride in August 1985, sending 135 people to the hospital, it led to Congress passing the Emergency Planning and Community Right-to-Know Act in 1986. This law provided local governments with information about toxic chemicals in order to support emergency planning measures. No such act came to India.[3]

After the Donora Fog in 1948, Americans began the fight to hold corporations accountable for pollution, and scholars see the roots of the 1970 Clean Air Act in that disaster. The Clean Air Act laid the groundwork for cleaning up America's air after a century of widespread and unchecked environmental degradation.[4] After the Clean Air Act passed, U.S. Steel had to clean up its factories, reducing smoke and pollution inside the workplace and emissions outside the workplace. Cities like Donora, Pittsburgh, and Gary, Indiana, became cleaner and healthier. When companies did emit toxins, as the West Virginia case shows, further legislation could tighten restrictions on their activities. Today, Americans do not die from a few days of air stagnation.

However, as the people of Bhopal found out, American corporations hadn't cleaned up their act. Instead they just moved their operations overseas to profit off of lax environmental laws. Modern capitalism encourages the movement of toxic risk out of the rich nations and into poor ones. Escaping American environmental restrictions means profitable pollution, breathed in, bathed in, and eaten by the world's poor. Sometimes corporations target the poorest communities in the United States to suffer for the nation's toxic history. Sometimes they move production overseas to impoverished nations. In both cases, corporations look to sever knowledge of the cost of industrialization from their comparatively rich consumers.

We don't hear about disasters the size of Bhopal every day. But smaller disasters happen all the time, sickening or killing one or a few people. They just don't attract news coverage. People die of cancer from toxic exposure and no one knows outside of their family and friends. American corporations have no more accountability to the people in the communities where they locate toxic plants than they did decades ago. Americans fought for a safe environment, and the corporate response shifted pollution to the world's poor, both within and outside American borders. Outsourcing toxic work means that Americans are safe from the costs of their consumption, but the world's poor live with the risk. Breathing in the particulate matter from heavy industry or choking on thick smog is one of the most powerful ways one can experience the environment. No one should need to choke to death on smog or suffer asthma in order to work, go to school, or walk in the neighborhood. Yet this happens to hundreds of millions of people in the world today.

From the moment American corporations were born in the late eighteenth century, they saw the natural world as a dumping ground. Within a few years of an industry arriving on a waterway, fish runs went extinct and waterways became disgusting dumps of foul-smelling water that made people sick. The air was no better: smoke coated nearby buildings, killed vegetation, and wiped out bird populations. Although the courts favored this behavior in nineteenth-century decisions, some citizens resisted. As early as the 1870s, residents of Newark, New Jersey, attempted to prevent a paper mill from dumping waste into the Passaic River, just upstream. In the early twentieth century, citizens in Pittsburgh and St. Louis demanded that corporations clean up their smokestacks. They knew that all this smoke and smog made them sick. Chicago passed the nation's first serious smoke law in 1881, giving citizens some legal rights to classify smoke a nuisance and authorizing a municipal inspection agency against smoke violations. While groundbreaking, it was also almost totally unenforced in an era of corporate domination of politics and society. The federal government was not ready to act.[5]

The fight was renewed during the Progressive Era of the 1910s. Settlement house workers including Jane Addams and Florence

Kelley lobbied to move Chicago's largest dump out of a poor residential neighborhood—already the nation had chosen to site toxicity in poor neighborhoods. Settlement worker Mary McDowell made it her mission to improve environmental conditions in Chicago's stockyard district, where meat producers polluted at will and thousands of people lived in horrifying conditions. The south fork of the Chicago River ran through there, known locally as "Bubbly Creek" because the decaying organic matter caused acid to bubble up in the water. The smell of this is unfathomable to modern Americans.[6] Reformers continued battling companies over smoke. Finally, St. Louis passed a major smoke control ordinance in 1940 that forced all fuel consumers to clean the smoke from fuel before it was released into the air. But nationally, gains were limited, and many Americans equated pollution with progress. It would take another generation for sizable numbers of Americans to question this ideology.[7]

Anger over the accumulated evidence of pollution combined with the greater political voice of the working and middle classes after World War II finally made pollution a major issue. The Donora Fog is only the most famous example in the United States (and the deadly London air pollution of 1952 served a similar function in Great Britain). The dumping of pollutants into Lake Erie, making the Cuyahoga River flammable, was emblematic of a general pollution problem throughout the nation's waterways. Suburban developers installed improper septic tanks for the nation's new middle class, and sewage and detergents leaked into the water supply. When home owners turned on their water, suds flowed out. By the 1950s, citizens across the nation had become increasingly concerned about what corporations were doing to the air and water. Even people in conservative areas such as rural central Florida began organizing against the fertilizer industry's phosphate pollution, which sickened cows, poisoned orange groves, and made citizens worry about their health. States were reluctant to challenge business. Corporations stalled, challenged the science, and demanded more testing, all while continuing the same profitable polluting practices.[8]

But Americans became increasingly angry about pollution. In 1966, 28 percent of Americans called air pollution a "somewhat serious" or "very serious" concern. By 1970, that number jumped to 69 percent. People began to demand meaningful federal action to control air pollution. Thomas True of New Iberia, Louisiana, asked Maine senator Edmund Muskie for help: "The black soot" from sugar factory emissions is "upon us in Southwest Louisiana. I have written my state and federal representatives, but have received no help." Muskie became a national leader in the fight against pollution because citizens like True demanded change. Corporations felt pressure to change their ways, and politicians less brave than Muskie were moved to crack down in order to save their political hides.[9]

Rachel Carson's groundbreaking 1962 book *Silent Spring* inspired the organizing against pollution. During World War II, chemical companies developed pesticides such as DDT to protect American troops from mosquitoes and other insects. After the war, chemical companies found ways to market these powerful pesticides at home. Between 1949 and 1968, pesticide use exploded by an average of 168 percent per year, despite an almost total lack of scientific research conducted on how the chemicals affected people, wildlife, or ecosystems. Our national bird, the bald eagle, became perilously close to extinction in the Lower 48 because DDT entered the water supply and became concentrated in fish and then in eagles' bodies after they ate the fish. This caused the eagles' eggshells to form too thin to hatch. *Silent Spring* brought this story to the American public. Showing how DDT and other pesticides moved up the food chain, Carson's book had tremendous impact. If eagle populations were in peril after eating DDT-laden fish, were humans not also susceptible? The chemical industry contested Carson's findings, using sexism to discredit her by calling her a hysterical woman who could not be a legitimate scientist because of her womanly emotions. But *Silent Spring* became a bestseller, motivating political figures such as President John F. Kennedy and Supreme Court Justice William O. Douglas to spearhead investigations that eventually led to bans of DDT and several other chemicals in 1972.[10]

Anti-nuclear-testing activists also brought air pollution into the national conversation during the 1960s. Atmospheric nuclear testing in the Soviet Union led to radioactive milk in Scandinavian cows, making people around the world worried about the effects of nuclear tests. Watching these tests became a tourist attraction in Las Vegas, with people viewing them from their hotel rooftops, but they also led to radiation spewed in the atmosphere to travel around the world, slowly falling on innocent people. In the United States, Women Strike for Peace led these protests, using their identity as mothers trying to raise healthy children and protect them from radioactive milk to fight against nuclear testing. They sent letters to Jackie Kennedy and Nina Khrushchev, urging them to pressure their husbands to stop the madness of nuclear testing. The American media were bemused—who were these women who appeared seemingly out of nowhere? Founded by Bella Abzug, later a leading progressive member of Congress, and children's book illustrator Dagmar Wilson, Women Strike for Peace mobilized fifty thousand women to protest. They played an important role in pressuring the United States and Soviet Union to sign the 1963 Limited Nuclear Test Ban Treaty, which ended atmospheric testing.[11]

Continued anger over corporate pollution led to the first Earth Day, on April 22, 1970. Today, we don't often think of Earth Day as a radical moment—our annual Earth Day celebrations now usually revolve around picking up trash along the river, if we do anything at all. But in 1970, the media saw it is a radical moment that could rival Vietnam as the center of protest in American life. Although its organizers wanted consensus and invited industry speakers, the audience did not care to listen to the people they blamed for the pollution crisis. At the University of Illinois, students disrupted a Commonwealth Edison speaker by coughing loudly so he could not be heard. Speakers talked of the "ecological catastrophe of the Vietnam War" thanks to chemicals such as napalm, made by American corporation Dow Chemical, and challenged corporate irresponsibility toward the earth and the people who relied on it to live.[12]

This energy transformed the nation. Congress passed the Clean

Air Act of 1970 by a nearly unanimous vote, establishing clear federal authority over the regulation of American air, creating federal standards on pollutants, and setting target dates for reducing or eliminating emissions. Congress followed by creating or amending other acts to crack down on corporate pollution such as the Resource Recovery Act of 1970, the Clean Water Act of 1972, and the Federal Insecticide, Fungicide, and Rodenticide Act amendments of 1972. Each of these expanded government authority and resulted from Americans angry over their despoiled landscapes. These new laws and regulations required a brand-new federal agency to administer them, so the Environmental Protection Agency (EPA) was formed in 1970. The EPA was the symbol of the new federal power to regulate corporate emissions.[13]

The 1970s saw an empowered American public demand more remediation from pollution. Citizen groups organized against pesticides, in favor of stricter clean air and water legislation, and in opposition to nuclear power plants. The Toxic Substances Control Act of 1976 required registration of chemicals, albeit only those introduced after 1979. Residents in Cincinnati, Ohio, passed a right-to-know amendment to the city's fire code after a newspaper series documented the city's high cancer rates. Shortly after, residents successfully fought a Standard Oil of Ohio proposal to ship benzene out of a terminal on the Ohio River where floods could sweep away a barge.

The exposure of a cancer cluster at Love Canal, in Niagara Falls, New York, outraged Americans. In the 1940s, the Hooker Chemical Company had buried 21,000 tons of toxic waste there. In 1953, Niagara Falls bought the land and built low-income and working-class housing, schools, and other buildings of the American dream. By the 1970s, locals began to realize they suffered an unusual amount of birth defects, cancers, and other health problems in their community. Led by home owner and mother Lois Gibbs, the people of Love Canal demanded government intervention. In 1978, President Jimmy Carter declared a federal emergency and moved the residents out of Love Canal. Continued outrage over Love Canal; a similar situation in Times Beach, Missouri; and other incidents of industrial pollution led to the establishment of Superfund in 1980, a federal program for long-term remediation of toxic sites. At first, a polluter tax paid for the program, amassing a $3.8 billion surplus for the program by 1996 and creating a very successful agency. Unfortunately, in 1995 Congress did not extend that tax, meaning the rapid depletion of that surplus and an underfunded agency, a defeat of successful government that became ever more common in that decade.[14]

The new environmental laws of the 1970s proved immediately effective. Between 1972 and 1978, presence of sulfur dioxide in the environment fell 17 percent, carbon monoxide by 35 percent, and lead by 26 percent.[15] Americans lauded a future of jobs and health, prosperity and beautiful nature. Unions such as the United Steelworkers of America, who represented many Donora workers, the United Auto Workers, and the Oil, Chemical, and Atomic Workers made alliances with environmentalists and promoted the Clean Air Act, Clean Water Act, and other core legislation that protected all Americans, whether members of the working class or wealthy, from the emissions and pollutants of industry. Environmentalists for Full Employment formed in 1975 to "publicize the fact that it is possible simultaneously to create jobs, conserve energy and natural resources and protect the environment."[16] When Ronald Reagan became president and cut OSHA and EPA funding, the AFL-CIO and Sierra Club created the OSHA/Environmental Network to organize resistance between the two movements.[17] Environmentalists and a Union of Needletrades, Industrial and Textile Employees local representing tannery workers in Fulton County, New York, overcame past differences and worked together on both the workplace environment of the tannery and tannery-created water pollution. By the late 1990s, workers reporting environmental violations and environmentalists helped the union develop plans to improve working conditions in the plants.[18]

The potential for a strong labor-green coalition to fight for healthy workplaces and ecosystems clean enough for people to enjoy in their free time was a threat to corporations. Companies responded to environmentalism's rise by taking advantage of a road the American government had already opened to them—moving their operations away from the people with the power to complain about pollution. They did this in two ways. Some industries scoured the nation, seeking the poorest communities to place the most toxic industries. They assumed those communities, usually dominated by people of color, would not or could not complain. The companies would work with corrupt local politicians to push through highly polluting projects before citizens knew what was entering their communities. Other industries went overseas, seeking to repeat their polluting ways in nations that lacked the ability or desire to enforce environmental legislation. Capital mobility moved toxicity from the middle class to the world's poor.

In 1978, Chemical Waste Management, a company that specialized in handling toxic waste, chose the community of Emelle, in Sumter County, Alabama, as the site of its new toxic waste dump. Corporations contracted with Chem Waste to handle their toxic waste. Sumter County was over two-thirds African American and over one-third of the county's residents lived in poverty, but whites made up the county political elite approving the decision. In Emelle, more than 90 percent of the residents were black. This is why Chem Waste chose Emelle. They worked with a local company led by the son-in-law of segregationist Alabama governor George Wallace to acquire the site. No one told local residents what was to be built there. Local rumors suggested a brickmaking facility. The company dumped polychlorinated biphenyls (PCBs) and other toxic materials at the site. Despite claiming it was safe, the company racked up hundreds of thousands of dollars in fines. Such activities were common for Chem Waste. It always chose communities like this to site its dumps—Port Arthur, Texas, in a neighborhood that was 80 percent people of color; Chicago's South Side in a neighborhood 79 percent people of color; and Saguet, Illinois, a 95 percent African American area.[19]

The racist actions of companies like Chemical Waste Management led to the environmental justice movement. By fighting for the environments where we live, work, and play, environmental justice has redefined environmentalism and connected capital mobility with environmentalism by focusing on how corporations make decisions about where to locate toxic exposure. Through the environmental justice movement, people of color began adapting the language of environmentalism to their struggles with toxicity and pollution. Scholars usually date the movement to an incident in 1982 when the state of North Carolina wanted to dump six thousand truckloads of toxic soil contaminated with PCBs in a predominantly African American section of Warren County. More than five hundred protesters were arrested. Civil rights leaders and community members began tying racism to environmentalism, noting how the Environmental Protection Agency in the Southeast had targeted African American communities for toxic waste dumping. A new social movement was born. Alabamians for a Clean Environment formed to fight the Emelle toxic waste site. Chemical Waste Management had built a toxic waste dump in Kettleman City, California, a 95 percent Latino town in a white majority county. When the company planned to add a toxic waste incinerator, residents fought back, forcing Chem Waste to withdraw its application in 1993. Residents and the company still battle over environmental justice there today. African Americans in Anniston, Alabama, won a lawsuit against the chemical company Monsanto, which paid $390 million in 2003 for contaminating their neighborhood with PCBs, while residents of Norco, Louisiana, defeated Shell Oil in court, forcing it to pay for them to move away from the neighborhood the oil giant contaminated.[20]

The environmental justice movement has not forced widespread changes in corporate strategies. Corporations still seek out the areas with the poorest people to dump toxic waste. The people of the Hyde Park neighborhood of Augusta, Georgia, have conducted a long campaign for environmental justice against a wood-preserving factory that dumped dioxin-laden wood-treatment chemicals into groundwater as well as against a ceramic factory that emitted dust across their yards, resulting in skin conditions, circulatory problems, and rare forms of cancer. The neighborhood near these factories is almost entirely African American, leading residents to believe their neighborhood was targeted for this exposure. African

American neighborhoods are routinely zoned for garbage dumps and landfills, and petrochemical companies locate cancer-causing chemical plants in black communities along the Mississippi River. Poverty and race too often mean toxic exposure and cancer in the United States. In a 2014 report, researchers at the University of Minnesota demonstrated that people of color in the United States breathe in air 38 percent more polluted than whites. In the Los Angeles metro area, 91 percent of the 1.2 million people who live less than two miles from hazardous-waste treatment facilities are people of color. Environmental inequality is a systematic problem made worse by intentional corporate decisions to profit off of poisoning minority populations.[21]

While some companies target sites within the United States to dump pollution, more commonly, corporations either move production overseas or ship waste abroad. Free trade agreements lack meaningful environmental standards. After NAFTA's passage, the American and Mexican governments engaged in meetings to plan for environmental problems, but corporations remained off the hook for their actions in Mexico. Twenty years after NAFTA, nothing has changed. Corporate control over the American government continues to ensure that trade agreements do not include environmental restrictions on corporate actions.

In the 1970s, with the first factories already going overseas, corporations began blackmailing workers, saying that increased environmental restrictions would force them to close their mills and move. This job blackmail provided a very effective strategy for corporations, allowing them to retake the pollution initiative from environmentalists and making workers scared pollution reduction would cost them their jobs. During a hearing for the Water Quality Act of 1965, St. Regis Paper Company president William R. Adams told a congressional committee, "The general public wants both blue water in the streams and adequate employment for the community. The older plant may not be able to afford the investment in waste treatment facilities necessary to provide blue water; the only alternative may be to shut the operation down. But the employees of the plant and the community cannot afford to have the plant shut down. They cannot afford to lose the employment furnished by the operation."[22] Such statements became ever more common after 1970, and workers believed them, fearing that placing scrubbers on smokestacks or limiting the dumping of chemicals in water would lead to the end of their jobs. They didn't want to get poisoned, but they needed to eat and buy their children clothes.

Companies began viciously using environmentalism as an excuse for shuttering plants they intended to close anyway. In 1980, the Atlantic Richfield Company (ARCO) announced the closing of its Anaconda, Montana, smeltery. It claimed it could not "satisfy environmental standards" the government now required of smelters. Workers were furious at environmentalists. But within a week, it came out that both the federal and state governments had offered to work with ARCO, granting it an extension or offering any concessions it wanted to stay in the state. The company refused. ARCO lied about a decision made to maximize profit. Usually, these nefarious lies went unchallenged, and environmentalism increasingly became seen as an elite movement unconcerned with the fate of American workers.[23]

Corporate mobility cleaved unions from environmentalists. In 1976, UAW president Leonard Woodcock noted that job blackmail was a "false conflict." However, "to a worker confronted with the loss of wages, health care benefits and pension rights, it can seem very real."[24] For example, in 1977, environmentalists and the United Mine Workers of America mostly agreed on an amendment to the Clean Air Act that would limit sulfur dioxide after environmentalists supported forcing corporations to place scrubbers on eastern smokestacks rather than mandating that lower sulfur coal be mined by nonunion labor in the West. But in 1990, the two interests could not agree on amendments for further emissions restrictions to fight acid rain. Coal companies increased their investment in the nonunion western mines as a result.[25]

Companies began playing states off one another in a national race to the bottom. When the Belcher Corporation announced the move of its Massachusetts-based foundry to Alabama in 2007, the company's chief financial officer stated, "The environmental regulations aren't as stringent in Alabama as they are in Massachusetts."[26] NAFTA and other trade agreements empowered corporations to follow through on their job blackmail internationally. A 1990s survey of American companies with factories in Mexicali, just across the U.S.-Mexico border, showed 25 percent moved to take advantage of lax environmental regulations, while 80 percent of furniture makers who moved from Los Angeles to Mexico in the late 1980s did so to reduce their environmental costs.[27]

American companies poisoned the water of northern Mexico. As Matamoros, just across the Rio Grande from Brownsville, Texas, grew with the arrival of American-owned factories in the 1970s and 1980s, citizens had new economic opportunities but were also sickened by the emissions no longer allowable in the United States. Near one chemical operation, xylene levels in the water were more than fifty thousand times the level allowable in the United States, and behind a General Motors plant nearby, xylene levels were six thousand times the American legal limits. The effects of this crossed the border—water and air pollution do not respect national boundaries. Birth defects in both Matamoros and Brownsville skyrocketed, particularly cases of anencephaly, a condition that leads to babies with undeveloped brains.[28]

NAFTA made these problems worse. In the years after NAFTA, more than 2,700 new maquiladoras were built along the U.S.-Mexico border. They rose without the infrastructure to service such large factories and the cities needed to house their employees exploded. Sewage disposal quickly became a major issue in northern Mexico. Air pollution meant both corporate profit and over 36,000 children in Ciudad Juárez emergency rooms between 1997 and 2001 due to breathing problems. Mexican federal spending on environmental protection fell by half between 1994 and 1999 at the same time that American corporations polluted that nation like never before. Mexican law mandates that toxic waste produced for other nations' companies be exported back to the home country, but only 30 percent of this waste is actually returned to the country of origin.[29] Corporations generate 80 million tons of hazardous waste in Mexico every year, and the economic costs of environmental degradation equal approximately 10 percent of Mexican gross domestic product. American corporations take little to no responsibility for any of this.[30]

When we think of air pollution today, we probably envision China, which exports its steel to the United States and other nations while its citizens literally choke to death on the legendary smog. Over the objection of environmentalists, labor organizers, and human rights advocates, China received most-favored-nation trading status in 2000 with the United States. The Clinton administration claimed that China would advance on environmental standards if the standards were voluntary. It was wrong. Mickey Kantor, President Clinton's chief trade negotiator, now calls the lack of environmental safeguards in the deals he worked on a "big mistake."[31] These agreements have helped worsen the greatest environmental crisis of the twenty-first century: climate change. A 2014 UN report from the Intergovernmental Panel on Climate Change showed that greenhouse gas emissions grew twice as fast in the first decade of the twenty-first century as in the previous three decades. Too often, Americans point to China or India as the drivers of these emissions to say there is nothing we can do at home, but in fact much of the emissions in Asia come from burning coal for factories producing goods for American and European markets. The UN report stated, "A growing share of CO_2 emissions from fossil fuel combustion in developing countries is released in the production of goods and services exported, notably from upper-middle income countries to high-income countries."[32]

In January 2014 alone, the United States imported 3.2 million tons of Chinese steel.[33] American corporate interests do not own these Chinese steel companies, but they do own thousands of other heavily polluting factories in China. These corporations want to avoid "environmental nannies," as Linda Greer of the National Resources Defense Council has been called.[34] The Institute of Public and Environmental Affairs, a leading Chinese environmental NGO, released a report in October 2012 detailing the massive pollution by apparel factories that contract with U.S. corporations, including Disney.[35] The report noted that subcontractors for Ralph Lauren discharge wastewater filled with dyes and other pollutants into streams and do not use pollution-reduction devices on coal boilers, releasing extra pollutants into the air. Chinese citizens protest the pollution, but their government has little tolerance for these protests, which pleases foreign investors.[36] A recent scientific estimate shows that in 2006, U.S. exports were responsible for 7.4 percent of Chinese sulfur dioxide, 5.7 percent of nitrogen oxide, and 4.6 percent of carbon monoxide. According to the World Health Organization, 2.6 million people in southeastern Asia, mostly in China, died of outdoor air pollution in 2012.[37] How many of those lives could be saved with better environmental standards on products imported to the United States? American companies may not be responsible for all the suffering of the Chinese working class from pollution, but they certainly contribute to it.

Although the United States has outsourced its air pollution to China, Americans still suffer the results. Some of the polluted Chinese air follows wind currents across the Pacific to the western United States. Although Los Angeles has done much to improve its smog in recent decades, Chinese air pollution is again making L.A. air unhealthy. A 2014 study published in the Proceedings of the National Academy of Science showed that 12 to 24 percent of sulfates in the American West come from drifting air pollution from Chinese production for the export market, enough to occasionally bring Los Angeles above federal ozone limits. As Steve Davis, co-author of the study, told the *Washington Post*, "We've outsourced our manufacturing and much of our pollution, but some of it is blowing back across the Pacific to haunt us."[38]

Americans may unknowingly deal with a smidgen of this pollution, but people who live near these factories deal with far worse. The people who live near the Rana Plaza factory site in Bangladesh where 1,100 workers died in April 2013 have to live with more than just the heartbreak of losing friends and family. They also have the daily struggle of massive pollution. Dyeing clothing requires water and creates pollution unless regulations force companies to clean it up. If the contractors American apparel companies use had to follow something similar to American environmental standards when producing for the American market, the dyeing problem could be mitigated, and the world's poor could have industrial jobs without being poisoned. The Clean Water Act includes regulations about dyes. This has made American waterways cleaner and people healthier. Alas, such an outcome was unacceptable for the clothing companies.

Many dyes use sulfur that creates rashes on workers' skin and remains in water supplies even after chemical treatment.[39] In the 1990s, the Mexican state of Puebla became a center of blue jeans production. Tehuacán was once known as the "city of health" for its natural springs. No more. The companies dumped blue dye into nearby water supplies. Soon the water ran a dark indigo, not coincidentally the color of a pair of dark blue jeans. The water was then used for irrigating fields, where the blue dye burned seedlings and destroyed crops.[40]

Today in Savar, Bangladesh, near the site of the Rana Plaza disaster, the water runs different colors from the textile factories, depending on what the factories are doing on a given day. Sometimes it is red. Sometimes purple. Sometimes blue. As they used to do in the United States before environmental reforms, the textile manufacturers just dump their dyes into the rivers, killing almost all aquatic life. Near the polluted canal in Savar is a school. But the students struggle to learn. The rank smell from the pollution wafts over the school, causing debilitating headaches. Nearby are two garment factories, two dyeing factories, a textile mill, a brick factory, and a pharmaceutical plant, almost all making products for the Western market.[41] Bangladeshi tanneries producing leather for China, Europe, and the United States impact the ecosystem in similar ways, with chromium and other pollutants contaminating groundwater, fouling rivers, and emitting benzene, hydrogen sulfide, and other noxious gases into the air.[42] Places like Savar are what some scholars call "sacrifice zones." Wealthy corporations have chosen these places to bear the environmental and health burdens of producing wealth for the world's elite. Local people do not benefit from this system. The limited benefits of low-paying, dangerous work are outweighed by the massive sacrifices the local residents pay in discomfort and illness.[43]

Corporations work with governments that lack accountability to citizens in order to avoid scrutiny of their polluting policies. The people who live near factories rarely have a voice in the environment of their communities. In China, the apparel industry knowingly dumps dyes into the water with impunity because it knows the Chinese state will do nothing about it. There are approximately 50,000 textile factories in China, but the nation's Ministry of Environmental Protection employs only 450 people. Compare that to the Environmental Protection Agency in the United States, which employs around 17,000 people. The EPA comes nowhere near having the resources to monitor American industry's environmental impact properly. China's commitment to enforcing environmental regulations is basically zero.[44]

Not surprisingly, a production system indifferent to the environment is also indifferent to both workplace safety and quality control. This is certainly the case in China. Chinese-made products for American consumers have poisoned children and pets because of their unsafe production standards. Since 2007, more than 5,500 dogs have gotten sick and more than 1,000 have died after eating tainted dog treats. Petco and PetSmart have decided to stop carrying pet treats made in China. Such incidents should make us ask not only about the standards of all products we ingest from China but also about what these poisons are doing to the communities in which the factories are sited. Of course we cannot know, because the process is concealed from us.[45]

The same failed supply chain standards that cause workers to die in fires and factory collapses also cause pollutants to sicken ecosystems and people. An April 2012 report by five environmental NGOs about the pollution problems of the textile industry in China did convince some brands, including Levi Strauss & Co., Nike, and Adidas, to extend their management of suppliers to dyeing operations, but the vast majority of American companies, including Disney, J.C. Penney, and Tommy Hilfiger, have so far done nothing. Residents near the Zhejiang Qingmao Textile Printing and Dyeing

Company face polluted wastewater and gases from factory operations. A resident named Ms. Lu said, "When it rains Qingmao dis-
charges black liquid into the river. One time they did this the whole
river was black. It rained last Friday and they did it again." Another
resident complained about the gases: "We can't stand it, it's killed so
many people. So many people have died from lung cancer."[46]

When nations do try to fight corporate despoiling of the environment, the companies use the courts of their wealthy home nations to counterattack. Latin American peoples have led the fight
against multinational corporations mining their land and polluting their water. Indigenous people in Peru have fought hard
against Colorado-based mining conglomerate Newmont opening
a gold and copper mine that they fear would make water supplies
undrinkable. El Salvador's former president Mauricio Funes cam-
paigned around a promise to not allow any metals mining, because
the cyanide used in mining poisons water, kills fish, and destroys
local ecosystems and economies.[47] The Commerce Group, a multinational mining corporation, owns a gold mine in El Salvador.
Like most gold mines, it leeches a tremendous amount of pollution
into local waterways, poisoning both fish and people. El Salvador
blocked the company from reopening the mine. Commerce Group's
response was to sue El Salvador for $100 million.[48] Ultimately, the
mining companies are more powerful than the governments of
poor nations.

Perhaps no industry sums up the problem of concealment and
pollution better than recycling. Most readers of this book probably
recycle. It makes us feel good. We get to separate out our recyclables
from our trash, put them in the blue bin, and then set the bin out
with the garbage once a week. When it gets picked up, the planet
is a little better off for our actions. It's the same with recycling old
phones and computers. Drop them off, they get reused or recycled,
and there's less garbage for our landfills. And recycling should be
an objectively good thing—recycling plastic bottles, glass, and paper saves resources and creates a more sustainable planet. Although
Americans had periodically engaged in reusing materials during
and before World War II, the modern recycling movement began in

the early 1970s, as environmentalists identified the massive amount of garbage the nation produced as a major problem. Recycling some of that material was an ecologically responsible thing any of us could do. By the 1990s, curbside recycling became common, and recycling moved into the American mainstream.[49]

But what actually happens to these recycled materials? Once again, out of sight, out of mind. Who actually separates the different recyclables? What are the conditions of work for these people? Who has to deal with the trash that ends up in there, the stale beer in the bottles, the sharp edges of metal cans, and the stench of rotting food bits? In December 2013, Pope Francis recorded a video tribute to the *cartoneros* of Argentina. *Cartoneros* means "cardboard people" but the term broadly applies to the people who sift through recycling. Francis called their work "dignified" and lauded their efforts toward environmentalism.[50] But Francis's public discussion of these people is rare, as they are invisible to us. Often that is because they live in another country. Most plastics, other than plastic bottles, are sent to Asia in bulk for recycling, although the actual disposal of the plastic is varied and much is burned for energy or just thrown away. In 2009, the United States exported 2.1 million tons of plastic recycling, over half of which went to China. We recycle our yogurt cups, but too often they just pollute another country.[51]

Half the world's car batteries are informally recycled through an international system that off-loads toxicity onto the poor. Approximately 20 percent of U.S. lead-acid batteries are exported to Mexico for recycling. Europeans export their batteries to Africa. China receives batteries from around the world. The damage to communities from battery toxicity can be significant. In Senegal in 2008, forty thousand people suffered from lead exposure and eighteen children died. In 1972, a San Diego metals company opened a Tijuana maquiladora that recycled heavy metals from lead-acid batteries and scrap metals. It closed in 1994, but neither the Mexican government nor the American company cleaned up the toxic waste left behind, which included seven thousand tons of lead slag. Local residents used the scraps to build squatter communities. The toxic materials led to an abnormal amount of birth defects, leading to the creation of the Environmental Health Coalition, an environmental justice group along the border organized to embarrass the Mexican government into cleaning up the mess, a process that is still ongoing.[52]

When it comes to recycling so-called e-waste, the problem is no better. In 1965, Intel co-founder Gordon Moore correctly predicted that the power of microchips would double every eighteen months.[53] Electronics become obsolete quickly. Like far too much else, recycling e-waste has been outsourced. The American government has almost no guidelines for recycling these materials. Eighty percent of American electronic recycling is shipped in bulk to Asia, especially China. A 2013 United Nations report called China the "largest e-waste dumping site in the world." The profit here is in the reuse of the so-called rare earth elements that electronics need to function. Workers literally pound computers and televisions to dust to extract the valuable metals, and in doing so they face massive exposure to these elements. Other processes involve dumping electronics in acid baths or burning the waste; these are also done without proper protection. Workers and nearby residents become exposed to lead, mercury, beryllium, and cadmium as well as chemicals such as hexavalent chromium and brominated flame retardants.[54]

Journalist Elizabeth Grossman provides an example of our out-of-sight, out-of-mind recycling of e-waste in her book *High Tech Trash*: "On the shores of the Lianjiang River in southern China, a woman squats in front of an open flame. In the pan she holds over the fire is a smoky stew of plastic and metal—a melting circuit board. With unprotected hands she plucks out the microchips. . . . Nearby a man sluices a pan of acid over a pile of computer chips, releasing a puff of toxic steam. When the vapor clears a small fleck of gold will emerge." E-waste recycling communities have undrinkable water, with lead rates 2,400 times the World Health Organization's safe level. People simply do not know what happens to their e-waste, and thus nothing gets done about it.[55]

None of this is to say we should not recycle. But our ignorance of the process of recycling, who benefits and who suffers, means that we need to think harder about our recycling streams to ensure justice and equity—out of sight, out of mind is not acceptable for corporations, and it should not be acceptable for consumers. Should the wealthy, consuming nations take responsibility for their own waste or ship it to the poor nations? At least some groups in the United States are fighting for responsibility as part of the larger struggle for environmental justice. The Computer Take-Back Campaign is a coalition of environmental organizations that seeks to make computer companies responsible for their products through the disposal phase. They have worked with groups in India, Taiwan, and other nations to document the damage the computer-recycling industry causes to Asians. They led a campaign against Dell after it contracted to use prison inmates in the United States to recycle computer waste, forcing the company to give up that practice in 2004. Greenpeace has also been a leader on this issue, famously stopping one ship delivering forty-two tons of Australian computer scraps to the Philippines.[56]

If recycling exports toxicity, there's the far more insidious trade in toxic waste from rich to poor countries. Beginning in the 1980s, after American citizens began demanding greater regulation of toxic waste in the wake of Love Canal and other public health disasters, corporations sought to export waste to poor countries to avoid regulatory costs. In 1986, the ship *Khian Sea* departed Philadelphia with fourteen thousand tons of toxic fly ash for delivery to the Bahamas. When that nation refused to accept the cargo, the ship floated around the Caribbean for months. It attempted to relabel the waste as fertilizer and dump it on Haiti, but that nation ordered it reloaded when the government found out what it really was. When Haiti rejected the fly ash, Robert Dowd, a representative of the Amalgamated Shipping Corporation, who owned the *Khian Sea*, ate a handful of the ash, saying, "See, it's edible. No danger." Despite the rejection, four thousand tons of the fly ash were left in Haiti. After voyaging around the world for twenty-seven months, attempting to dump the fly ash in several nations, including Cape Verde, Guinea, Indonesia, the Philippines, and Sri Lanka, the waste mysteriously disappeared somewhere off the coast of Southeast

Asia, probably dumped into the Indian Ocean. In 1996, the U.S. government finally had the fly ash dumped in Haiti removed in response to local people protesting over it killing their goats. This and many similar events around the world led to the 1989 Basel Convention of Transboundary Movements of Hazardous Wastes and Their Disposal. This was a useful first step, but it only controlled, rather than banned, the toxic waste trade. Plus, the convention redefined exporting toxicity as "recycling," making the process much more difficult to regulate. This was addressed by a further agreement in 1995, but hazardous-waste companies have fought to rescind or weaken it.[57]

Some environmental justice activists have opened their communities for what is called "toxic tourism" in order to build the public attention necessary to engage activists to help them. Mostly this is happening in the United States, such as in the predominantly African American community of Newtown, Georgia, where a variety of toxic industries have created a cancer cluster. Sometimes human rights organizations like Global Exchange will sponsor tours to polluted communities in Mexico. While these tours do open the eyes of those who can take them, the need to travel and work through an agency to witness the realities of modern pollution speaks to the effectiveness of corporations in placing toxicity away from the daily lives of American consumers. These are no Santa Barbara oil spills or Cuyahoga River fires that will tap into the consciousness of millions. For the worst pollution, in nations ranging from Haiti to Bangladesh, almost no Americans see it at all.[58]

Unfortunately, the Obama administration has not prioritized fighting the insidiousness of international trade exporting pollution around the world. Obama wants to pass the Trans-Pacific Partnership (TPP), a twelve-nation free trade agreement covering nations from Chile to Brunei, would continue allowing American companies to operate without consequences. So far Congressional Democrats have rejected the TPP because it would ship even more American jobs overseas and increase the environmental impact of American manufacturing. Organized labor has pointed out the environmental impact of such a deal. Says the International

Brotherhood of Boilermakers, "Let's not exacerbate the pollution problems of the world and perpetuate human exploitation by including nations like Malaysia and Vietnam in a free trade pact, as the TPP would do."[59] The Boilermakers are correct. These trade deals export not only American jobs, they also export environmental problems. The American government should not be facilitating environmental injustice. Trade deals should serve the citizens of both nations, not just corporate elites. Global trade has its benefits, but wanton pollution for the sake of profit is not an acceptable cost.

4

CONCEALED FOOD, BROKEN WORKERS

W hen you think of the globalized economy, you might not think of food. But capital mobility and the legal framework facilitating it have tremendously shaped the food system. It has transformed where and how our food is produced, who grows it, and how it affects the ecosystem. NAFTA's agricultural provisions allowed American farmers to dump their products on the Mexican market while raising animals fed on cheap American corn. This transformed Mexico. Mexican pig farmers went out of business because pork prices dropped so low. In 1995 Mexico imported 30,000 tons of pork from the United States, and in 2010 it imported 811,000 tons. Mexican hog farmers had to leave their farms to make a living. Some migrated north, becoming undocumented immigrants in the United States. A group of those people found work in a Smithfield Foods processing plant in North Carolina. Smithfield used these immigrants to bust a union-organizing campaign in the plant. When some of those immigrants in turn joined the union, Smithfield called the Immigration and Naturalization Service to report itself for immigration violations. One morning, twenty-one workers were individually called to their supervisor's office, arrested, imprisoned for using false social security cards, and then deported. Hundreds of other workers fled town, fearing they would be deported next. For Smithfield executives, the fines for hiring undocumented workers were the price of a union-free workplace. This actually backfired on Smithfield because the company had to replace those workers with union-supporting African Americans, and the United Food and Commercial Workers International Union, the nation's largest food worker union, won an election there in 2008. But Smithfield's strategy often does work. An Iowa slaughterhouse turned itself in for immigration violations in 2008 in a similar attempt to disrupt union organizing. Immigration and Customs Enforcement officials entered the plant and arrested 389 of its 970 workers. This time, the union drive stalled.[1]

Many of the Mexican workers in North Carolina came from the state of Veracruz, on the Gulf Coast. Those who stayed behind in Veracruz also found themselves fighting Smithfield. NAFTA rules facilitating land privatization allowed American agricultural companies to create U.S.-style agribusiness operations in Mexico. Smithfield built a pork-processing facility in Veracruz, and it treated the people who lived around that facility as poorly as the workers in North Carolina. The company buried dead pigs in un-lined pits. When those pigs decomposed, they contaminated the local water supply. Local residents organized to stop Smithfield from expanding the new facility and won.[2]

This Smithfield story tells us much about food's role in the glo-balized economy. First, it shows that the food industry outsources production for the same reasons as other industries—to pollute and to exploit workers while minimizing resistance from empowered locals with labor and environmental organizations. Hog and poul-try factory farms cause horrifying pollution when their lagoons of manure seep into waterways, and their workers are treated no better than the animals. This creates resistance, which can manifest itself in both environmentalism and unionism. The meat industry already locates its facilities in antiunion states such as North Carolina, and even politicians in more progressive states, like Maryland gover-nor Martin O'Malley, oppose regulations demanded by citizens to keep their water clean because they fear that the meat industry will move to another state.[3] If the regulations in all the states become too strict, NAFTA has opened up Mexico to American agribusiness. States compete with states and nations with nations in a race to the bottom. Ecosystems and workers suffer.

Smithfield also shows how the food industry creates a cheap labor force for other American companies investing in Mexico or hoping to attract low-wage immigrant labor in the United States. American companies exploit NAFTA's provisions on agricultural products to flood Mexico with cheap corn, beef, pork, chickens, and other products, creating the agricultural and labor conditions that allow companies like Smithfield Farms to exploit Mexicans both in Mexico and the United States. As food anthropologist Steve Striffler writes, "Mexican immigration in particular has been about ensuring a steady supply of cheap food" for American consumers.[4] Since undocumented workers fear deportation, they have little leverage to negotiate with employers. Smithfield is not the only company to report its own immigration violations when threatened with unionization. Agricultural policy and corporate migration have uprooted families and decimated communities while effectively hiding the impact of food production from consumers.

Words such as *globalization* and *outsourcing* obscure a central issue here: capital mobility is not strictly an international phenomenon. Corporations do not care about national borders so long as they can accomplish their objectives. Whether the slaughterhouse is in North Carolina or Veracruz, most of us never see where our food comes from. When it makes sense to invest in Mexico, agribusinesses do so. But they can also move to the vast Great Plains or the South, where environmental regulations are few and labor unions weak. As Timothy Pachirat writes in his powerful first-hand account of working in a Nebraska slaughterhouse, "Distance and concealment operate as mechanisms of power in modern society."[5] Hiding food production protects companies by concealing how the industry treats animals, what it dumps into the ecosystem, and how it treats workers. But the rise of political movements fighting for food safety and local food can reshape the food system and eliminate some exploitation if they focus on the justice, not just the quality of ingredients, behind the food. Today's consumers might eat organic food, but that does not mean the food is produced in a way that contributes to social justice. It does not mean that the people growing the food, butchering the meat, or serving you in the restaurant are treated humanely. Food activists must incorporate capital mobility and worker justice into their critique of industrial food. Peeling off the food industry's concealing blindfolds can empower consumers to again fight for labor and nature.

The history of food is the history of globalization. Domesticated animals and plants are all native to a specific place and slowly spread over the continents. Corn was first cultivated in the deserts of Mexico, and coffee comes from Ethiopia. Potatoes originated in the Andes and black pepper in southern India. Today, much of the world's population cannot fathom living without those foods.

The modern period of food globalization began when European explorers arrived in the Americas in 1492. When European ships returned, they brought American food with them. Tomatoes entered Italian cuisine, chilies became central to Thai food, and potatoes became the staple food of Ireland as the global trading networks moved these foods around Europe, Asia, and Africa. The introduction of maize to the Old World vastly improved nutrition, particularly transforming southern Europe and Africa. Europeans brought wheat, barley, rye, olives, and, most important, domesticated animals, including cows, horses, pigs, and chickens, to America.[6]

This movement of food is part of a broader process known as the Columbian Exchange—the exchange of biology between the New World and Old World that began in 1492. It includes humans, animals, plants, and diseases. Not only was this exchange why Europeans succeeded in conquering the Americas—because indigenous peoples lacked the resistance to European diseases, which rapidly reduced their populations—but it also transformed both hemispheres. Old World organisms rapidly altered New World ecologies: most indigenous American dog species went extinct, introduced plants outcompeted native plants, rats and up to sixty new species of earthworms decimated small animal species. Even today, diseases, plants, animals, and humans continue to travel around the globe, ranging from the emerald ash borers threatening the future of ash trees (and thus baseball as we know it, since bats are made from ash) in the United States to diseases such as HIV, West Nile virus, Ebola, and swine flu creating worldwide health scares.[7]

Globalization in food continues. Today, we keep finding new foods we want to eat. Quinoa from Peru and Bolivia has become so popular in Western countries that shortages have developed. Açaí from Brazil became a global phenomenon just a few years ago as Western consumers looked for a new superfood; it has faded back into obscurity almost as rapidly. Meanwhile, Coca-Cola, Pepsi, and McDonald's export their products into indigenous communities and developing nations around the globe, providing food with American cultural cachet but also undermining local food traditions and contributing to an increased global crisis of diabetes and obesity.[8]

Two other recent events in the globalization of food should concern us. First, the impact of American and European capital mobility on the land and people of the developing world has benefited local elites and multinational corporations at great cost to the rural poor, leading to desperation, alienation, and migration away from farms and into cities by impoverished people. Second, globalized agricultural corporations, based around transportation and chemical technologies that allow food to be delivered anywhere within the United States rapidly and cheaply, have increasingly moved production out of our sight, even if it remains within domestic borders. Just like our clothing, we don't know the conditions of work, the pollution caused by food production, or even what we are really putting into our bodies.

Let us move through the food system from farm to plate to show the impact of capital mobility and concealment. The American land is incredibly fecund. Our grains, vegetables, and meat provided the raw fuel for workers building industrial America. With new technologies, by the mid-twentieth century American farms produced so much that the nation needed new outlets for its produce.

The federal government could use this food to push its geopolitical agenda, such as when it saved the Soviet Union from a famine in 1972, but this surplus needed a more permanent solution. In stepped the growing international ideology of neoliberalism and the accompanying free trade agreements that facilitated a global agricultural marketplace.

Mexican elites were as susceptible to neoliberal ideas as Americans. During the 1970s and 1980s, the Mexican government began ending government-guaranteed price support of agricultural products, making the status of Mexican farmers shaky even before NAFTA's passage. Then NAFTA's free trade provisions allowed American agribusiness to dump cheap corn, milk, pork, and other agricultural products on the Mexican market. Free trade created 700,000 industrial jobs in Mexico but also forced 2 million Mexican farmers off their land and generated the labor force for modern corporations.[9] Following NAFTA, the prices for Mexican-grown crops fell between 44 and 67 percent. The centuries-old tradition of small farming for rural survival went into rapid decline. One out of every three Mexican hog farmers went out of business between 1994 and 2001. There were crops that Mexicans could farm for the wealthy U.S. market instead of subsistence corn or pork agriculture—but these were capital-intensive crops that required enormous tracts of land. Snow peas, broccoli, and cauliflower needed a capital investment of $3,145, $1,096, and $971 per hectare, respectively. Average Mexican farmers could not come close to affording such a venture.[10] This meant that millions of farmers could no longer work on their land. Between 2001 and 2008, agricultural employment in Mexico fell from 10.7 million to 8.6 million people.[11]

Those that tried to stay on their land were subject to the capricious international market for commodities. One farmer told journalist Susana Baumann that her family had a contract with Nestlé for her farm's milk, but in 2003 Nestlé lowered the price paid and stopped picking up the milk, leading to spoilage. Her family had to leave their land and became undocumented immigrants to the United States.[12] She and millions of others started a migratory path to the big cities of Mexico, to the U.S.-Mexico border to work in the maquiladoras, or into the United States as the workers on our farms, in our restaurants, and on our construction sites.

Theoretically, the import of cheap American farm goods should at least have provided Mexican consumers cheap food, but it actually left them vulnerable to international commodity prices. The home of maize became a corn-importing economy. When I was in Mexico City over the winter holidays in 2007, the newspaper headlines were emblazoned with fears over rising tortilla prices because that formerly cheap American corn became expensive after American agribusiness began using it to make ethanol, high fructose corn syrup, and other industrial products. Tortilla prices tripled in some parts of Mexico in 2006. The average Mexican family consumes one kilogram of tortillas a day. So when prices rose as high as $1.81 for that kilogram in a nation with a minimum wage of $4.60 a day, the protests in Mexico created a brief but major political crisis for the Mexican government. What happened in Mexico happened around the world. Between 2007 and 2008, the world's least developed countries saw their food import costs increase by 37 percent. Prices later declined, but the connection between free trade agreements and food insecurity became apparent.[13]

In 2009, there were 6.5 million undocumented Mexican immigrants in the United States. As farmers themselves, many of them found jobs on American farms. American fruit and vegetable farms require a lot of labor. Agribusiness would love to automate it, but machines bruise tender produce. Instead, corporations wrest every cent of profit from a migrant labor force with little concern for the workers' health or lives. They have done so for a century, fighting to exempt farmworkers from federal labor legislation, supporting exceptions to immigration law to ensure cheap labor, and brutally crushing farmworker strikes. Today, farmworkers in south Texas and California's Central Valley die of heat exhaustion, yet even this receives little public attention. In May 2008, an undocumented seventeen-year-old named Maria Isabel Vasquez Jimenez picked in a grape field near Stockton, California. It was 95 degrees, and the nearest water cooler was a ten-minute walk away, too long for her brief break. She died of heatstroke. In addition, a recent Human

Rights Watch report excoriated American tobacco farmers for the conditions on their farms. Children as young as seven work ten- to twelve-hour days during the harvest. Three-quarters of the children interviewed suffer from green tobacco sickness, a syndrome caused by handling tobacco plants for long periods that causes vomiting, dizziness, and headaches. Yet most tobacco-producing states explicitly exclude agricultural labor from their child labor laws, and North Carolina lacks any state-level child labor law at all. The federal government could intervene, as it has prohibited "hazardous" work on farms for children under the age of sixteen, but it has not declared work on tobacco farms hazardous.[14]

When employers care little about their employees' health, poisoning them through toxic chemicals becomes common. In an industry as exploitative as farming, this happens far too often. Since World War II, the chemical industry has developed increasingly toxic pesticides and herbicides to eliminate pests and improve agricultural outputs. But farmers have poisoned their workers through pesticide exposure. One study of California Latino farmworkers showed they had a 59 percent greater chance of developing leukemia and a 70 percent greater chance of developing stomach cancer than the Latino population in the United States as a whole. Farmworkers frequently complain about pesticide exposure and understand that their work makes them sick. One Mexican-American woman who worked in the fields said, "This year, we had much irritation of the legs, back and face while thinning sugar beets. This did not happen in other years. They must be using something new and bad." Cancer clusters developed in farmworker towns such as McFarland, California, as pesticide poisoning created unusual cancer deaths among children.[15] But global corporations make $30 billion a year off these pesticides, providing little incentive to implement the regulations necessary to grow food and protect people at the same time.

These poisons helped drive unionization. In the 1960s, the United Farm Workers (UFW) briefly became a force in the California fields, partly through organizing workers and partly through mobilizing its national supporters in boycotts. But due to internal strife, by the 1980s the UFW had faded from the lives of most California farmworkers, easily ignored by agribusiness. Newer farmworker unions such as the Coalition of Immokalee Workers (CIW) in Florida and the Farm Labor Organizing Committee (FLOC) in North Carolina and the Midwest have made progress, but most farmworkers remain unorganized today.[16] Still, these newer farmworker unions have made a major difference in the lives of their members. The CIW spent a decade organizing against the terrible conditions of Florida tomato workers, including leading a boycott of fast-food chains that used these tomatoes. This paid off, as it has pressured 90 percent of tomato growers to raise wages and follow standards that ban verbal abuse and sexual harassment while also convincing Walmart to follow the group's labor standards in monitoring its tomato suppliers on the East Coast.[17]

Typically, consumers mobilized around pesticides when the threat affected them. As discussed in chapter 3, Rachel Carson's 1962 book *Silent Spring* helped create the modern environmental movement by pointing out the impact of DDT on the ecosystem, leading to its ban in the United States in 1972. Environmentalists around the country organized to fight against pesticide use in the late 1970s, highlighting the connection between the profits of chemical companies and diseases in our bodies. When investigators discovered that pesticide residue ended up in the vegetables consumers purchased, the outrage grew. This finally forced chemical companies to respond. They developed so-called nonpersistent insecticides. Unlike DDT, which remains in the ecosystem, nonpersistents such as parathion break down quickly.[18]

But this was a direct result of consumer pressure, not worker pressure. Consumers needed to be placated, but workers can be ignored. Nonpersistent insecticides allowed companies to transfer the effects of poisons from the rich to the poor. The effects of nonpersistents largely disappear by the time the broccoli gets to market, but they have an intense immediate effect after their application. That means workers face all the risk. Consumers no longer had to worry, but the poisons went straight into workers' bodies. When agribusinesses move vegetable production to Mexico, it only makes exposure worse, due to the lack of worker protections. Once again, when a labor hazard did not personally involve consumers, the conditions of work disappeared from the conversation. At least 20 million cases of pesticide poisoning are reported every year in the developing world. People suffer from skin conditions, breathing problems, damage to the nervous system, and many other medical problems. A 1985 UN report estimated twenty thousand fatalities a year, a number the World Health Organization estimates has changed little in the twenty-first century, although precise numbers are almost impossible to verify due to poor monitoring and reporting practices. Today, more than 90 percent of pesticide poisonings occur in developing nations.[19]

In the 1940s, an American scientist named Norman Borlaug began conducting research in Mexico on disease-resistant and high-yield strains of wheat. His success in this research was combined with new mechanized technologies and enormous amounts of chemicals, including nonorganic petroleum-based fertilizer and pesticides, to produce colossal quantities of food in the developing world. In 1968, U.S. Agency for International Development director William Gaud coined the term Green Revolution to describe how this rapid growth in food production could transform the world. Nations like Mexico and India wholeheartedly embraced the Green Revolution, leading to greater food production and growing populations. Borlaug won the 1970 Nobel Peace Prize for his work.[20]

There's no question that the Green Revolution saved lives and filled bellies. India struggled with famine for centuries before Borlaug brought Green Revolution technology to the subcontinent in the mid-1960s. That technology also helped create the labor force for global corporations by driving farmers off their land. As Vandana Shiva has convincingly shown, the Green Revolution has come at enormous costs to workers' health, the stability of millions of small farmers, and rural ecosystems. The "miracle seeds" provided by American companies undermined genetic diversity and took control of farming away from the people who had developed agricultural practices specific to their homes for thousands of years. It created monocultures that led to destructive plant diseases. Into that fray came American chemical companies, such as Union Carbide and Monsanto. Big Chemical allied with local elites for mutual advantage; the former saw new markets and profit, the latter personal wealth. Enormous quantities of pesticides were dumped into water supplies and poisoned workers. (It was pesticides for Green Revolution agriculture that created the Union Carbide disaster at Bhopal discussed in chapter 3.) Between 1972 and 1985, pesticide imports rose 261 percent in Asia. Corporations in the global North had found a new way to profit off the bodies of the global South.[21]

The Green Revolution also led to the rapid decline of small family farms, which prior to then had dominated agriculture through the history of human civilization. Family farmers did not have the money to purchase the fertilizer, machines, and chemical pesticides necessary to compete in the global marketplace. In the New Deal of the 1930s, the Agricultural Adjustment Act helped drive thousands of American sharecroppers off the land, sending many of them to California, as chronicled by John Steinbeck in *The Grapes of Wrath*.[22] With the Green Revolution, capitalist land centralization spread into Latin America and Asia. By the late 1960s, American observers in India noted that the Green Revolution was throwing farmers off their land, leading to conflict in villages. Today, millions of farmers struggle to hold on to their land in the face of worldwide commodity markets that are fueled by technologically driven development. Family farmers simply cannot pay off the debt they incur for the technologies they need in order to sell in a world marketplace that privileges big landowners. In the Indian state of Maharashtra, 3,926 farmers killed themselves in 2005, up from 1,083 in 1995. Farmer suicides have risen in China and Mexico as well. Many kill themselves by drinking the pesticides they purchased to use on the crops.[23]

Although not without significant benefits, the Green Revolution contributed to several of the problems discussed in this book. The inability of the poor to stay on their farms has forced them to migrate to find work. This urban migration provided a needy labor force willing to accept almost any wage from American manufacturers and contractors. When you need a job because American chemical companies have helped throw you off your land, you will take what you're offered. The Green Revolution has created the beautiful produce sections of American supermarkets but at an enormous cost to the health of the people growing the food. We, as consumers, do not see the impact of this system when we purchase broccoli or lettuce in January. We see the tasty salad we will have for dinner, but the labor that goes into the food disappears, as does its impact on the ecosystem. For the industrial food system, this obfuscation is intentional and profit-generating. They want us to buy their food not knowing how many fish have died from poisoned waters or how many workers have gone to the hospital.

A corporate system that does not value workers' lives also does not value treating animals with dignity. Concealment hides the conditions of animals from consumers along with the conditions of human labor. As consumers, we buy our hamburger or chicken or fish, but what do we know about the animal? Do we even recognize it as the same animal in the barnyard? Cows and chickens are cute. What do they have to do with the ground beef at Safeway or the chicken nuggets at McDonald's? We can laugh at Chick-fil-A commercials with the cows trying to get us to eat chicken, but the vague awareness that we are eating actual animals goes little further than the notion that cows can't spell. In the nineteenth century, there were slaughterhouses right in New York City, and Chicago had its enormous meatpacking district. The animals at those facilities were not necessarily treated well, but at least consumers knew more about their meat. Today, corporations have turned animals into industrialized products, unconcerned with their health, comfort, or treatment.

More than 99 percent of our chickens, 92 percent of our beef, and 97 percent of our pork comes from domestic production.[24] But the principles of concealment that incentivize the outsourcing of production dominate this industry, too. Each year, Americans grow about 9 billion broiler chickens, 113 million pigs, 33 million cows, and 250 million turkeys on factory farms. Companies purposely locate these facilities far from cities. The feedlots and processing plants of the modern beef industry are on isolated roads in

Nebraska, Iowa, and Kansas that tourists rarely use. Chicken operations in southern Delaware and pork factories in rural North Carolina also remain out of sight and out of mind. There are a few exceptions, such as the large concentrated animal feeding operation on Interstate 40, west of Amarillo, Texas, or the Harris Ranch Beef Company feedlot along Interstate 5 in California. You can smell these for miles.

Outside of those exceptions, farm animals have disappeared from our view. Undercover investigations by animal rights activists have shown horrible and cruel treatment of animals in America's meat production facilities. Workers are underpaid, understaffed, and stressed, and they often abuse the animals in frustration. Workers have to breathe in the gases from animal feces, stand in pools of blood, and risk their lives working with the machines of factory farming. Turkeys are bred with huge breasts that prevent their natural reproduction, nesting hens are caged so tightly that they develop debilitating bone conditions, and pigs are penned in cages so small the wires cut their snouts. It's a filthy, disgusting, horrifying system that does not have to exist. We can eat meat, raise animals with some level of respect, and train workers to treat animals correctly. But Smithfield Foods and Tyson Foods find the current system tremendously profitable and have no interest in reform.[25]

These meat factories also have enormous environmental impacts. A 1997 report showed that the United States produced 1.4 billion tons of animal manure a year, about 130 times the amount of human waste.[26] In a new phenomenon that was first reported in 2009, the large pits that companies use to collect the manure have developed foam up to four feet thick that rises to the top. The foam traps methane and can lead to explosions. One manure pit caused a barn to explode in Iowa in September 2011, killing fifteen hundred pigs and severely burning one worker. Scientists have not yet been able to explain why this foam has started to develop.[27] Nutrient runoff from agricultural fertilizers and factory farming is also causing algae blooms in western ponds that lead to deformed frogs with eight hind legs.[28]

Public knowledge of working conditions and animal treatment is the food industry's worst nightmare. This is the motivation behind a series of so-called ag-gag bills to criminalize undercover footage of industrial farming operations. Iowa, Utah, and Missouri have these laws, and Idaho joined them in February 2014. In Idaho, it is now illegal for anyone not employed by the farm—and for anyone who misrepresented themselves to get hired—to make video recordings of what happens on that farm without the express consent of the owner. Violators could receive a year in prison and a $5,000 fine. Agribusiness pushed for the law after an undercover video showed workers beating and sexually abusing cattle at an Idaho dairy operation. Animal rights groups are challenging on constitutional grounds, but it is a dangerous advance in the concealment of industrial activity. If laws protect what happens in meat factories from view, why would they not give all factory owners legal standing for concealment? Why not make the documentation of violations of workers' rights or the dumping of pollution in any industry a crime? Although court challenges will result, if these laws are held up, they are a very scary legal aid to corporations concealing their operations.[29]

We once knew more about who raised our meat and how it was processed. Until after the Civil War, most Americans lived on farms or in small towns. Food production was largely local, supplemented by larger national and international markets for foods like sugar and coffee. Meat was especially local. People wanted to see the meat they bought, particularly their beef. Given that fresh beef goes bad quickly, consumers did not trust anything that was not butchered locally. Until the late nineteenth century, people raised their own animals, bought meat from nearby farmers, or went to butchers who knew where the animal came from. Even big cities like Boston and New York had slaughterhouses to provide freshly slaughtered beef.

When American cities exploded in size after 1880, local food production became harder. A city of a million people could not easily grow its own food or slaughter its own meat. The advent of refrigerated railcars in the 1880s turned meat into an industrial product and played a major role in separating the production of food from everyday lives. Refrigeration meant that meatpackers could precut beef and send it across the country without concern about spoilage. To overcome people's concerns about its quality, the companies took a loss in selling their meat, undermining local butchers and creating new markets for cheap meat that would generate profit after the smaller competitors shut down. Millions of cows that grazed on the Great Plains rode trains to Chicago where they went into huge stockyard pens. They were killed in enormous slaughterhouses, processed into a variety of products, and then shipped by train to consumers across the country. By the early twentieth century, beef was not from a cow but from a package you bought at a local market. Once Americans became used to refrigerated or canned beef, they assumed it was good meat. That assumption was often mistaken.[30]

The gargantuan meatpacking district of Chicago achieved fame and became an international tourist attraction. But, as Upton Sinclair described in his famous 1906 novel *The Jungle*, these factories created treacherous work conditions and nasty food. The novel's detailed description of the factories killing rats with poisoned bread and then mixing the dead rats and bread with the beef horrified meat-loving Americans. President Theodore Roosevelt responded by signing the Pure Food and Drug Act and the Meat Inspection Act, establishing federal authority to regulate the national food system. Over the following decades, government inspectors ensured a safer, cleaner food product for Americans.[31]

Sinclair wrote his novel to expose the terrible lives of workers and convert readers to socialism. But Americans mostly ignored those messages. Slaughterhouse workers stood on floors soaked in blood and water in very cold temperatures, with flying hooks and knives risking their limbs and lives every second. They began forming unions in the 1890s to improve their lives, but it was not until the creation of the CIO-affiliated Packinghouse Workers Organizing Committee (later the United Packinghouse Workers of America or UPWA) in 1937 that they achieved major gains in pay and working conditions. Organized labor increasingly played a big role throughout the nation's food economy after the 1930s. UPWA members cut beef in Chicago. The milkmen delivering glass jars of fresh milk to doorsteps were Teamsters. Thanks to the unions, the conditions that led Sinclair to write his novel faded. By the 1960s, unionized meat cutters made 28 percent more money than average workers made for nondurable manufacturing.[32]

While meatpackers came to terms with the unions, unionization and good wages were bad outcomes for trucking companies, grocery store chains, and the Republican Party. A 1955 union contract won by the meatpacker unions that put a collective $50 million in workers' pockets begins the recent history of capital mobility in meat production. This contract frustrated Eisenhower administration officials, who faced heat over high beef prices. Secretary of Agriculture Ezra Taft Benson and his undersecretary Earl Butz, who later created the modern farm subsidy system while Secretary of Agriculture under Richard Nixon, wanted to raise farm profits without increasing consumer costs. Their answer was to undermine unions and squeeze wages by moving meat production out of the cities and into nonunion plants in the countryside, near where the cows and pigs were farmed.[33]

New upstart meatpackers, with the support of trucking and grocery chains who profited from cheaper meat, introduced refrigerated trucks that allowed meat processing in union-free rural areas. This undermined the big Chicago packinghouses and their unions. The new rural corporations had ruthless antiunion mentalities. Iowa Beef Packers (IBP) became a leading meatpacker in the 1960s. Today part of Tyson Foods, IBP rapidly consolidated the rural meatpacking operations in the Midwest, built enormous feedlot operations on the Great Plains, and created nonunion workplaces with low wages. In 1969, IBP workers in Dakota City, Iowa, went on strike. IBP hired scabs to replace them. Violence broke out on both sides and one person was killed. When unionized butchers in New York City refused to sell IBP beef, the company made a deal with the Mafia to break the boycott, undermining the strike. IBP wages were soon 50 percent lower than in the Chicago plants. The big meatpackers could not compete, closed their unionized slaughterhouses, laid off twelve thousand workers, and moved their operations to the

Plains as well. Further IBP hard-line antiunion strategies led to the rapid weakening of the UPWA, which became the United Food and Commercial Workers (UFCW) in 1979.[34]

The new geography of meatpacking, with its decentralized production, low wages, and poor working conditions, meant that farm owners earned more money and consumers maintained low beef prices. Workers—never seen by consumers—were caught in the middle. Nonunion factories demanded vastly increased production from their workers. Fatigue, repetitive-motion injuries, serious accidents on the job, and high turnover followed. One IBP manager considered an average annual turnover rate of 96 percent at a plant "low," showing how little the corporation cared to provide labor dignified enough conditions to keep workers on the job.[35]

The companies might not have wanted unions, but many in the new rural workforce did. Poultry truck drivers joined the Teamsters in North Carolina. The UFCW had major successes organizing southern poultry factories during the 1980s. The largely African American workforce in these plants took major personal risks by unionizing to improve the low wages and unsafe working conditions. Companies responded by closing unionized factories and opening new nonunion plants nearby, intimidating new hires into signing union-decertification petitions, or declaring bankruptcy and reopening the plants without union contracts. They also began replacing African American workers with immigrants, often undocumented, from Mexico and Central America. An Immigration and Naturalization Service investigation in 1991 led to accusations that Tyson Foods paid smugglers to bring employees up to their plants from Mexico and Guatemala. Most unionized plants faded in the face of this determined antiunion effort.[36]

With union-free workplaces and undocumented workers, employers created an exploitative system of labor in the Plains states that looked more like the outsourced maquiladoras of Mexico than the unionized shops of Chicago. In 2005, Human Rights Watch released a report saying the American meat industry violated basic human and worker rights because of the terrible workplace safety, violations of freedom of association, and exploitation of undocumented immigrants. A decade later, little has changed. Meatpacking is a dangerous, nonunion, polluting industry that fights worker organizing through hiring, intimidating, and firing vulnerable workers, and it avoids pollution standards through threats to move operations.[37]

Conditions are arguably even worse in the international fish industry. At Walmart, you can buy inexpensive bags of frozen crawfish and shrimp. As with clothing subcontractors, Walmart signs contracts with suppliers that provide shellfish at low cost. And as in the apparel industry, Walmart's pressure for low prices means seafood suppliers squeeze every cent out of labor. In 2012, the Worker Rights Consortium issued a report excoriating Walmart for contracting with C.J.'s Seafood, a crawfish processer that brought guest workers from Mexico to its Louisiana processing facility. C.J.'s forced them to work sixteen- to twenty-four-hour shifts and locked them in the plant. Workers were threatened with deportation if they complained. Despite these threats, a worker named Ana Rosa Diaz, who had left her four children at home in Tamaulipas, Mexico, to find work, called the National Guestworker Alliance and reported the conditions. This started a series of investigations, including by the U.S. Department of Labor. Scott Nova, executive director of the Worker Rights Consortium, said, "The extreme lengths of the shifts people were required to work, the employer's brazenness in violating wage laws, the extent of the psychological abuse the workers faced and the threats of violence against their families—that combination made it one of the most egregious workplaces we've examined, whether here or overseas." This pressure and bad publicity led Walmart to suspend the contract, but not to change its own labor practices or take any responsibility for the manufacturing of its products.[38]

States such as Louisiana promote themselves as "business friendly," attracting corporations with the unstated promise that companies like C.J.'s can operate with little state interference. Increasingly, though, companies like Walmart want to avoid even the possible threat of a reduction in supply through regulations. Shellfish production has moved decisively overseas over the past two decades. More than 80 percent of shrimp eaten in the United States comes from other nations, with Bangladesh, Vietnam, and China increasingly providing Americans with their inexpensive shellfish. Those governments do not enforce labor laws in fish-processing sites. Immigrant workers in a shrimp factory in Thailand's Song-khla Province that supplies Walmart went on strike in 2012. They struck over their filthy barracks and a reduced food allowance that left them starving. The Cambodian and Burmese workers cannot read Thai, are in debt to traffickers for their expenses in getting to Thailand, and have little recourse to improve their lives. Walmart originally claimed it had told the Songkhla supplier this behavior violated its labor codes, but it later denied ever having received products from that factory, despite overwhelming physical evidence to the contrary. Thai police fired gunshots in the air to break up the strikers, demonstrating that the government's interest was in protecting the fish elite and foreign contracts, not ensuring basic human rights. The new government in Thailand, following the 2014 coup, is even worse in its contempt for workers and the poor.[39]

On fishing boats, conditions are even worse. Labor brokers sell migratory workers from around Southeast Asia to the mackerel fishing industry until the immigrants pay off their debts. Fifty-nine percent of these workers have witnessed the murder of another worker. One ship owner killed all fourteen of his workers rather than pay them. Meanwhile, fish exports continue to grow in importance to the Thai economy. Thailand is now the third-leading exporter of fish in the world. The United States imported $2.5 billion in seafood from Thailand in 2012, including more than 20 percent of the nation's mackerel and sardines.[40]

The food products we buy in the middle aisles of the supermarket are even more obscured from their real costs than vegetables and meat. American companies have engaged in the same union busting, outsourcing, and subcontracting in processed food as in apparel or toys. These workers are subjected to the same problems of poisoning, poor conditions, and capital mobility as workers in every other industry. In 2013, Kellogg's locked out its majority-black workforce at a Memphis factory that makes Fruit Loops and

Frosted Flakes in order to crush the union, Bakery, Confectionery, Tobacco Workers and Grain Millers International Union Local 252G. The company recently moved 58 million pounds of cereal production from Memphis to a new factory in Mexico where workers are required to live in company housing. It then hired a union-busting agency in Ohio to bring in scab laborers to Memphis. This one action is part of a larger move by Kellogg's to eliminate most of its American factories and all of its unions. The company has recently closed union plants in Australia and Canada, shifting production to nonunion sites. In July 2014, a federal judge ordered an end to the lockout and the workers returned to the job, but the long-term outlook for the union members keeping their jobs does not look promising.[41]

What happens when Kellogg's wins its fight and processed food is outsourced overseas? Let's look at the candy industry to find out. In November 2013, an explosion rocked the Dulces Blueberry factory in Ciudad Juárez, Mexico, which made candy for several leading American companies and produced some of our favorite treats, including Sour Patch Kids, gummy bears, and jelly beans. At least seven workers died. Another seven remained hospitalized a month later with severe burns. While Mexican authorities say these factories are well inspected, as is their claim regarding all maquiladoras, at least two large fires at the plant occurred in the past decade, and inspectors found flammable candy components stored improperly. The fines incurred for these violations totaled $9,000—peanut candies for contractors working with American companies. Essentially, the drive for cheap candy created a Triangle fire in food.[42]

Sometimes it makes political and public relations sense for food companies to keep some work in the United States. In these cases, companies want to bring the labor conditions of the developing world back to their home factories. Take Hershey. The famous chocolate company is so connected to Pennsylvania that leaving it entirely would be a difficult decision rife with bad publicity. Hershey can, however, move Jolly Rancher, a company it bought in 1997, across the globe, as it did when it shut Jolly Rancher's Golden, Colorado, factory in 2002 after fifty-three years as an economic anchor and icon of that Denver suburb. At first Hershey moved production to Reading, Pennsylvania, and then, in 2009, it moved production of Jolly Ranchers, along with York Peppermint Patties, to a new factory in Mexico. Hershey closed other factories in the United States and Canada as well. Plants in Guadalajara, Mexico, and São Roque, Brazil, replaced those in Smiths Falls, Ontario, and Oakdale, California. It kept some production in its Pennsylvania home for good public relations but wanted cheap labor as in Mexico and Brazil. In 2011, it became clear that the workers at the company's Palmyra, Pennsylvania, plant should not have been workers at all; they thought they were coming to the United States as foreign exchange students from nations ranging from China to Poland. No one told them they would labor in a chocolate factory when they received their student visas after paying up to $6,000 for the experience. They were told they would experience American culture. Indeed they did—the American culture of labor exploitation, where they had to pick up fifty-pound boxes and were threatened with deportation if they resisted. They went on strike over low pay and harsh conditions. It took great bravery for the students to say they had had enough, making their story public. Who knows how often this happens without being reported? Hershey had to pay the workers $213,000 and received a $143,000 fine—a mere trifle for a highly profitable global corporation.[43]

Many food workers are much less empowered than foreign students. Like farmworkers and meatpackers, many of our food workers are undocumented immigrants who lack the language skills and legal standing to demand enforcement of workplace regulations. Employers seek these workers out to maximize exploitation and profit. A political system that has empowered corporations to attack and destroy unions created this exploitative system, and the ability to avoid or violate pollution regulations makes it worse. Our food system reflects our declining democracy writ large.

Restaurants are yet another place where concealment allows for exploitation, even though this is work that cannot be outsourced. The kitchen door itself is enough for employers to hide terrible working conditions from diners. Some of those migrants leaving Mexico end up cooking our food while others grow it. We eat at restaurants and probably assume that the cooks receive decent treatment, or we don't think about it. Most of us tip, some less well than others. But workers rely on those tips to eat, because the tipped minimum wage in the United States is $2.13 an hour. Their pay keeps them below the poverty line. People of color are routinely discriminated against in restaurants and cannot advance in the industry. Restaurant workers are forced to work when sick, making your food unsanitary through no fault of the worker. Labor violations are rampant. It's all right there, just behind a swinging kitchen door. Food justice has to include the cooks and the servers. Ending the tipped minimum wage is one way we can help. There should be no difference between minimum wages for restaurant workers and other workers. In fact, seven states have equal minimum wages, and people still go out to eat in those states.[44]

There's also a tremendous amount of exploitation in our grocery stores. In many cases, this situation is actually worse in stores that market themselves as alternative and sell organic foods. Many big grocery store chains are organized with the United Food and Commercial Workers. UFCW representation has helped its members achieve good wages and union contracts at those stores. But at the places where many people who think of themselves as food-conscious environmentalists shop, such as Whole Foods, the conditions are quite different. Not only does Whole Foods co-founder and current co-CEO John Mackey deny global warming and hate even mild health care reform like the Affordable Care Act, he is also strongly antiunion. When President Obama was elected, labor hoped the Employee Free Choice Act would pass, which would have made union organizing far easier by allowing a majority of workers to sign a union card instead of forcing a National Labor Relations Board–administered union election that routinely allows employers time to attack the union. Fearing this would pass, Whole Foods store supervisors began threatening workers with their jobs if they joined a union. This was not the first time Whole Foods had attacked unions. When drivers at its San Francisco distribution center voted to join the Teamsters in 2006, the company fired two drivers and engaged in systematic harassment of other employees. The company has also suspended Spanish-speaking workers for violating its English-only policy on the store floor, in effect not allowing its workers to communicate with one another. For consumers who care about healthy food, it's also important to know whether the stores who sell it treat workers fairly and allow them the choice to have union representation. Ignoring this issue means contributing to the unjust food system.[45]

But here's the thing about food: because it is so important to our lives and our health, it is one set of products where we can effectively resist the concealment of production. Eating is a profound, if everyday, experience that affects our health and our happiness. The explosive growth in farmers' markets, concerns about genetically modified organisms, and fears of pesticides have challenged the industrial food complex, just not over its treatment of workers. Free-range chickens and cattle have become highly desirable and expensive products, both for taste and for health and safety concerns, but less so because of the workers injured and killed in the meatpacking plants. Consumers have demanded country-of-origin information for meat. This all frustrates the food companies. They were outraged by 2013 Agriculture Department regulations that forced meat companies to include labels identifying the country of origin of the dead animal. The American Meat Institute, a meatpacking trade group, even referred to these regulations as "segregating" the animals, perverting the racialized history of the United States to promote the concealment of meat production. The meat industry has filed suit against the new law, but at present it is still in effect.[46]

It's not just Americans who have become outraged at the food system that poisons them and treats animals as if they do not feel pain. While obscured and hidden food production is a central tenet of modern food capitalism, for American fast-food companies to profit they need to find new markets. So they have expanded around the world, pushing a vision of the United States as a consumer paradise to which other nations' middle classes can aspire. While this strategy has proven quite successful for McDonald's, Burger King, and other American fast-food corporations, it has also inspired resistance. Probably the most famous example was in 1999 when the French food activist and slow-food movement leader José Bové tore down a McDonald's under construction in Millau, France. Most people, whether in France or China, are not going to go to such extremes. But when they find out how the system of concealed food production leads to abuses that affect them, they act with the same fury Americans have felt when they experienced the horrors of the industrial system. In July 2014, a Chinese news report exposed a Shanghai meat-processing plant sending expired and rotten meat to American-based fast-food companies across the country, as well as for use in McDonald's chicken nuggets in Japan. What's especially notable about this case is that the Chinese meat company is actually owned by OSI Group, an American agricultural conglomerate based in Illinois. For all that Americans complain about unsafe Chinese products, in this case it was American meat-production methods exported abroad. McDonald's has, of course, decided to stick with the supplier, leaving no reason for Chinese consumers to believe that American fast food is safe to eat. This story once again shows the power of concealment and how throwing back the curtain on food production causes demands for change.[47]

We can see the current local food movement as a backlash against corporations' efforts to hide their operations from us. We cannot control very much about our relationship to the larger economy. But regional food networks, with production ranging from rooftop gardens to large farms on the outskirts of cities, can bring a significant amount of food democracy back into cities while providing enormous environmental benefits compared to the current system. Eschewing monocultures for diversified food crops would cut down on the pesticides and herbicides needed, meaning less fertilizer, less pollution, and healthier rivers, lakes, and oceans as well as small farmers who could afford to live and farm without expensive chemicals.

Promoting local food production that encourages sustainability over corporate profits might also help farmers in the developing world stay on the land if they choose to do so. German milk exports threw ten thousand Dominican Republic dairy farmers out of their jobs in the 1980s and 1990s.[48] Where did they go? To Santo Domingo, to the United States, to greater poverty. Dominican milk drinkers lost their food security and became dependent on the international milk markets. Greater local ability for Dominicans to feed themselves would help everyone except big agricultural companies and the corporations who take advantage of the cheap labor provided by people forced off their land. Fair trade food would also help spur local production in the hands of small farmers but still serve a global marketplace of aware consumers who care about the environmental and labor conditions that produce their food.[49]

But food movements also need to be justice movements and connect to bigger issues—food justice, worker justice, and animal justice are interconnected. If we are serious in thinking about a democratic food system, we have to support good working conditions throughout the food industry. It means we need to support farmworker and meatpacker unions. We have to end the tipped minimum wage and demand greater funding for OSHA and the FDA to inspect our food factories. *New York Times* food writer Mark Bittman uses his platform to routinely call for sustainable food. But he also sees true sustainability coming only when both the price of food rises enough that farmers can make a profit and the poor make enough money to buy it. That means, in his words, "Unionization, or an increase in the minimum wage, or both. No one would argue that canned tomatoes should be too expensive for poor people, but by increasing minimum wage in the fields and elsewhere, we raise standards of living and increase purchasing power."[50] Supporting farmworker justice is one concrete way that we can encourage sustainability and justice in food.

Food demonstrates the complexity of capital mobility and the structural changes globalization has wrought on people and nature. Capital moves, but capital also moves people. Corporations allied with governments created vast new supplies of food through technology, but they also imposed policies that separated people from the land, forcing them to move and become the working class of the new capital mobility. The sweatshops of Mexico, Honduras, and Bangladesh could not exist without the Green Revolution. Concealing food separates consumers from producers. Meanwhile, production takes place behind barbed wire fences, in locked factories, in the depopulated Great Plains, and across the Mexican border.

Ultimately, our food problems stem from the same lack of democracy that plagues our society. In our food system, animals are abused, workers die, waterways become polluted with animal waste, and wildlife dies. Yet most of us have no idea this is happening. If we can demand ethically produced food that allows consumers insight into food production, we can go far to reshape the world into a more just and sustainable place. Food corporations, from Monsanto to McDonald's, hope this never happens.

5

THE CLIMATE IS FOR SALE

In 2012, José Antonio Zamora Gutiérrez, Bolivia's minister of environment and water, spoke at the United Nations Framework Convention on Climate Change in Doha, Qatar. Gutiérrez forcefully stated, "The climate is not for sale." He rejected market-based solutions for carbon emissions and noted how the international market was destroying the planet's fragile life.[1] Under the presidency of Evo Morales, Bolivia has become an international leader in fighting for climate justice, asking why a poor country in an arid environment with a shaky water supply should have to suffer for the wanton energy use of the world's rich nations.

Unfortunately, the climate is absolutely for sale, and in this marketplace, rich nations have hidden the costs from consumers through concealing energy production. Petroleum corporations extract dirty energy from all around the world, sending it to American consumers. The energy industry is predicated upon consumers not having to think about where their power comes from. When we fill up our car, we fret over fuel prices, but what is the impact of oil production on the countries that produce it? We have a vague sense that it comes from the Middle East, but little more. But this search for energy has driven the geopolitical agenda for decades, radically transformed societies, ravaged ecosystems, and subjected the people living in its production and processing zones to cancer and pollution. As energy consumers we are almost completely isolated from the effects of this system, unless supplies become limited.

The connection between fossil fuels and climate change makes this issue all the more urgent. Increased carbon emissions are drastically raising the planet's temperatures, melting the polar ice caps, raising sea levels, destroying coastal ecosystems, and inundating coastal communities. Drought will expand deserts and imperil our food supply while fires destroy forests. Like all environmental crises, climate change will disproportionately affect the world's poor, who have contributed little to the problem. Economic injustice and environmental injustice combine to create catastrophic climate change. ExxonMobil's drill sites in Kuwait, processing plants in Texas, and gas stations in New York outsource the effects of this system to Inuits in Alaska, Bangladeshis living on the Ganges River delta, and the residents of low-lying island nations like Kiribati and Tuvalu, all of whom are among the first people directly affected by the changing climate.

When oil is produced in Nigeria, Saudi Arabia, or Venezuela, its horrible effects are out of sight for Americans. But petroleum companies can outsource only so much production because they have to follow the fossil fuel deposits. When oil is produced in the United States or other Western nations, the filthy industry can create flash points of resistance. Experiencing the impact of energy production opens the eyes of those who witness it. Once again, knowledge has the potential to transform politics. If those resisting fracking and the Keystone XL pipeline can build upon those efforts to connect domestic and foreign energy production, they can do much to build national and international pressure for a clean energy infrastructure that stops outsourcing the harms of our energy consumption onto the world's poor and takes a strong stand against climate change. For wind and solar energy to replace oil and coal would require sacrifices from wealthy first-world consumers in having wind turbines and solar cells in sight; in fact, nothing would ensure responsible energy production more than us seeing it.

For most of human history, we had few energy needs and we

met those needs locally. The Industrial Revolution created growing populations and spiraling energy demands. Still, for the first century of the Industrial Revolution, the United States produced most of its energy and lived with the consequences. Americans and Europeans nearly drove whales to extinction by harvesting whale oil for lamps. A growing demand for oil during the Civil War led to a boom in crude production in the following decades in vast oil fields in Pennsylvania, Texas, Oklahoma, and California. Oil exploration was haphazard, wasteful, and polluting. Careless exploration methods led to oil gushers that went uncapped for days, wasting tens of millions of barrels of crude oil.[2]

Until the mid-twentieth century, little grassroots resistance to energy production existed in the United States. Americans saw energy production and environmental degradation as signs of progress. The extermination of the vast flocks of passenger pigeons was a sign that we were turning wild land into productive farms. Deforestation meant transforming useless timberland into productive agriculture. Oil spills, smog, and toxic rivers were acceptable by-products of building America.

However, it did not take long for Americans to react against the rapacious business practices of energy companies. John D. Rockefeller's Standard Oil dominated 90 percent of the national oil market by 1900 through ruthlessly driving competition out of business. Ida Tarbell, the daughter of one of Rockefeller's onetime competitors, got her revenge when she wrote a series of influential articles beginning in 1902 exposing Rockefeller's dealings that led to a 1909 government antitrust suit against Standard Oil and the company's eventual dissolution in 1911. The coal industry's dangerous labor practices, murder of union organizers, and total domination over the lives of its employees made it a target for labor reformers throughout the twentieth century.[3]

After World War II, Americans became less patient with the environmental disasters of energy production. As unions won contracts with increased wages and fewer working hours, the rising standard of living led to increased disposable income. Free time meant American workers started vacationing, and when they traveled, they did not want to see oil wells, clear-cut forests, or mining pits. By the time of the 1969 Santa Barbara oil spill, Americans' beliefs about the environmental cost of energy production had changed. But so had American oil exploration. While domestic production was still important to corporate bottom lines, American oil companies had spent the previous decades investing heavily in the Middle East, Indonesia, Venezuela, and Nigeria. As in manufacturing, American oil companies found it profitable to separate Americans from the costs of unregulated production.[4]

The U.S. government went to great lengths to ensure access to this foreign oil. The CIA orchestrated the 1953 coup in Iran after democratically elected president Mohammed Mossadegh tried to nationalize his nation's oil wealth. Mossadegh did not oppose selling oil to the West. He just felt that his people, not British and American oil companies, should reap the profits. During the Cold War, protecting oil supplies and fighting communism went hand in hand, with the U.S. government supporting brutal dictators around the world as long as they would supply us with oil. This included Mohammad Reza Shah Pahlavi of Iran, who replaced Mossadegh; Saddam Hussein in Iraq; Suharto in Indonesia; and dozens of other dictators who routinely murdered their people with armies and police trained by the United States. Effectively, American taxpayers subsidized oil company profits through military operations and foreign aid for governments friendly to American oil companies.[5]

Meanwhile, Americans transformed their infrastructure following World War II to create suburbia. The American dream required a lot of oil. Single-family housing, subsidized by federal loans in new developments, replaced the dense urban living of the pre-war decades. The government built the interstate highway system to ferry suburbanites from home to their now-distant jobs in the cities. Public transportation systems died from neglect. Suburban shopping malls with thousands of parking spots emptied out downtowns. Automakers constructed large cars with low gas mileage. Millions moved to the Sun Belt, made possible thanks to energy-intensive air-conditioning. Corporations delivered on a promise of consumerism unknown in human history, but it was at the cost of making the nation dependent on huge energy inputs. This infra-structure makes a widespread transformation to clean energy more difficult today.[6]

Americans received a rude awakening in 1973, when the nations of the Organization of the Petroleum Exporting Countries (OPEC) launched a boycott of oil imports to the United States after it sup-ported Israel in the Yom Kippur War against Egypt and Syria. The embargo lasted for five months, leading to long lines for gasoline, a crisis in confidence about the nation's future, and the first serious questions about the nation's energy choices. American car compa-nies were slow to respond, and fuel-efficient Japanese cars became increasingly appealing to pinched consumers. After his 1977 inau-guration, President Jimmy Carter promoted conservation and al-ternative energy, even putting solar panels on the White House, but he too faced the perils of angry citizens of oil-producing nations. In 1978, Iran's Islamic revolution overthrew the American-supported shah. The shah had proved to be a loyal ally, and he had allowed American corporations to export oil after the 1953 coup, but his brutal repression of dissent led to widespread discontent in Iran. Oil prices skyrocketed following the revolution after Iran cut off its oil, and Americans were once again angry over vulnerable gaso-line supplies. But when oil prices plummeted in the early 1980s, Americans' attention to energy issues disappeared. The era of the SUV followed, with no thought to where oil came from or what costs our habits had upon the world. Our chance to reckon with energy production and forestall climate change passed. Despite ris-ing oil prices in the 2000s that reached $4 for a gallon of gasoline, Americans have made few fundamental changes to their energy consumption.[7]

Outside of gas prices and shortages, the only times in recent decades when Americans have seriously considered the impact of oil consumption have been when disaster occurs in their nation. I have already discussed the role of the Santa Barbara oil spill in spurring the environmental movement. Outrage again grew after the *Exxon Valdez* disaster in 1989, when an oil tanker spilled up to 750,000 barrels of oil in pristine waters just off the Alaskan coast, leading to catastrophic wildlife deaths; some populations have still not recovered today. Oil-covered sea otters and birds were visceral symbols of the cost of oil production. Public pressure and exposure of Exxon's safety failings led to a $5 billion ruling against Exxon, although successive appeals reduced it $507 million.[8]

The 2010 Deepwater Horizon spill again demonstrated the wanton irresponsibility of the oil industry when it comes to both worker safety and environmental damage. The spill spewed more than 4.1 million barrels of oil into the Gulf of Mexico in the eighty-seven days before British oil company BP could cap the well. Transocean, which operated the oil rig for BP, was responsible for 73 percent of the accidents in the Gulf between 2007 and 2010 despite operating less than 50 percent of the oil rigs. BP has fired union activists trying to organize the rig workers and achieve a safe workplace. In drilling the well, BP cut corners and took risks in order to maximize profit and speed up the drilling process, submitting a drilling-permit plan that included a wildlife expert who had been dead for several years.[9]

BP paid dearly for the spill, $42.2 billion as of February 2013. Yet even though eleven workers died, concern for the dangers faced by oil rig workers has completely disappeared from the public conversation. The federal government placed only a six-month moratorium on the risky drilling methods that led to the explosion, and BP regained its ability to drill in federal waters in March 2014 after a four-year ban. Yet little evidence suggests that BP has solved the problems leading to the spill. Scientists have only just begun understanding the impact of the Deepwater spill on marine life, with researchers recently making connections between the spill and cardiac arrest in tuna. The conditions for another disaster remain. Effectively, nothing has changed.[10]

Louisianans have long dealt with the impact of fossil fuels, but even though this part of the industry is domestic, it is still concealed from most Americans. Petroleum production in the Gulf of Mexico has left widespread environmental problems in its wake, not only with the Deepwater Horizon spill but also in the so-called Cancer Corridor of Louisiana between Baton Rouge and New Orleans, where petrochemical corporations have located production facilities. In 2012, the refineries there had 327 accidents, an average of 6.3 per week, mostly the release of pollutants such as benzene into the air and the dumping of chemicals into the water supply. When an oil refinery releases ten pounds or more of benzene into the air, it has to file an accident report within an hour. An ExxonMobil refinery in Baton Rouge had a single benzene release of 31,000 pounds. The people living next to these plants, largely African Americans, suffer from high rates of cancer and other illnesses, and while they have organized to fight the oil and chemical companies, their poverty and isolation largely keep their struggles out of the headlines.[11] Louisiana has a major tourism industry, but most tourists either stay in New Orleans out of sight of the chemical plants and refineries or, if they do see them, usually only comment on their ugliness, oblivious to their impact on the land and people nearby.

It's much the same in Appalachia. West Virginia, Kentucky, Tennessee, southeast Ohio, and Pennsylvania have suffered from 150 years of coal production. The coal industry spent decades ordering the murder of union organizers, fighting against compensation for black lung disease, and running the mountains like a feudal fiefdom. West Virginia is indeed wild and wonderful, as its license plates claim. But today, mountaintop-removal mining reshapes the state, dumping millions of tons of contaminated soil into valleys, poisoning waterways, and sickening residents. Coal companies claim mountaintop removal is the most cost-effective production process, but it forces the long-term costs of mining onto local communities. It poisons waterways with mercury, lead, arsenic, and selenium. Improper storage of coal waste also leads to polluted waterways. A Duke Energy coal ash leak in North Carolina in 2014 turned at least 27 million gallons of water in the Dan River into a toxic soup, polluting the water source for Danville, Virginia.[12] Yet few Americans see the destroyed mountains and polluted waterways that are the cost of the dirty electrical system that American consumers use.

Perhaps no place shows the connection between energy production and poverty more effectively than the Navajo reservation in the Southwest. Few places in the United States are more remote than the Navajo Nation. While coal companies mine 7.8 million tons of coal per year off Navajo lands, everyday people living in this region often do not benefit at all. The Navajo Generating Station is one of the most polluting power generators in the country. Not only do the coal companies force Navajos to move from their homes, but more than eighteen thousand Navajo homes lack electricity, despite providing the energy that powers the Southwest.[13]

Like residents of West Virginia or the Navajo Nation worried about the impact of energy production on their communities, Louisiana residents were deeply concerned about the Deepwater spill and the impact of the oil industry on their land.[14] The BP oil spill devastated Louisiana's tourism and fishing industries, which faced 88,000 square miles of the Gulf closed to fishing and public perceptions of polluted, ill, and deformed seafood.[15] Louisiana and its residents have long suffered to allow us cheap oil. The oil industry has chopped canals through the bayous, leading to the oceans eroding the low-lying Mississippi delta into the sea. A canal called the Mississippi River–Gulf Outlet was completed in 1965; it provides a highway of ocean water for hurricanes to suck up on their way to New Orleans. Twenty-five acres of Louisiana slide into the ocean every day, and swamps that used to protect New Orleans from the full brunt of hurricanes are gone, making the city more susceptible to inundation like it experienced during Hurricane Katrina in 2005.[16]

We should be angry with oil companies for despoiling our natural heritage. What Exxon did to Alaska and BP to Louisiana is outrageous. But the fossil fuel industry's actions in the United States pale in comparison to what it does in Nigeria and the Middle East. Oil companies work with dictators that stamp out dissent against the companies. In the 1990s, the Ogoni people of Nigeria led a nonviolent movement against Royal Dutch Shell for the contamination of their land in the Niger River delta. In response, the Nigerian government, far more concerned about pleasing the oil industry than an ethnic minority, executed the movement's leader, the writer Ken Saro-Wiwa, and eight others. Everyday people in Nigeria have received no benefits from the oil industry. Nigeria exports 2.5 million barrels of oil per day yet has developed no refining capacity and has to import the fuel processed from the oil drilled there.[17]

The Niger River delta is now an environmental disaster zone. Poisoned water, wildlife depletion, and heavy metal contamination continue to be major problems. Between 1976 and 2001, the Nigerian government reported 6,817 oil spills, more than one every other day, and this is no doubt undercounted. Oil companies operate with impunity in Nigeria, showing little to no interest in responsible extraction.[18] In 1999, Shell pumped a million gallons of wastewater into an abandoned well near the town of Erovie, Nigeria; a mysterious illness that caused vomiting and stomach problems and killed ninety-three people soon followed. In 2002, the people of Ubeji, Nigeria, complained of their spoiled fishery and the deaths of several people from poisoning from oil pollution.[19]

The terrible treatment Nigeria has received from oil companies has garnered international attention from activists. The Saro-Wiwa execution led to calls for a boycott against Shell.[20] There are Western environmentalist and human rights activists who ally with locals around the world to resist the oil industry. These alliances are especially strong between rich world environmentalists and South American indigenous peoples. Texaco and Gulf Oil discovered oil in the Ecuadoran Amazon in 1967, and by 1972 they were polluting and stealing land from the five indigenous groups living in the forest. Texaco pulled out of Ecuador in 1992, but not until it had constructed unfenced and unlined oil pits that leaked crude into water and poisoned soils with barium, cadmium, and chromium-6. Pipelines broke and oil oozed through the forest. Indigenous peoples organized to fight Texaco during the 1970s, and this caught the attention of the growing number of Americans interested in indigenous rights and environmentalism. Those allies have provided publicity, funding, legal support, and consumer activism in the corporate countries of origin.[21] American and European lawyers have spent two decades fighting for Texaco and then Chevron—which merged with Texaco in 2001—to pay for the pollution. In 2011, an Ecuadoran court finally granted the indigenous tribes a major victory, requiring Chevron to pay $18 billion, although a court later reduced that to $9.5 billion. Chevron has fought the judgment, and in March 2014 a U.S. district court judge barred the Ecuadoran people from pursuing the fines in the United States, claiming the lawyers for the plaintiffs bribed the judge. Still, the fight continues to make Chevron pay for its pollution.[22]

Today, the United States produces slightly more than half its oil because of the recent boom in domestic oil shale extraction.[23] Thanks to decades of environmental law, the oil industry cannot pollute in the United States as openly as it can in Ecuador. Outsourcing energy production allows for even greater arrogance toward people and the planet than it does in the United States, with its real, albeit too lax, regulations. Yet American environmentalists have struggled to produce long-term alliances with local communities around fossil fuel production in the United States.

The root of this problem is the geographical subterfuge of mobile capitalism. Oil, natural gas, and coal jobs pay well compared to jobs at Walmart or McDonald's. Many Louisianans see no alternative but to embrace the oil industry as a job creator. It employs more than one thousand people in both Lafayette and Terrebonne Parishes, and in areas with few other job options it is difficult for workers to attack the industry that is feeding them.[24] The job blackmail that corporations used to cleave labor from environmentalists in the 1970s still has power. Driving around West Virginia or eastern Kentucky today, you might see dozens or even hundreds of signs and bumper stickers bemoaning President Obama's supposed "war on coal." It's not that West Virginians want the coal companies to pollute their land, but if the coal companies leave, what other jobs are there for people without college degrees? Walmart? During World War II, hundreds of thousands of people left Appalachia for jobs in northern factories. Where are the jobs they can take today? In China and Bangladesh.

But our increasingly comprehensive search for every drop of oil and gas on the planet has brought energy extraction and production to parts of the United States that had not experienced it for a long time. This is creating a new front in the struggle against dirty energy, especially in reaction to the process of natural gas extraction called hydraulic fracturing, more popularly known as fracking. Corporations inject a mixture of water, sand, and chemicals into rock at high pressures, breaking it and freeing the fossil fuels for extraction. The energy industry has embraced fracking despite almost no testing of its environmental and even geological impacts. Driving that fluid underground causes earthquakes in areas that rarely experience them. Between 1975 and 2008, Oklahoma experienced between one and three earthquakes of magnitude 3.0 or higher; between 2009 and 2013, when the area was being fracked, it experienced forty per year. Similar earthquake clusters have developed in fracking zones in Texas, Ohio, and Colorado. Arkansas suffered more than seven hundred earthquakes in a six-month period in 2011, including its strongest in thirty-five years. As in coal country, many residents often fear opposing fracking because it provides well-paying jobs, and they have few alternatives. For the state of Ohio, racked by job losses thanks to capital mobility, any jobs in fracking seem like a blessing, despite the earthquakes. Fracking in water-hungry states such as Texas takes precious resources away from farmers and people and potentially causes long-term damage to aquifers.[25]

Yet the earthquake clusters, fear of water contamination, and unwillingness of companies to inform residents what chemicals are being injected into wells have led to significant resistance. Ohio placed new restrictions on drillers in 2012 after a rash of earthquakes near Youngstown. Opposition to fracking in the Marcellus Shale in New York is a major statewide political issue. New Yorkers Against Fracking has led the fight against the process in the Empire State. They have connected with California activists to protest fundraisers for New York governor Andrew Cuomo in the Golden State in order to pressure him to maintain New York's fracking moratorium ban. Americans Against Fracking has built a national coalition of dozens of organizations opposed to the practice. With every earthquake and polluted water source, more local residents find the practice irresponsible. As in other industries, the frackers look to conceal their operations from the American public. Twenty states have mandated that fracking companies disclose their chemicals so that citizens may be aware of the potential pollutants. Now the companies are fighting back. North Carolina Republicans have introduced a bill to make it not only a crime but a felony for individuals to disclose the contents of a company's fracking chemical blend to the public.[26]

The return of oil production to Americans' lives adds to this resistance. With the rise in oil prices over the past decade, both the Bush and Obama administrations have presided over a Bureau of Land Management that has approved fossil fuel production at irresponsible rates, angering environmentalists. In the United States, the Canadian effort to build the Keystone XL pipeline, which would send oil from the tar sands—a form of petroleum with even harsher climate consequences than most petroleum—of Alberta to refineries in Texas, has spurred resistance led by Bill McKibben and his 350.org movement. Anti-Keystone activists have engaged in huge rallies and civil disobedience to pressure Obama to reject the pipeline, making this decision the most visible climate-related issue of his presidency.[27]

Oil train crashes and pipeline ruptures reinforce the anti-Keystone message. An oil train crash in Quebec killed fifty people in July 2013. Such events are becoming more common in the United States as well. A pipeline ruptured in March 2013 near Mayflower, Arkansas. Resident Sherry Appleman said, "I could smell that horrible smell. I got really scared." Residents suffered from nausea and headaches. ExxonMobil and the Arkansas Department of Environmental Quality assured residents there was nothing to fear, despite the illnesses.[28] A train carrying crude oil derailed near Casselton, North Dakota, in December 2013 and exploded, causing a huge fireball and four hundred thousand gallons of spilled oil.[29] Most of the town of Milford, Texas, was evacuated in November 2013 when a natural gas pipeline exploded. No one was hurt, but this should serve as another reminder of the dangers of fossil fuels in the present and in the future.[30] Meanwhile, oil executives are actually touting this pollution as a good thing. Canadian oil company Kinder Morgan argued that the inevitable spills from an oil pipeline would stimulate the Canadian economy, or, in its words in a document arguing for pipeline expansion, create "business and employment opportunities for affected communities, regions, and cleanup service providers."[31]

On the West Coast of the United States, local citizens are resisting the coal industry's attempt to export millions of tons of coal from Wyoming's Powder River Basin to China through the ports in their towns. Allowing American coal to ship to China through West Coast ports would cause pollution in the United States, contribute to the massive air pollution in China, and add to the ever-growing carbon dioxide emissions transforming the climate. The proposed Gateway Pacific Terminal in Cherry Point, Washington, could export 48 million tons of coal a year. But local people in Washington and environmentalists nationwide have challenged it, submitting 125,000 comments in opposition to the project.[32]

With the expansion of energy production in the United States, the chance of a major accident occurring in a heavily populated area grows. This is terrible, but it's also worth noting that this is the point where widespread resistance is likely to develop. The production of the fuels themselves has created little resistance. The Powder River Basin is transformed beyond recognition, but it's a place where very few people live or have reason to visit. There has been some attention paid to the tar sands mining in Canada that will fill the Keystone pipeline because of its climate impact, but it's the pipeline itself that has become the focus. People become motivated about environmental problems when they are personally affected.

This resistance has begun to have an impact on the political system. Knowledge leads to protest, which leads to attracting lawmakers' attention. It is a good sign that Senators Jay Rockefeller and Ron Wyden have called on the Obama administration to take "prompt and decisive" action to investigate increased oil train derailments. A call for reform from two senators does not make a reform movement, but the more attention the issue receives, the more Americans will be safe from the dirty energy industry. And without the grassroots opposition to Keystone, President Obama almost certainly would have already approved the pipeline since it is such a priority of the Canadian government. As of writing, the future of Keystone remains in doubt despite growing Canadian anger.[33]

Of course, not all of the world's oil, natural gas, and coal ends its journey in the United States. But much of the energy used in other nations is the raw fuel that allows for the outsourcing of the world's industrial labor. Moving raw materials and finished goods across the world requires enormous energy inputs. Cotton grown in China, India, and the United States is sent to factories around the world, processed into clothing, and then sold across the globe. Transportation is the third-highest environmental impact of cotton, behind only soil erosion and chemical use.[34] China's carbon dioxide emissions have increased from 13.8 percent of the world's total in 2005 to 22 percent in 2006. But as Vandana Shiva writes, "Much of China's 6.2 billion metric tons of CO_2 emissions could just as easily be considered U.S. emissions because U.S. companies have outsourced to China the manufacture of goods that are eventually consumed in the United States."[35] Imports as a total of U.S. carbon dioxide emissions rose from 12 percent to 24 percent between 1997 and 2004, a result of American companies outsourcing production abroad and importing the finished goods back to American consumers. It's the same in Great Britain. Between 1990 and 2008, British carbon dioxide emissions fell by 19 percent. The British government could claim it was taking the lead on climate change, but most if not all of that reduction came through outsourcing production. The overall carbon footprint of what the British people actually consumed grew 20 percent during the same period. Again, by moving production around the world, corporations shield everyday people from the true cost of industrial production, undermining any challenge to the industrial system transforming the climate.[36]

Because of the potential for resistance around power generation, corporations will outsource production when they can, just like an apparel company. In the aftermath of the 2000–2001 California energy crisis, energy providers in California began building new plants in northern Mexico to ship power back to California. Because they were in Mexico, the plants did not have to go through the rigorous environmental permitting of U.S. plants, even though the emissions from the plants drifted across the border and affected people in California's Imperial Valley. One of these new plants alone would emit 378 tons of nitrogen oxides, 376 tons of carbon monoxide, and nearly 4 megatons of carbon dioxide each year. As of 2008, energy companies had proposed at least seventeen similar facilities on the Mexican side of the border for American energy consumption. The differences between the two nations are profound: for liquefaction of natural gas, the United States requires remote siting because of the danger of leaks and accidents, but Mexico does not, exposing Mexican citizens for the sake of American consumption. Citizens on both sides of the border have fought against this energy boom with some success, but the desire of energy companies to avoid environmental regulations through building in Mexico is strong.[37]

The Mexican power plant example is the outlier, not the norm. Fossil fuels produced in the United States provide sites of resistance for American companies because of their relative lack of mobility. Given the threat of catastrophic climate change, the ability to protest at the point of energy production is absolutely vital. The rapid warming of the Earth is the greatest threat humans face today, and in order to mitigate its effects we have to strike at those most responsible for it—the dirty energy companies. This requires understanding the connections between fossil fuels and climate change, making connections between rich world climate activists and people from developing nations fighting for their own future, and using the geographical centers of energy production as sites of protest to bring national attention to what is causing the world to boil.

The impact of climate change is likely to be the greatest catastrophe in world history. The Earth Summit in Rio de Janeiro, Brazil, in 1992 led to general principles on a climate change convention that resulted in the Kyoto Protocol, creating an outline for worldwide emissions reductions. However, most nations have failed to meet these targets, and the 2012 return to Rio led to no such agreement. The impact of this lack of action is tremendous. Climate change is already having major repercussions on the poor around the world. In South American nations like Bolivia and Peru, indigenous populations have lived in the dry climate of the Altiplano for centuries by having access to drinking water from melting glaciers. This is changing rapidly as a drying climate and disappearing glaciers reduce the region's water supplies at a time when the population of Bolivia is exploding. Future water supplies in Bolivia are imperiled.[38] Other nations will have far too much water. Low-lying and densely populated Bangladesh already deals with great suffering from monsoonal rains. Scientists predict 18 million Bangladeshis will be displaced due to rising sea levels by 2050. A sea level rise of one meter will lead to a loss of 18 percent of Bangladesh's land. But Bangladesh produces only 0.3 percent of climate-change-creating emissions, mostly to run factories that produce goods for foreign companies. Island nations such as Tuvalu, Kiribati, and Maldives will simply cease to exist as rising sea levels drown them. Around the world, we will see tens of millions of refugees, creating economic, social, and humanitarian crises never before seen in world history outside of war.[39]

While we cannot say that a single weather or climate event is directly caused by climate change, there's no question the impacts of hotter, dryer weather in the American West, higher ocean temperatures in the waters off our shores, and more extreme weather events are already being seen in the United States. Much of Florida is probably doomed. Over 2.4 million people live at an elevation of six feet or less above sea level in southern Florida. "Climate change is no longer viewed as a future threat round here," noted University of Miami professor Ben Kirtman. "It is something that we are having to deal with today." Seawater is already inundating the area's sewer systems and flooding streets on a regular basis. Even conservative estimates of sea rise make Miami's future seem doubtful. Sea levels have risen eight inches since 1870 and will likely rise one to four feet by 2100. Yet Florida politicians like Marco Rubio and Rick Scott continue denying climate change is a problem or even that it is caused by humans. The United States is in no way prepared to deal with the reality of millions of people flooded from their homes. Yet every day we do nothing on this issue is another day closer to a certain and unprecedented disruption of our economy and population, not only in Miami but also in New Orleans, New

York, and other major cities. Nowhere has this nation even begun seriously preparing for climate change.[40]

The twenty-first century has witnessed a seemingly significant increase in extreme weather events. On September 12, 2013, nine inches of rain fell on Boulder, Colorado, creating disastrous flooding. Is that an event we can connect to climate change or is it an isolated incident? We don't know. What about Hurricane Sandy? Hurricanes happen, of course. But in late October in New York? The water temperature was five degrees above normal, the highest temperature ever recorded in the Atlantic Ocean off the northeastern United States at that time of year. Ocean temperatures do not fluctuate nearly to the extent of land temperatures. Those five degrees can spawn the kind of destructive storms the Northeast has seen in recent years. We know that climate change is going to lead to significantly warmer oceans. We also know that not all five of those degrees are explicitly attributable to climate change. So we can't tell exactly to what extent Hurricane Sandy happened because of climate change, but we can say that warming oceans make these events more likely.[41]

Then there is the issue of drought. Perhaps the biggest climate story in the United States in the 2010s has been the almost unprecedented drought in the American Southwest. Researchers at Utah State University have shown connections between amplified wind patterns, human-caused climate change, and the drought. From Texas to California, catastrophic drought has made people question the future of this region. The year 2013 was the driest year on record in California; 2014 was the third driest, as the winter rains and snows never came. Fires and insects race through the forests, permanently altering the ecosystem. The water supplies for this arid region are drying up rapidly. The great reservoirs behind the dams constructed in the mid-twentieth century to channel every drop of scarce western water to agriculture, industry, home owners, and Las Vegas casinos fueled the rapid growth of the Southwest after 1950. Yet millions of people continue to move to Texas, Arizona, Nevada, Colorado, New Mexico, and California. The water supplies absolutely do not exist for continued growth in Denver, Las

Vegas, Phoenix, and other regional cities. It is entirely possible that the wet years of the late twentieth-century West will not return. As world-renowned climate change expert Jonathan Overpeck of the University of Arizona says, "Climate change seldom occurs gradually." The West is no more prepared for the impact of catastrophic climate change than the rest of the nation.[42]

Climate change is transforming the oceans with incredible rapidity. Coral reef bleaching is destroying one of the world's most unique and varied ecosystems. Other issues, such as starfish disintegration on the northern Pacific coast, presently have unknown causes but can likely be traced back to climate change in oceans.[43] The impact on oceans will mean a major decline or even extinction of many fish that are today part of our diet. Many of the harshest impacts of climate change will be inconvenient for the world's rich but devastating for the world's poor. Few of us in America rely on fish for survival, but this will devastate the people who fish for a living. We will probably switch the fish in our diet to chicken or beef or pork. Where will the fishermen go? To the maquiladoras? The slums of urban capitals? Migrate to the United States to serve as undocumented and therefore easily exploited labor?

Even within the United States an often-hidden geography of poverty blinds us from the impact of extreme weather. Substandard mobile homes without foundations topple during tornadoes, insurance rates and property values push the poor to build on flood plains, even while the federal government subsidizes the rebuilding of rich California communities when wildfires ravage them. The impacts of climate change will exacerbate these problems as the rich seek to protect themselves, leaving the poor in areas prone to flooding and without the stable jobs that would allow them to build proper homes that protect them from weather events. Climate change will affect the urban poor disproportionately as well, as hotter summers lead to more cockroaches, which researchers have linked to skyrocketing asthma rates in poor urban communities because many people are allergic to them.[44]

*   *   *

As we have seen, individuals and groups can enact change. But individual action is very difficult with an issue as complex as climate change. Part of the problem is that climate change's effects are spread over the globe, mirroring the dispersed production and consumption that drives it. American and European corporations have created climate change, but they do not suffer the impacts. In essence, we have outsourced the problem. When people think about climate change, they think about what they can do personally to help out. Should they buy a hybrid car, put LED lightbulbs in their house, give up meat? These suggestions reflect Americans' current identification of themselves as consumers who make individual buying choices that will help change the world. In the past, consumer choices have helped in environmental struggles—seeing the forest where they hiked or hunted being logged motivated citizens to join environmental organizations, write a letter to their congressman, or sign a petition. Land preservation efforts long benefited from consumer activism.

It's hard to blame Americans for thinking this way. We are a consumer nation. Corporations both promised us the American dream and ensured for a very long time that we did not see the social and ecological effects of our consumption. Driving an SUV, having a large suburban house, flying around the country or world for vacations—this is the definition of the good life in the United States. We have so committed to this lifestyle that reengineering our vast infrastructure to save energy is very difficult. Public transportation struggles to work in suburbs because of the dispersal of single-family homes across a vast area of land. As a nation of high-end consumers who value individual choice, we want to believe that our individual choices can make a difference.

But our choices are limited because of the powerful forces seeking to do nothing about climate change. Corporations control the narrative around responsibility for climate change. The oil companies do everything in their power to undermine any fight against climate change. They influence news outlets like Fox and spend millions of dollars planting doubt in people's minds about an incontrovertible scientific fact. Energy giant ExxonMobil has led this charge, funding "research" and reports that suggest climate change is a hoax, an appealing message for politicians who support the oil industry. The company pledged publicly to stop giving money to climate-change-denial groups in 2007 (I heard an ExxonMobil vice president pledging to do this in a conference call to bloggers that year). But it immediately broke this pledge, giving $1.5 million more to these groups in 2009.[45] ExxonMobil CEO Rex Tillerson told his shareholders at a 2013 meeting that the oil economy would never disappear even if climate change is real because "what good is it to save the planet if humanity suffers?"[46] It's not just ExxonMobil. The American Petroleum Institute, Royal Dutch Shell, BP, and the enormous oil-infrastructure companies that do the drilling, construction, and transportation, whose names you will never hear—companies such as Oklahoma-based Continental Resources, Inc., the largest producer of oil in North Dakota's Williston Basin oil boom—all contribute to ensuring the status quo continues.[47]

The impact of this media blitz has profoundly shaped the climate debate, or lack thereof, in the United States. Ninety-seven percent of scientists believe that climate change is happening, and 95 percent believe people cause it through CO_2 emissions from the burning of fossil fuels.[48] This is about as close to a consensus as one can see on any issue in science. Yet polls consistently show that large numbers of Americans do not believe climate change is happening. The media give equal time to those debunking scientific fact as to those warning Americans about the world's greatest crisis. People are busy and have little time to sort out complex scientific debates. Every time it snows or we go through a cold snap, conservatives laugh about the climate change hoax, and because we filter our beliefs through what we are witnessing, whether the horrors of Triangle or an oil spill or the weather outside right now, they convince people that climate change is either nonexistent or something that Americans don't need to worry about. A 2013 Pew poll showed that only 40 percent of Americans thought climate change was a global threat, the lowest number in the world.[49]

Because of this effective corporate propaganda blitz, not to mention enormous corporate donations to political campaigns, politicians have no incentive to act to fight climate change. The most obvious example is the Republican Party in the United States, which is chock-full of climate deniers like Oklahoma senator James Inhofe, the ranking minority member of the Senate Environment and Public Works Committee, who simply say human-caused climate change is not happening and continue to serve the interests of the fossil fuel industry. But it's not just in the United States. Corporate lobbying has made a major difference in Australia as well. At one time an international leader on fighting climate change, Australia has elected the right-wing Tony Abbott as prime minister. Abbott has dedicated himself to repealing all the ecologically responsible energy and climate legislation passed by his predecessors. Australia had a $23.50 tax per metric ton of carbon production until July 2014, when Abbott and his right-wing Liberal Party repealed it, a major blow to one of the best hopes we had that rich nations would fight climate change.[50]

Oil companies could lead the way to a clean energy future by changing course and investing in wind and other clean forms of energy, but they refuse to do so, not only because of the business difficulties but also for ideological reasons. Wind and solar is hippie energy, after all. Wind energy development has plummeted in the United States since 2012, just as it needs to be skyrocketing. In 2012, the United States brought thirteen gigawatts of wind energy online. In 2013, that number fell to only one gigawatt after Congress refused to extend wind energy tax credits for manufacturers. Wind energy is getting cheaper and cheaper to produce, but because it is not the dirty energy that Republicans prefer, they refuse to fund it.[51]

Only drastic coordinated action around the world will mitigate the effects of two hundred years of corporations spewing climate-change-causing gases into the atmosphere. Capital mobility makes this much harder. If a nation, whether the United States or Bangladesh, in the present system of extreme capital mobility unilaterally cracked down on corporations emitting climate-change-inducing gases, the corporations would just leave. Even a growing economic powerhouse like China is vulnerable. Theoretically, if

China placed carbon emissions restrictions on the foreign companies producing in that nation, those companies would just leave for another nation that allowed them to emit without restriction. The economics incentivize doing no such thing and instead encourage opening your country to wanton corporate exploitation in exchange for low-paying jobs and widespread pollution.

Climate change is the ultimate environmental justice battle. It is about creating an energy regime that treats people with respect and ensures equity of burden when producing power. It is about ensuring that those who cause climate change bear their share of the effects. It is not only about forcing corporations like ExxonMobil and Shell to not decimate the Niger River delta and coastal Louisiana but also about preventing them from erasing entire nations, and major metropolises, including Miami, from the planet. In the beginning, the environmental justice movement consisted primarily of affected people in a particular place organizing themselves against a single company or issue. They fought a long-term fight to protect their homes, often without much in the way of publicity or alliances from larger national or international organizations. Much remains the same, but the larger awareness of the systemic nature of corporate exploitation of the poor has created greater infrastructure to publicize and support local movements. Climate activists and everyday citizens need to connect the local with the national and international, connecting fights over oil company exploitation in Ecuador, Nigeria, and Louisiana with the larger struggle to save the planet's climate, ecosystems, and possibly its humanity. The system that oppresses the Ogoni, steals land from the Ecuadoran tribes, and causes cancer in people living near petrochemical plants is the same system preventing us from saving our climate from massive alteration. The worldwide system of oil production, thriving far out of sight, enriches corporations and encourages us not to ask too many questions about it.

Fighting this must include a massive transition to clean energy production, even if we, the rich world consumers, bear some burden. Energy production and class go hand in hand. Oil and coal are mined far from the homes of the wealthy. The rich want to keep energy production out of their sight, while the poor rarely have that choice. But this environmental inequality cannot continue if we want a clean energy world. The response to wind turbines has been telling. Many areas with high winds are also places that people like to visit. Sometimes, as in the Great Plains, you can have fields of wind turbines that spark no opposition. Huge areas of west Texas now produce wind energy. But while Europeans have largely embraced big wind power, much of it offshore, wealthy New Englanders have protested plans to place large turbine projects in the sight lines of their multimillion-dollar summer homes. For years, residents of Massachusetts's wealthy resort island of Nantucket have fought a project that would build 130 turbines off the coast. The project would provide 75 percent of Cape Cod's energy needs with a clean and renewable fuel. But the rich do not want to see it. Opponents claim the turbines will ruin the natural beauty of Nantucket Sound.[52] That's possible, of course, but what about the beauty of the Niger delta or of the Louisiana bayous? Why should the wealthy escape the consequences of their energy use?

Any effective strategy that fights climate change is going to have to include a wide variety of energy sources, some of which will have to be produced near the communities where the energy is used. Some of these might be less intrusive, such as solar panels or wind turbines on roofs. In Portland, Oregon, for instance, apartment buildings can market themselves as having a wind turbine, playing off some liberals' desire for a hip green consumerist lifestyle. But we also need energy produced on a more industrial scale. It is impossible to create energy on a large scale without some environmental trade-offs. Hydroelectric dams kill fish and have helped endanger wild salmon stocks in the Pacific Northwest. The deep blackness of solar panels comes through a chemical process with nasty by-products. Creating solar panel banks in high enough numbers to create a significant amount of our energy will require the environmental degradation of some desert areas. Wind turbines kill birds. Nuclear power has all sorts of problems that make it too dangerous to use. Biofuels lead to widespread deforestation or the planting of enormous monocultures of corn that don't burn cleanly. Biomass, algae, geothermal, hydrogen: these are all far away from providing a meaningful amount of our energy and, like the above, will almost certainly have unintended negative consequences.

The question therefore is going to be what the new energy world looks like. Responsibly produced green energy is necessary. Moreover, we need to see the production of that energy, for it is only when citizens are activists that the energy will be produced responsibly. If the energy companies continue concealing the impacts of energy production and we continue to encourage them to do so by refusing to lift the veil, then we are all complicit in outsourcing what is likely to be the greatest catastrophe of all time: climate change.

6

THE WAY FORWARD

In the mid-twentieth century, General Electric was the prime economic engine for its hometown of Schenectady, New York, and the surrounding region. It made Schenectady a home of good jobs for researchers and scientists, mechanics and assembly-line workers. GE located its electrical capacitor plant in Fort Edward, New York, about forty miles northeast of Schenectady. For decades, the plant used polychlorinated biphenyls (PCBs) to make the capacitors safe and reliable. Unfortunately, PCBs also cause cancer, fetal disorders, and cognitive dysfunction. The industry knew of the effects of PCB exposure after workers in a New York factory died of liver failure in 1936, but for decades GE dumped the PCBs into the Hudson River watershed. By the time the federal government banned PCBs in 1976, 1.3 million pounds polluted the Hudson River and 7 million pounds poisoned local landfills. PCBs entered the bodies of fish and birds and then the bodies of the people who defied the ban on Hudson River fishing to feed their families. In 1983, the EPA declared two hundred miles of the Hudson a Superfund site. Workers in Fort Edward and people throughout the Hudson watershed had to live with the consequences of PCB exposure. They also needed jobs in a place that promised limited potential for new economic development, thanks to GE poisoning the land.[1]

In 2013, GE announced it was moving capacitor production to

the now-ironically named Clearwater, Florida, where it can enjoy a nonunion workforce, a favorable regulatory climate, and, because of this, higher profits. The United Electrical, Radio and Machine Workers of America (UE) represents the Fort Edward workers. UE political director Chris Townsend said, "It shouldn't be this easy to close this plant. The General Electric Corporation has been shown every imaginable consideration. . . . Our members have worked with this company to keep this plant profitable. Now the company decides to walk off, leave hundreds of people stranded with no jobs, no income."[2] You might argue, "This is America and corporations have property rights to move their operations wherever someone agrees to host them." Why do we allow corporate property rights to trump the rights of everyday citizens to jobs, good schools, safe neighborhoods, and the investment in their homes and communities? What happens to the property values of Fort Edward home owners, left with no hope for jobs and a polluted landscape? What happened to the home owners of Detroit, Cleveland, and Scranton as jobs disappeared? Why should a corporation be able move anywhere it wants for any reason it chooses? We do not really ask these questions, but we should. We might bemoan corporate mobility, but we rarely challenge the fundamental right of corporations to move.

What is happening to Fort Edward and other cities around the United States was not inevitable. Rather, it was a series of political decisions made by politicians beholden to the rich, sacrificing the lives of everyday Americans for the interests of shareholders and CEOs. It certainly wasn't always this way. Let's think about the United States in 1970. It was a society undergoing rapid upheaval, suffering from political tension and discontent. Some of our popular memories of the time revolve around sex, drugs, and rock and roll; Woodstock and Altamont had just taken place. Some young people had opted out of society and joined communes. Others had joined radical organizations such as the Weather Underground or Black Panthers. The Vietnam War continued with no end in sight. President Richard Nixon's invasion of Cambodia led to campus protests and the killing of students at Kent State and Jackson State.

Building trade union members in New York attacked antiwar protesters on the streets of lower Manhattan. Second-wave feminism
challenged entrenched patriarchy throughout American life. The
Stonewall Rebellion had taken place a few months earlier and the
gay rights movement had started to grow. The conservative backlash against the gains of the civil rights movement had begun to
transform national politics, and emboldened conservatives put
their hopes in rising politicians such as Ronald Reagan.[3]

During this period of Americans standing up for their beliefs in
new ways, many people also expressed their discontent toward corporations. They could do so because they felt economically stable.
The early 1970s was the peak of Americans' demand for corporate
accountability on the job and in the environment. The economy
had expanded almost every year since World War II, and thanks
to union contracts and high taxes on the wealthy those gains were
shared fairly with working Americans. Rising salaries had created the middle class. More and more Americans owned their own
homes. Strong unions in auto, steel, and dozens of other industries
had given working-class people a respectable living. Public sector
union organizing was growing rapidly. Americans' demands for
safe work and a clean environment meant that everyday citizens
became part of broader social movements and created a great political wave. In 1969, coal miners fought and won passage of the
Federal Coal Mine Health and Safety Act, granting a comprehensive government program for black lung disease for the first time.
The Occupational Safety and Health Act of 1970 created OSHA,
the first overarching federal agency to monitor workplace safety
and health. Twenty million Americans came out to the first Earth
Day in 1970, a sign of the growing demand to hold corporations accountable for their ecological damage. The National Environmental
Policy Act passed Congress in 1969, committing the U.S. government to environmental policy planning. Richard Nixon created
the Environmental Protection Agency to administer the panoply
of new environmental regulations. The Environmental Quality
Improvement Act, the Lead-Based Paint Poisoning Prevention Act,
and a major expansion of the Clean Air Act all came along in 1970

and 1971. In just three years, the nation became a safer and cleaner place to live.[4]

In the 2010s, it's become all too common for disappointed progressives to claim Nixon as more liberal than Barack Obama because he signed all this legislation. But this facile analysis ignores why Nixon signed that legislation. Nixon's priorities were foreign policy and fighting the Vietnam War. Because these laws were so popular, he knew he could not veto these measures without costing him the political capital he needed for his real aims. The real story is not that Nixon signed the legislation, it's that the National Environmental Policy Act passed unanimously in the Senate and 372–15 in the House. The Clean Air Act passed the House 375–1. The Occupational Safety and Health Act passed the Senate 83–3. Popular sentiment to clean up the environment outmuscled corporate pressure to weaken or reject these bills. Americans decided they could have good jobs and clean air, a robust economy and wilderness protection. The richest nation in the world could have it all.[5]

The nation has moved sharply to the right since 1970. The labor movement's hope that Obama and a Democratic Congress would pass the Employee Free Choice Act, which would have allowed for card-check unionization with a majority of signatures and faster collective bargaining procedures, died by the end of 2009. The same happened to environmentalists' hope for a cap-and-trade bill to fight climate change. Income inequality continues to grow. Political gridlock and an extremist Republican Party determined to stop all Democratic legislation have made many cynical about politics. The idea of holding the same job for thirty years and retiring with a respectable pension is a relic of the past. Government regulatory agencies are underfunded and controlled by pro-corporate political appointees. Instead of the inexpensive higher education of the 1970s, we have students leaving school with crippling debt that hamstrings their decisions for decades, made worse because borrowers cannot discharge these loans through bankruptcy. Even with that debt, they have no guarantee of job security after graduation. Corporations have retaken control over American politics and consolidate their power with each passing year. A right-wing Supreme Court eviscerates a century of progressive legal advances with each court session. The postwar promises to Americans are broken dreams of the past.

What happened? That's the question that progressives have asked themselves for years. The answers are complex. But corporate decision making is the most important reason for the collapse of the middle class. The increasingly organized and aggressive business lobby following the 1971 Powell Memo combined with individual corporations' decisions to bust unions and send work around the globe to new, low-paid, and more pliant workforces. By the mid-1970s, business started flexing its muscles in politics, and new legislation to expand the progressive gains of the early part of the decade became much harder. Corporations responded to citizen demands by moving operations abroad, and politicians let them. The overwhelming legislative victories that had held corporations responsible for their actions rapidly became a thing of the past as economic fears became a new part of life for millions of Americans.

The effects of globalized production and capital mobility are cumulative, and the slow nature of these effects helps blind us to the system's incredible transformative power. Each lost union job takes a lot of money out of an American worker's pocket, a little out of her union's budget, and undermines her ability to play a role in the political process. Labor unions have done more than any institution in American history to provide working people a voice in American political life. Destroying them eliminates that voice— a vacuum corporations then fill with their own loud voices and fat pocketbooks. Outside of the immediate profits that arise from lower wages abroad and fewer environmental regulations in poor countries, this is the upside of mobility for corporations. With each unionized factory closure, labor unions have less dues money, less political power, and less ability to influence American politics.

Over time, year after year, the impact of individual factory closings compounded. The great industrial unions of the New Deal disappeared or became a shell of themselves. Environmental issues became less important to the American public as citizens grew more worried about their jobs. The need for political parties to listen to unions or environmentalists declined. Corporate cash replaced citizens' voices in influencing politicians. Republicans stopped pretending they cared about working people and openly embraced their billionaire benefactors. Democrats could just assume they had locked up the votes of labor and greens and went chasing campaign donations to keep up. Former industry lobbyists took jobs at the EPA and OSHA, undermining the effectiveness of government regulation. Opponents of unions staffed the National Labor Relations Board. Federal budgets cut funding for regulatory agencies. Jobs kept fleeing from America. Emboldened corporations lost the pretense of caring about their workers, and the quarterly profit margin became more important than the American middle class. And so the cycle continues. Another year, more union jobs lost, more corporate control over politics, an endangered middle class.

Supporters of globalization say the decline of social and political institutions in the United States is worth it. They talk about "economic freedom" for the rich and the new job opportunities given to Bangladeshis, Sri Lankans, and Hondurans by Nike, Walmart, and Gap. But the lives of most of these workers is hard, degraded, and poisonous, marked by occupational illness, sexual harassment, forced pregnancy tests, and plant closures when the multinational corporations find an even cheaper country in which to produce their goods. Capitalism forced people off their farms and into the cities, where they were desperate for work and forced to accept any wages and working conditions. Yes, some people have benefited from this system: a global elite and small middle class service the system of global capitalism. But the masses remain entrenched in deep poverty, a situation difficult to improve when their employers can move to yet another country if they unionize.

"The Gilded Age" was the name given to the period in the United States after the Civil War by Mark Twain for the crassness of the time, hidden by the thinnest layer of gold. It was marked by extreme income inequality and callous indifference for the poverty afflicting millions of Americans. In 1860, the top 1 percent possessed about 24 percent of the nation's wealth, and in 1900 they had in the range of 26 to 31 percent. (In 2014, the top 1 percent controlled around 30 percent of the wealth).[6] Horatio Alger stories comforted the rich who wanted to hear that everyday people could rise in society if they just worked hard enough. Widespread political and financial corruption not only made the age cynical but also toyed with workers' lives as financial bubbles burst and sent millions into unemployment. Strikes were met with the guns of the military, and the wealthy responded to demands for economic justice with contempt and scorn. The project of modern conservatives is re-creating the Gilded Age. Writers such as the *National Review*'s Amity Shlaes argue that the minimum wage is immoral and defend actions like Andrew Carnegie's crushing of the Homestead Strike as ideal corporate behavior. Karl Rove believes the United States went off the free market rails when Americans began reforming capitalism during the Progressive Era. Glenn Beck has called Theodore Roosevelt a "socialist" for his mild reforms enacted a century ago.[7]

Shlaes's, Rove's, and Beck's dreams are coming true. Wealth disparities unseen in more than a century have developed. The U.S. government began keeping income records in 1913, when the Sixteenth Amendment created the federal income tax. In 2012, the top 1 percent of earners became the richest in recorded history, earning 19.3 percent of American income, surpassing the previous record of 18.7 percent, set in 1927, just before this income inequality contributed to the Great Depression.[8] Between 1979 and 2007, the 1 percent captured 53.9 percent of the increase in U.S. income. During that time, average income for our elites grew by 200.5 percent versus just 18.9 percent for the bottom 99 percent.[9] Between 1978 and 2011, CEO pay rose 726.5 percent versus 5.7 percent for workers.[10] Using Organisation for Economic Co-Operation and Development statistical analysis, the United States now has the fourth-worst income inequality of any developed nation, trailing only Chile, Mexico, and Turkey—nations far less wealthy overall than the United States.[11] The critique that Occupy Wall Street (OWS) made had many objects, but its heart was income inequality as personified by the corporations based near OWS's home of Zuccotti Park in lower Manhattan.

Corporations have re-created the dangerous, poisonous, deadly society of the Triangle Fire but have spread it around the world to take advantage of the poorest nations while concealing knowledge of these conditions from consumers. No American consumers will see these factories burn or those rivers run foul. In the United States, the stable jobs and economic growth that gave Americans the confidence to challenge corporate control in the twentieth century have slipped away. The institutions that forced corporations to give American workers a fair shake are dying a bit more every day. These are all victories for the plutocrats, as they move closer to re-creating on a worldwide scale the power they held in the United States in the late nineteenth century.

In May 2014, Senator Bernie Sanders of Vermont asked Federal Reserve Chair Janet Yellen, "Are we still a capitalist democracy or have we gone over into an oligarchic form of society in which incredible economic and political power now rests with the billionaire class?"[12] The answer is clearly the latter and becoming more so every day. The income inequality in a United States with ever-fewer good jobs means that for millions the American dream is impossible to live. Instead of creating a level playing field for the poor, the wealthy have sought to concentrate riches in their offshore bank accounts or move their corporate headquarters abroad, even though all their business is done in the United States. This protects them from the government taxing their income, even though they demand the government serve their interests in promoting their businesses. Between 1951 and 1963, the top marginal income tax rate was 91 percent. Not at all coincidentally, this was the period of greatest equity for the American working class. It remained no lower than 70 percent until 1981, when Ronald Reagan gave his wealthy friends enormous tax breaks as he dismantled the postwar welfare state. Today it is a mere 35 percent for the nation's richest people.[13]

The disparity between CEO and entry-level pay today has grown so wide that it would take a McDonald's worker making $8.25 an hour more than a century of nonstop work to make the $8.75 million "earned" by the CEO of McDonald's in 2011.[14] Do the business owners use their growing wealth to create jobs for Americans? No. Instead, they create gargantuan compensation packages for high-level executives and use capital mobility as a cudgel against the remaining unions standing in the way of even higher profits. For example, Boeing was the iconic corporation of Seattle for decades. The airplane manufacturer has thrived off government and commercial airplane contracts, building the planes of the military-industrial complex. In the first quarter of 2014 alone, Boeing produced a $965 million profit, down from $1.1 billion in the first quarter of 2013.[15] But this is not enough for Boeing executives who demanded that workers represented by the International Association of Machinists and Aerospace Workers (IAM) give up enormous parts of their contract. Under threat to move production of the 777X jetliner to its South Carolina plant, where workers make only half of what the Washington union members do, the IAM had to sign a contract canceling workers' pension plans, slashing benefits, and granting only a 1 percent raise every other year. Epitomizing the arrogant modern capitalist that hearkens back to the J.P. Morgans and John D. Rockefellers of yesteryear, Boeing CEO Jim McNerney is not satisfied with decimating the future of his own workforce. McNerney also needs to kill the idea of retirement for American workers. He heads the Business Roundtable, a corporate lobbying group that is calling to raise the retirement age to seventy years of age. McNerney's own retirement pay as of November 2013 was $265,575 a month.[16]

With each passing year, the structure of American employment becomes more rigged against working people. Americans work harder, produce more, and receive fewer benefits than they did thirty years ago. Between 1980 and 2005, manufacturing productivity increased 131 percent, but mean hourly wages remained lower than in 1973.[17] When workers lose their jobs, finding a new one can be almost impossible, especially for those out of work for several months. In the immediate aftermath of the 2008 recession, an unemployment insurance extension gave the jobless ninety-nine weeks of benefits. That ended in 2014 when Republicans refused to extend it. Kentucky senator Rand Paul said, "When you allow

people to be on unemployment insurance for 99 weeks, you're causing them to become part of this perpetual unemployed group in our
economy."[18] The idea that meager unemployment benefits extended
to less than two years are so generous that people will choose to live
off them is absurd, but Paul serves his corporate masters by making
these statements. He's far from alone in this position, as the failure
of the legislation demonstrates.

With factories moving away or subcontracting abroad and
unions in decline, corporations are able to double down on their
assault against the workplace regulations of the twentieth century.
Republican judges are leading this charge. In late 2013, the Fifth
Circuit Court of Appeals in New Orleans effectively ruled that employees could not use class action lawsuits to improve conditions
in the workplace—a strategy used to combat racial and sexual discrimination. Instead, workers would have to sign contracts with
employers—at the price of keeping their jobs—agreeing to individual arbitration for all complaints, making individual workers stand
against the collected power of their employer. Former National
Labor Relations Board member Craig Becker editorialized after
this decision that the United States is rapidly becoming a place with
a "rightless workplace."[19]

Wanton violations of labor law and repeal of workplace rights have
become so bad that the International Trade Union Confederation
ranked the United States alongside nations such as Iran, Pakistan,
Botswana, Haiti, El Salvador, Mexico, and Thailand in its rankings
of nations violating workers' rights under the category of "Systemic
Violation of Rights." According to those rankings, Thailand, the
home of the Kader toy factory fire, respects the rights of its workers
as much as the United States. The same violations of rights in the
countries where American work is moved have returned to haunt
the remaining American workplaces.[20] American work has become
much safer since OSHA's establishment in 1971, but that does not
tell the whole story. Much of the improvement in safety has come
from the most dangerous labor being outsourced abroad in conditions where workers are injured and die on the job. Today, OSHA
could be more effective, but corporations and their political lackeys

keep the agency underfunded and employer-friendly. Ultimately, it should not matter to us where workers suffer. The fact that they suffer making products for us to buy is outrageous. When workers in Bangladesh die making our clothes, that is no less a tragedy than if the worker were in New York.

The petrochemical industry is particularly indifferent to workers' lives. Twenty-three workers died in a 1989 accident in Pasadena, Texas; eight at Sterling, Louisiana, in 1991; fifteen at Texas City, Texas, in 2005; and eleven on the Deepwater Horizon drilling rig that caused the BP oil spill in 2010. After the Texas City incident, British Petroleum claimed it would improve safety, yet it was fined $87 million in 2009 for not correcting the problems that had led to the 2005 disaster. That fine did little to change BP's practices, as the Deepwater Horizon accident shows. Oil production deaths are rising, with 545 dead oil field workers between 2008 and 2012—216 in the weak regulatory state of Texas alone.[21]

OSHA fines are absurdly weak in the current antiregulatory climate. This means that employers have little incentive to make safety improvements. Workers die as a result. In 2011, Daniel Collazo, a worker at the Tribe Mediterranean Foods hummus plant in Taunton, Massachusetts, died when he got caught in the gears of a grinder, slowly crushing his head as he screamed in terror. In 2009, OSHA inspectors had fined Tribe for its "extreme safety risk," but the company did not make the changes because the fine was only $9,500, far less than the safety upgrades would have cost. When Collazo died, OSHA fined Tribe $540,000, but that was a risk worth taking because the fines for mere violations were so minuscule.[22] The major institutions pressing for stronger OSHA fines are unions, and they are in a desperate decline.

Even the hired thugs of the Gilded Age workplace are returning. In an event reminiscent of how mining companies treated workers a century ago—when coal plutocrats ruled West Virginia and eastern Kentucky like a medieval fiefdom, murdering union organizers, kicking strikers out of company houses, and intimidating workers—in 2013, the Gogebic Taconite mine in northern Wisconsin hired Bulletproof Securities, a private security firm from Arizona, to provide guards armed with semiautomatic rifles in order to intimidate environmentalists opposing the mine. There was no reason why the company needed a heavily armed paramilitary force. But in today's pro-business climate, why not?[23]

What's more, there is little evidence that American political leaders have seriously questioned the wisdom of continuing the promotion of job migration from the United States. One of President Obama's major policy goals is to sign the Trans-Pacific Partnership (TPP) into creation. The TPP is a proposed agreement creating free trade between twelve nations around the Pacific, including rich nations like the United States, Canada, and Japan, and poorer nations such as Vietnam, Malaysia, and Peru. Like NAFTA, the TPP would effectively encourage American corporations to move operations into countries with terrible human rights, labor rights, and environmental records, providing no legal framework to make companies responsible for what happens in outsourced factories. It allows companies to take advantage of Vietnam's 28-cent-an-hour minimum wage and buildings that might collapse or burn. It continues the outsourcing of American jobs, the increase in income inequality, and the reversal of a hundred years of victories by the American working class to ensure a fair piece of the pie.[24] This would continue to allow American companies to operate without consequences. *Washington Post* columnist Harold Meyerson wrote of research by former Federal Reserve vice chairman Alan Blinder stating that if Obama gets to create the TPP, 22 to 29 percent of all American jobs could be outsourced to Asia. Twenty-five percent of American jobs mean 36 million people out of work. How can the American working class survive this? There is absolutely no reason we should have the slightest bit of confidence after twenty years of NAFTA and nearly a decade of recession and stagnation that corporations and politicians are telling the truth when they call the TPP a job creator. The immediate future of the agreement is in doubt as many leading congressional Democrats oppose it, but even if it is defeated, that President Obama and his advisers have pushed so hard for this legislation demonstrates the hegemony of free trade without consideration for American workers among the nation's economic and political elite.[25]

* * *

It is impossible to create a just society in a world of unrestrained capital mobility. Without stable work, the United States' increasing income inequality gap, persistent unemployment, and high personal debt loads will not improve. Without guarantees of corporate stability when foreign-owned factories open, the people of Honduras, Bangladesh, and Vietnam cannot win the victories the American working class did in the twentieth century. Progressives must develop a plan to keep well-paying jobs in the United States and to ensure that workers making products overseas for American markets are treated with dignity and respect.

It is not hard to envision what the United States needs: fair-paying jobs, environmentally responsible business practices, sustainable economic growth, government action to fight climate change, reformation of the corporate food system, restoration of tax rates to 1960s levels, and immigration reform would restore a great deal of justice to this nation. We need new federal programs to take on these problems, rebuild the nation's crumbling infrastructure, and reinvigorate the welfare state of the New Deal and Great Society. It shouldn't be hard to envision this kind of federal agenda, because it is what we had a mere few decades ago. But enacting these programs is difficult without the stable work of yesteryear. Similarly, it should not be that hard to imagine American companies contributing to improving the lives of the world's workers rather than merely exploiting them. When companies do move, requiring them to follow basic pollution and safety standards is hardly unreasonable. Bangladeshis and Cambodians should have work that does not kill them or cause tumors to grow in their children. We have to strive for a world that is economically, socially, and ecologically sustainable. These are basic principles of justice. In order to move toward these goals, we have to fix or replace the system of capitalism escaping the restraints to irresponsible behavior that American citizens placed on it in the twentieth century. This requires regulating capital mobility and crafting global regulations with consequences for corporate misbehavior that empower workers wherever companies are located to fight for their own rights.

If we are trying to find a starting place to show us how to fight these problems, we can do worse than the antisweatshop movement. For decades, labor unions talked about overseas workers stealing their jobs, an ineffective strategy that pitted workers against one another. The antisweatshop movement of the 1990s brought a more compassionate lens to the problem by focusing on the conditions of work, built alliances with workers around the world, created long-standing organizations to publicize and build solidarity with the oppressed, and forced some limited corporate changes to labor practices, convincing some apparel corporations to agree to voluntary standards with mild monitoring.

The sweatshop movement was composed of a few activists on a few college campuses spreading information about conditions in sweatshops abroad. One by one, other students said it was intolerable that clothing companies made their school's apparel under these conditions. They organized and demanded that their university administrations find ethical suppliers. Given how small this movement was, it achieved wonderful things. It continues to do so. In 2013, the University of Wisconsin sued Adidas, its apparel supplier, to pay $1.8 million in severance pay to workers at an Indonesian factory. The University of Wisconsin could do this because its contract with Adidas included a provision that the company pay all promised benefits to workers.[26] Since the Rana Plaza collapse, United Students Against Sweatshops has protested in front of Gap stores, with people lying like corpses on the sidewalk, emblazoned with signs reading, GAP: DEATH TRAPS and WORKERS SHOULDN'T DIE FOR FASHION.[27]

Consumer awareness of the global apparel system is the worst-case scenario for Adidas and Gap. A single individual can make a difference. To mark the one-year anniversary of the Rana Plaza collapse, a woman named Liz Parker went to an outlet of the British clothing store Matalan carrying a signboard shaped like a coffin that read MATALAN PAY UP! LONG OVERDUE FOR RANA PLAZA VICTIMS. Parker presented a letter to the store manager demanding

Matalan offer compensation to the victims. Local newspapers reported Parker's protest, bringing knowledge about this issue to anyone reading at home or online around the world. Parker provides a concrete example of what any of us can do, anytime.[28]

College students are well positioned to lead this charge because university administrators have to at least pretend to care what students think, whereas employers do not have to care what their employees think. The same goes for other organizations to which you belong: your church, your high school, or your food co-op. Professional sports fans could organize to demand the NBA or NFL have jerseys and hats produced under fair trade conditions. A group of Harry Potter fans have formed the Harry Potter Alliance to demand that Warner Bros. not make its Harry Potter–themed chocolate from cocoa produced by West African child slaves. Warner Bros. contracts with Behr's Chocolate in Orlando, which received a grade of F on the ethics of its chocolate sourcing from Free2Work, an organization that investigates industries with reputations for using slave labor. Warner Bros. initially claimed sympathy with the Harry Potter fans but has since stonewalled any information about its relationship with the chocolate company. But Warner Bros. has felt the heat on this issue, attracting media attention it doesn't want. This helps improve the lives of the world's workers.[29]

Our awareness should contribute to social justice. Opting out of the global production system does nothing for the workers. It only makes us feel good about ourselves. Saying that you will buy clothes at thrift stores to avoid supporting Nike or Walmart is not a solution to the problem. Bangladeshi apparel union activist Kalpona Akter urges Americans and Europeans to avoid boycotts because the people in these factories need to work.[30] Seeing the connections between different forms of progressive change also helps us link our actions to larger ideas. You might want organic peanut butter in your college dining hall, but you can also demand that the peanuts are grown on a farm that treats workers fairly. Also, are the dining hall workers, janitors, and dormitory workers treated well? Many universities have subcontracted this work to companies specializing in large-scale service, such as Aramark and Marriott, who slash workers' wages, provide few if any benefits, and intimidate and harass them on the job. When I was a student at the University of Tennessee in the late 1990s, the student group I worked with began fighting for a living wage campaign for UT workers. That quickly became a unionization campaign when workers, angry about their treatment by the university, expressed interest in organizing. Today, that union is United Campus Workers–Communication Workers of America Local 3865, with branches at campuses across the state.

Fighting outsourcing and supporting local economic justice campaigns are two sides of the same coin. The same corporate power that exploits workers in Bangladesh exploits workers at your local Walmart. The union movement, weakened by decades of corporate attacks and shuttering of union shops, still does more than any other American institution to fight for workers' rights. This is precisely why conservatives hate unions so much and why we need to support local union campaigns and buy union-made products when possible. Alternative labor organizations have also sprung up. Workers' centers fight for the rights of those difficult to organize, especially undocumented immigrants, fast-food workers, and those who labor at low wages in small shops.[31] The fast-food workers' movement and the fight for a $15/hour minimum wage are starting to change the country. Fast-food workers around the country have engaged in daylong strikes over the past year, bringing attention to their plight. As of writing, they have decided to escalate their demands, including protesting at shareholder meetings, which led to the arrest of 430 workers and their supporters during protests in September 2014.[32] Each of these fights builds the activist infrastructure necessary to take control of the country back from corporations. By lending a hand to these struggles, or even by honking a horn when you see fast-food workers picketing, you provide important support that builds those movements. President Obama has come out for a $10.10/hour minimum wage, and several states and cities have or are moving toward minimum wage increases. Would this have happened without the Occupy movement protesting over income inequality or the fast-food workers striking? Almost certainly not.

Organized labor has lent key support for the fast-food workers' struggle, and this should remind us of its central role in advocating for and empowering working people. The labor movement is complex and diverse, with some unions supporting social movement unionism and others looking out only for their own members. The relationship between labor and other social movements has sometimes been tense or even hostile, going back to the 1960s. Too many on the left today view unions with hostility; there was much talk among Occupy activists of labor "co-opting" the movement, without evidence that labor would try to do that.[33] Today's labor unions are far from perfect organizations, but they do more than any other institution to push for policies that benefit the working class. Without their organizing capacity, the chances of any progressive revival plummet. For example, the Service Employees International Union, the nation's largest labor union, has taken a lead on fighting for immigration reform, helping to empower undocumented immigrants and their families. Working America, an affiliate of the AFL-CIO, has started a series of workshops across the nation to explain how poverty is not an individual affliction but a national phenomenon stemming from corporate choices. It hopes to educate a million people. There is not an institution that can replace this.[34]

Organized labor can also do much to publicize the conditions of workers in the developing world. In the past, American unions have made horrible mistakes when it comes to international solidarity. During the Cold War, the AFL-CIO allowed itself to become a tool of the CIA. The anticommunists leading the American labor movement worked with the CIA to undermine leftist unions and governments, supporting right-wing military coups that repressed and murdered unionists. This terrible history cannot be erased, yet it's also important to move beyond it and support overseas labor movements irrespective of U.S. foreign policy.[35]

On the other hand, since the Cold War ended, American labor's alliances with Latin American labor movements have led to an increase in labor laws in those nations. This began during the 1990s despite the pressures of outsourcing. Even if those labor laws were not frequently enforced, they set important legal precedents.[36] The

administration of George W. Bush hoped to again use the labor
movement to push foreign policy agenda, creating the American
Center for International Labor Solidarity, better known as the
Solidarity Center. But while still funded by the U.S. government and
thus subject to its influence, the Solidarity Center has attempted to
move beyond this devastating past by supporting not only unionization but also women's rights, community health, child labor prevention, and labor law revision. It has been particularly active in
Bangladesh, providing needed publicity to the survivors of the 2012
Tarzeen factory fire in Dhaka and directing international attention to the struggles of the Bangladeshi working class. A Solidarity
Center report on the conditions of work in Bangladesh's shrimp
industry stripped away some of the concealment from the lives of
the workers who provide us with the seafood we love. Other reports
on women workers in Tunisia and the role of unions in working toward democracy in Zimbabwe build important solidarity between
progressives in the Western world and workers struggling in international anonymity to make better lives for themselves.[37]

This support from American organized labor abroad is necessary
because it is much harder for citizen-activists to fight for concrete
changes to labor conditions when the workers live across the world.
Companies contracting work out in a global supply chain can and
do enforce standards on the cost and quality of work. They can also
set standards for safe work and wages. They choose not to do this.
They can ensure that electronics workers handle chemicals with
gloves, that those sandblasting distressed jeans have proper breathing guards and the factories have functioning ventilation systems,
and that workplaces have fans and bathrooms for workers. But they
do not because no one forces them to do so. To do that, we have to
demand that governments mandate change.

The only way to reverse the global Gilded Age is to empower
workers to have power on the job that matches that of their employers. Workers and consumers in the United States and throughout
the developed world need to fight for international standards for
corporations that follow them wherever they go. We must demand
our governments create and enforce these laws. We need to use

international agencies and independent monitors to regulate the factories. Workers must have the political power to demand that their employers treat them with dignity without losing their jobs. Workers should have the right to sue their employers or the companies contracting with their employers regardless of where the site of production is located. This is the only way to ensure that workers in the United States and in the developing world can prevent catastrophes. Otherwise, with the incentives of the global race to the bottom, the companies will just keep moving. If Bangladeshi workers unionize, the companies can move to Indonesia, South Africa, Mozambique, or wherever. There's always another country with lower wages and less legal enforcement. Without mandated and enforceable standards following companies, corporations will never allow a middle class to exist anywhere.[38]

These principles might sound utopian in an age of unfettered corporate mobility, but in fact there are lots of precedents in U.S. and global history to help guide us. There are international laws disallowing products made by slave labor or from endangered species. There is no meaningful difference between these restrictions on global trade and ensuring that corporations do not pollute rivers, destroy ecosystems, decimate workers' lungs through exposure to hazardous materials, or belch chemicals into the air and give children cancer. Americans have already made choices about acceptable conditions for production. As a nation, we decided to not accept the importation of ivory or crocodile handbags. The Convention on International Trade in Endangered Species of Wild Flora and Fauna (CITES) went into effect in 1975. CITES provides for international monitoring of trade in wild species to ensure that such trade does not create endangered or extinct species. Today, 176 nations have signed the accord. The U.S. Fish and Wildlife Service ensures American compliance with CITES. CITES is hardly perfect; enforcing environmental treaties depends on the individual nation. China's black market in endangered species from impoverished Asian and African nations threatens to drive many animals to extinction. People even still smuggle endangered species into the United States. But the law's weaknesses do not suggest its impracticality. It is true that no single law will solve all problems. But the illegal trade is still *illegal*, with penalties for violators. It has certainly reduced the trade in endangered species. Laws that restrict corporate activity have the ability to be far more effective if workers are empowered to monitor employers' behavior. After all, animals cannot report violations, but humans can speak up and call for laws regulating labor conditions or pollution.

Americans can also look to Europe for ideas. In 2013, the European Union created a new logging code on sourcing timber from tropical nations. Throughout the tropics, rain forests are declining in the face of cattle ranches, mining operations, and illegal logging. The EU code harshly penalizes those trafficking in illegal timber. Timber suppliers must provide documentation of where and how the timber was harvested, keeping detailed paperwork for five years about the traders selling the wood. This forces timber companies to take responsibility for the actions of their suppliers. For us, it provides legal precedent for national and regional governance over corporate behavior in a contracting regime. This far outpaces any U.S. law on the timber trade and provides an excellent example of how government can force companies into compliance on standards of sourcing products. There is no reason the United States cannot do the same thing with timber, as well as with apparel and electronics.[39]

The U.S. government has, in fits and starts, paid attention to how the low labor standards of other nations undermine American labor and has sought to intervene, not to hurt foreign labor but rather to raise standards for all. In the early twentieth century, low wages and brutal working conditions plagued international shipping. Ship bosses ruled ocean labor with an iron hand, meting out corporal punishment. Workers could not quit their jobs. Contracts bound them to employers for a period of one to three years. If they did quit, they would lose their wages and be imprisoned at hard labor. Improved conditions on American ships just made them uncompetitive with unreformed European shipping.

As historian Leon Fink has shown, International Seaman's Union of America (ISU) president Andrew Furuseth worked closely with reformist politicians across the political spectrum, most importantly Wisconsin senator and leading Progressive Robert La Follette, to fight this problem. The ISU publicized the horrors of what happened on the ships, far out of sight from American consumers. It used the Triangle Fire to make its case: "No one will claim it is safe to crowd people into a theater or a shirtwaist factory and then to lock the doors." Furuseth furiously lobbied President Woodrow Wilson to sign what became known as the La Follette Seaman's Act, which he did in 1915. The law banned corporal punishment on ships, gave seamen the right to break their contracts in exchange for half their wages earned to that point on a voyage, and, most important, made the law applicable to any vessel sailing to an American port. As Fink states, this law created a "race to the top," as the U.S. government used its power to force foreign nations to agree to American working standards if they wanted to trade in American ports. Conditions for seamen improved around the world, as they had the option to walk away any time their ship landed in the trading behemoth that was the United States.[40]

U.S. import law has long banned goods made by slave labor. The McKinley Tariff Act of 1890 first pioneered this principle and was significantly enlarged in the Smoot-Hawley Tariff Act of 1930. In 1997, the Treasury, Postal Service, and General Government Appropriations Act added goods from forced or indentured child labor to the banned list. Today, we attempt to use this law against Chinese imports made by prison labor. It's not always easy for American customs inspectors to know for sure if a product came from prison labor, and because they are prisoners in a totalitarian state, the workers have no ability to reach out for help. Chinese workers have become so desperate that a few have slipped notes into the products they know are exported to the United States. An Oregon woman found a note from a Chinese worker in a toy she purchased detailing the horrible conditions of life in the factory. China openly violates the Smoot-Hawley forced labor provisions through using third-party contractors to sell the prison-labor-made goods to American contractors. American professor Stuart Foster served seven months in a Chinese prison. While there, he and his fellow inmates were forced to make Christmas lights for export to the United States with sadistic guards beating prisoners who worked too slowly. This is why we need more than just laws—we need the will to enforce the legislation, which takes a movement centering on labor rights around the world pressuring the government. Independent inspectors are necessary to ensure the goods are not made in prisons; without inspections and consequences for failing those inspections, all the laws in the world won't stop exploitation. But without the legal framework, we have no place to start.[41]

But then again, the United States has moved toward the Chinese prison labor model rather than fight it. Undercutting free labor with prison labor is an attractive option for states and private contractors. Immigrants suspected of immigration law violations, even if they are legal U.S. residents, are forced to work for a dollar a day in detention centers. The private corporations running these prisons use this system to avoid paying for outside labor, taking millions of dollars out of the hands of American workers. This is effectively slave labor and should be banned by the Thirteenth Amendment. A movement of workers and progressives must force the government to follow responsible labor practices both domestically and with regard to imports before the maquiladoras and prison labor systems of the developing world are the imports themselves.[42]

Even within the context of globalization, the U.S. government can act to promote labor rights. In 1976, the federal government instituted the Generalized System of Preferences (GSP), a system of tariff preferences for developing nations that was part of the government's larger promotion of globalization. But it also gave nations import advantages to the United States if they recognized labor rights. Twelve nations lost GSP-beneficiary status, and this helped put pressure on military dictatorships in Chile and Paraguay to introduce democracy and grant more freedom for workers, while in Guatemala the fear of losing GSP status helped stop a military coup in 1993 and helped stimulate the first unions and collective bargaining agreements in the nation's maquiladoras.[43]

The federal government has also acted in the apparel industry. The Multifibre Agreement, created in 1974, checked some outsourcing by placing textile import quotas that discouraged a race to the bottom. This was an international agreement and an exception to the domination of the principles of free trade over world economics during these years. It spread textile production among seventy-three nations, placing limits on how much one nation could invest in apparel factories and undermining companies playing nations off one another for lower wages and less regulation. In 1995, the international community began to phase it out, and its end on January 1, 2005, led to the modern explosion in textiles fleeing to the cheapest country, at first China and then Bangladesh, Sri Lanka, Vietnam, and Cambodia.[44]

Labor unions were angry with President Clinton for signing into law the North American Free Trade Agreement. They pressured Congress to act to revisit the law. When the House of Representatives initially rejected Clinton's request to negotiate new trade deals in 1997, Clinton had to show he took labor's concerns seriously. So as part of a new trade deal with Cambodia, Clinton agreed to a union proposal to provide the Cambodian government incentives to improve the conditions of apparel workers. The final compromise between the Clinton administration and labor allowed workers to unionize in return for an increased export quota. They received $50 a month for a forty-eight-hour week, a dozen federal holidays, vacation days, sick leave, and maternity leave. The Cambodian deal became the only free trade agreement with an enforceable labor provision.

The plan worked. With oversight from the International Labour Organization (ILO), Cambodian clothing exports and union density grew together. Apparel makers signed union contracts with workers. It was not a perfect system—factory owners tried to avoid the regulations and coached workers on what to say to ILO inspectors. But it led to enormous improvements and showed how government could improve workers' lives. Like most trade agreements, this one came to an end. The U.S.-Cambodian trade pact ended with the Multifibre Agreement's demise. Cambodia now had to compete with the rest of the world without inspections or union contracts. Within weeks of the quota ending, underground sweatshops appeared with terrible working conditions. Companies were more free than ever before to concentrate in nations with the worst workplace standards, and Cambodian labor saw its union pacts quickly scuttled and its working conditions and wages plummet to some of the lowest in the industry. Wages fell by 17 percent for Cambodian garment workers between 2001 and 2011.[45]

Even the threat of U.S. legislation regulating labor on imported products can move industry to action. In 1992, Iowa senator Tom Harkin introduced the Child Labor Deterrence Act, which would have prohibited importing goods made with child labor to the United States and called for both civil and criminal penalties for violators. Indian carpet makers, reliant upon child labor, began moving toward an independent monitoring system with the assistance of German unions, although when it became clear that Harkin's bill would not pass, the Indian carpet industry resisted meaningful monitoring and the system was weakened and easily avoided by the carpet makers. Unfortunately, Congress has never passed the Child Labor Deterrence Act, but the actions of the Indian carpet makers suggest suppliers and importers are watching American labor law and will react positively to mandates.[46]

Admittedly, these stories are anomalies in a long history of government indifference to workers' rights. Despite these occasional efforts of government, for most of U.S. history the government has not supported workers' rights. The Department of Commerce, controlled in the 1920s by Republican presidents who opposed such legislation, undermined the Seaman's Act by creating lax enforcement provisions on ships and assuming that ships from nations with standards similar to American laws would not need inspection, regardless of the actual conditions on the ships. The anti-immigrant laws passed in the 1920s meant that seamen could not take advantage of the ability to quit in an American port if they were from China or Italy or Russia because they couldn't immigrate to the United States. In the 1950s, the Supreme Court ruled the international provisions of the Seaman's Act unconstitutional during a period where the growth of trade agreements and the need to rebuild western Europe in the face of the Cold War made the court uncomfortable with the United States mandating labor conditions abroad.[47]

The Senate's unwillingness to pass international treaties, including United Nations conventions guaranteeing basic human rights, remains a major impediment for labor rights, human rights, and environmental protection. The Basel Convention of 1989 provided regulatory control over hazardous-waste trading between the global North and South and prohibited the export of hazardous waste to many countries. But the United States is one of only a handful of nations, including Myanmar and Haiti, to refuse to ratify the treaty. Instead, the United States has explicitly exempted electronic waste from the very limited laws the nation does have to protect countries from toxic waste. With the United States undermining the treaty through its active role in the toxic waste trade, the entire treaty becomes almost impossible to enforce, and also illegal imports and bribery are now a major part of the international toxicity trade.[48]

The Supreme Court has also limited the actions citizens can take to support workers overseas. U.S. shipping unions supported a strike by Italian workers flying under a Liberian flag for better working conditions. In 1963, the Supreme Court ruled this action a violation of legitimate union activity, in part because it would be damaging to American foreign relations if American unions could affect ships flying under foreign flags.[49] Recent decisions are more concerning. International groups have sued U.S. corporations under the Alien Tort Statute (ATS), enacted in 1789. Under the provisions of this law, U.S. district courts have the right to hear claims from foreign citizens if they have suffered from actions "in violation of the law of nations or a treaty of the United States." Beginning in the 1980s, people around the world began filing lawsuits in U.S. courts for human rights violations, even when an American was not directly involved. Lawsuits against Texaco for its environmental damage in Ecuador are an example of people using the ATS to try to hold corporations accountable for the wanton damage they create. Similarly, Nigerians sued foreign oil companies in American courts for aiding the Nigerian government in torturing and killing civilians protesting oil exploration. But in *Kiobel v. Royal Dutch Petroleum*, the Roberts Court found for the oil companies by a 5 to 4 margin, severely undermining the ability of human rights activists to use U.S. courts to push for international standards. However, it remains unclear whether American companies can be sued on these grounds.[50]

Despite these problems, activists and citizens need to force the government to act for the benefit of people rather than corporations. Some commentators argue that globalization has lessened the power of the state, severely restraining the possibility of using state power to control global corporations.[51] While outsourcing has introduced a new dynamic to the world, states can still control the corporations residing or doing business within their borders. The reason for using state power to create progressive change is simple—the vast majority of victorious social struggles in American history have been won only after they forced the government to codify their demands into law. The labor movement triumphed when massive strikes pressed the federal government to level the playing field between workers and corporations in the 1930s. The civil rights movement could not achieve its basic goals without the Civil Rights Act of 1964 and the Voting Rights Act of 1965. The women's suffrage movement needed the Nineteenth Amendment to succeed, and the failure to ratify the Equal Rights Amendment in the 1970s takes an important legal tool away from the women's movement today. Environmentalists forced corporations to reduce their polluting of American water, soil, and air only when the government mandated it. Gay marriage proponents require legal transformations, and they are winning because of their brilliant strategy.

Dealing with the outsourcing plague will require reshaping the government's priorities, because many politicians today care little about economic inequality. Republicans openly support whatever their corporate masters want, opposing nearly all regulations, giving the wealthy tax breaks, promoting corporate influence over politics, and encouraging union busting. Democrats usually support higher minimum wages, environmental regulations, and a more robust social safety net. These are important differences between the parties. On the other hand, Democratic presidents have pushed job-killing free trade agreements with as much vigor as Republicans. Bill Clinton signed NAFTA. Barack Obama wants the Trans-Pacific Partnership. In a post–*Citizens United* nation, corporate leaders are buying elections. The two-party system seems hopeless for creating progressive change.

But there has never been a successful third-party movement in U.S. history. As we saw after 2000, Ralph Nader's success in drawing enough voters from Al Gore in Florida and New Hampshire to swing the election to George W. Bush did absolutely nothing to move the Democrats to the left, nor did it help build a long-term left-leaning challenge to the Democratic Party. The last third party to have any lasting impact was the Populist Party in the 1890s, but it collapsed after Democrats co-opted a few of its positions, leaving the small farmers who engaged in that rebellion against corporate exploitation in no better shape than before it began. Some have called the early Republican Party a third party, but this is inaccurate. It filled a gap in the two-party system after the Whigs declined in the face of sectional tensions over slavery.[52] The winner-take-all American political system simply makes a third-party challenge an enormous mountain to climb.

This leaves one political tool—taking over the Democratic Party. We have to make it stand for working people, for environmental justice, for economic equality, and for fair-trade agreements. We can turn Democrats who support polluting and union-busting corporations over unions and greens and prioritize Wall Street over workers out of office. We can run for city and county Democratic Party offices, bringing a pro-worker agenda into the party. We can pressure candidates to support higher minimum wages and to hold corporations accountable for their actions both inside and outside American borders. We can show candidates that embracing working people is a ticket to victory. We can turn the Democratic Party back into the force that it was in the 1930s and 1960s, when it fought for working Americans because working people themselves had the political power to make the party elites listen.

Even on the local level, progressives dominating government can make a big difference. In 2013, the Portland, Oregon, city council adopted a resolution divesting city resources from Walmart, a plan it is currently implementing. It did this after evaluating city holdings that cause "health and environmental concerns, abusive labor practices, and corrupt corporate ethic and governance." Walmart's labor practices fit these standards and the city acted. If other cities followed, it could make a real impact on Walmart and potentially force it to treat its workers with some semblance of respect. Similarly, the city government of Madison, Wisconsin, has instituted an ethical-sourcing program for the city, committing its vendors to fair labor practices modeled on International Labour Organization guidelines. This is how government can create change if citizens demand and fight for it.[53]

Taking over the Democratic Party is no easy task, as any activist will tell you. Today, the federal government is less responsive to the needs of working people and the cause of economic justice than at any time since the 1920s. But while the challenges of taking back the American government are great, conservatives have shown us it is doable. The structures are in place. Ultimately, however we manage to do it, we have to challenge corporations and their uncontrolled mobility that dominates our modern economy. Nothing else will allow Americans to create stable jobs for working-class people or allow people of the developing world to claw their way out of poverty.

Some will argue that focusing on the American government is wrongheaded. Wealthy American supporters of the current economic model might say, "What about the governments where this stuff happens? Doesn't Bangladesh have a responsibility to crack down on Gap and Walmart instead of us innocent consumers with busy lives?" They will even argue that lower safety standards are good for Bangladeshis because they mean the country will attract more jobs.[54] The Bangladeshi government is absolutely at fault for the Rana Plaza collapse. The factory owners dominate Bangladeshi politics and have no incentive to change the system. They kill organizers and repress unions. But making these claims that safety standards are strictly the responsibility of the government and people of the nation of production is immoral, particularly since American business funds and supports the oligarchs who control politics in these countries. In 2006, Vietnamese workers struck in protest against the conditions in their factories. The government threw the strike leaders into prison. In 2013, Cambodian garment workers protesting for rights from their government found themselves at the wrong end of a gun. When Cambodians and Bangladeshis and Vietnamese workers find themselves oppressed by a combination of their own governments and their Western-based employers (or the companies who contract with them), the American people must demand better.[55]

The weakness of the 1990s antisweatshop movement, through no fault of its own, was that it lacked the size and power to force corporate compliance with a strict regulatory code. Instead, the apparel companies agreed only to voluntary codes of conduct and self-monitoring guidelines. The Clinton administration pressed for the creation of the Fair Labor Association (FLA) in 1999 in response to the antisweatshop movement. But the FLA uses monitors known for their sympathy for the companies and has no enforcement standards, meaning companies face no penalties for noncompliance. Unions originally joined the FLA but quit soon after it became clear the corporations had no interest in improving conditions. When, in 2008, FLA member Russell Athletic closed a factory in Honduras rather than accept the union its workers organized, the FLA did nothing to reprimand the company. To quote Global Exchange co-founder Medea Benjamin, private monitoring "leaves the fox guarding the hen house."[56] One FLA monitor, Social Accountability International, gave a Pakistani factory a positive rating in August 2012. The next month, three hundred workers died when that factory burned. Apple asked the FLA to evaluate the Foxconn operation in China where it makes its goods. Even though this factory's dormitories have suicide nets to prevent workers from jumping off the top floors to their deaths, the FLA investigator called it "first-class."[57]

Even when companies have expended a bit of energy on reforms, they have ultimately failed to make a big difference because of the lack of repercussions for noncompliance. After United Students Against Sweatshops exposed Nike's labor practices in the 1990s, the company, stung by the criticism, sought to increase monitoring of its suppliers. It developed its own code of conduct, trained suppliers, and sent out monitors to inspect factories. Yet the effort failed because it lacked mandatory penalties for noncompliance and because workers received no political or labor rights that would allow them to report violations without fearing for their jobs. The only incentive for compliance in a voluntary system is the corporation's maintaining its contract with the supplier. But subcontracting with stipulations for the low costs encourages labor violations. Nike is not going to cut ties with successful suppliers. Profit margin and shareholder value will always defeat labor conditions and environmental responsibility in corporate decision making.[58]

We must demand and mobilize for a more just global labor regime that would require the American government to prioritize the needs of workers as much as those of companies, giving workers around the world tools to improve their lives. Consumers can do a lot. From Triangle to Rana Plaza, outraged consumers have placed great pressure on apparel companies to reform. Other industries have faced similar pressure after they caused catastrophes. But in the United States of an earlier time, workers and reformers could unite for political change because they lived in the same country. Today, international reformers allying with overseas workers run into the problem that the two groups are rallying different governments to act. American reformers have little to no impact on the governments of Bangladesh and Honduras, but those governments don't listen to their own workers either and engage in open union repression. We have seen in this book that when apparel workers fight for unions, the companies simply close the factories and move. Without international labor standards, this will continue. We need to push Western governments to recognize a broad set of standards that require corporations to take responsibility for the behavior of their suppliers and subcontractors. They must recognize the right of workers to organize, the rights of women in the workplace to not be victimized with sexual harassment or assault, the rights of communities to not have pollution spewed into their rivers and air, and the right to labor in a healthy space. These are basic rights and the broad principles we need to fight for our government to impose upon corporations if they sell goods in the American marketplace.

Corporations that avoid responsibility to their workers define the modern American economy. They do so in many ways—through outsourcing work overseas, through contracting with temp agencies, through supply chains, and through a variety of other means intended to protect corporate interests from people demanding a just and dignified life. All of this protects corporations from workers organizing into unions, suing them over workplace-safety issues, or doing anything else. Unless workers have the right to legal action against their employers, they will not have the power to fight back. We have already won important victories. In July 2014, the general counsel of the National Labor Relations Board ruled that McDonald's was a "co-employer" of the workers at its franchises. This potentially has widespread ramifications because now McDonald's could be held legally responsible for the wages and working conditions at its restaurants. The fast-food workers' struggle for $15 an hour could now reach a new stage, with the government opening up a door for them to express worker power through the legal system.[59]

This is just one of many possible ways the government could improve the lives of American workers. Modern global capitalism is talked about as if it is a natural force, like gravity. It's not. These are political problems with political solutions. If the government can protect American workers, which it absolutely can, it can do the same for foreign workers laboring to make products for the American market. We must demand that our government take the lead in crafting international labor standards that force corporations to treat workers with dignity no matter where they locate their production sites. Concealment must end. The only way to do that is to give workers the power to use American courts to press their cases. If an apparel factory making clothing for Walmart and Gap turns local rivers red with dyes, uses brutal supervisors who sexually abuse female workers, or kills workers through poor safety standards, those workers in Bangladesh, Honduras, and the Philippines should have the right to sue the parent or contracting companies in American courts. This is perhaps the best way to discourage companies from continuing to move in response to workers demanding dignity. By using innovative legal strategies such as suing American companies under the Alien Tort Statute for violations by their suppliers or by federal or state governments passing laws mandating new standards of corporate behavior internationally, workers could have the ability to appeal to the nations where the products and profits they generate with their labor travel. If American corporations and American CEOs want the privilege of basing their corporations or their homes in the United States, they should have to abide by fundamental rights, perhaps set by the International Labour Organization, the closest thing the world has to a nonpartisan labor organization.

Founded in 1919 and integrated into the United Nations in 1946, the ILO sets international standards on labor conditions. ILO standards are the best universal declaration of labor rights we have to go on, and American companies operating overseas routinely violate them. The ILO certainly is not perfect; like other UN agencies, it is vulnerable to pressure from big countries and it is not democratic. Nor is the ILO antiglobalization; in fact, it tends to promote globalization for the sake of efficiency. On the other hand, it has a nearly century-long history of trying to set concrete standards for workers, and at least it is an international agency with workers' rights clearly at the heart of its mission, unlike, say, the World Bank or International Monetary Fund. It lacks the ability to punish violating countries, but the United States can do that for products entering its borders. The United States needs to ratify ILO conventions and empower workers, activists, and journalists to uncover abuses committed by American corporations wherever production is sited.

Working with ILO standards concerning the right to organize, ending child labor, improving occupational safety, and protecting workers and citizens from toxic exposure, labor unions and companies can cooperate in a system that brings some jobs to developing nations under safe and dignified standards while keeping some jobs at home. In 2000, Faber-Castell, an office supply manufacturer, signed an agreement with the Building and Wood Workers' International union to extend basic ILO principles throughout its global factories, including a large one in Brazil, that would require overtime pay, guarantee decent working conditions, and ensure a workplace free of intimidation or sexual harassment. That union has signed other international framework agreements with companies in Germany, Sweden, the Netherlands, Italy, and France, helping to export workplace rights along with capital. Implementing these standards is often difficult with subcontractors and suppliers, but this far surpasses any model to which American companies have agreed. If the government were to mandate that American companies follow ILO conventions, that would go far in creating agreements similar to the one to which Faber-Castell has committed.[60]

We must also fight to keep corporations in place long enough that workers can win basic rights without fearing for their jobs. The scourge of constant capital mobility every time workers win a campaign to improve their lives has to end. It simply should be illegal for a corporation to close or move when its workers form a union. When a company chooses to site a factory somewhere or contract operations to a subcontractor, it needs to sign a legally binding agreement to stay in that location for a particular amount of time. Perhaps a twenty-year contract is a sensible length, with some escape clauses if a company stops making a product or goes out of business. Entering bankruptcy, however, should not be enough, as corporations today use bankruptcy proceedings to rid themselves of pesky union contracts, such as most of the major American airlines have done in the past decade.

The United States needs a law, let's call it the Corporate Responsibility Act, that sets basic environmental, wage, workplace safety, and sexual harassment standards for all products produced by American companies and sold in the country. It could be based on an ILO framework that protects a wide range of labor and environmental rights. Moreover, it should specifically attack the principle of capital mobility to avoid labor and environmental standards. It needs to include not just companies based in the United States, but also those who use tax inversions—purchasing foreign companies in order to move their official headquarters abroad for tax reasons while continuing to operate in the United States, as Burger King did by buying the Canadian fast-food company Tim Horton's in 2014.[61] It also needs to give workers the right to sue corporations in American courts.

A central feature of the law would be stringent reporting requirements. Corporations would have to file reports with the federal government detailing where they produced all of their products. Walmart would have to know precisely where everything made for its stores was produced, discuss the working conditions of those factories, and open their records for government inspections. It would be legally liable for all of the goods it contracted out for production. Yes, it would create more paperwork for corporations. Good—they need to keep better records about production. Business always complains about government regulation, but it is only with such regulation that we can hold corporations legally responsible for their behavior. If it costs one dollar more for a pair of jeans, keeping workers alive is well worth the additional cost. Such a law would go further to police illegitimate corporate behavior than any law in American history. This might sound radical and impractical, but it is necessary to create a global legal framework around labor and environmental law to match the radically globalized economy of the twenty-first century. Anything short of this will allow corporations to continue oppressing workers and plundering the planet with little recourse for those who are fighting for dignity and sustainability.

No, this law is not going to pass in the current Congress. But we have to enter the national political conversation concerning economic, trade, and environmental issues by demanding the kind of accountability from corporations that no one, not even labor unions or environmentalists, has talked about in a very long time.

Only by placing pressure on corporations and their politician lackeys can we shape a twenty-first century that respects workers and ecosystems around the world rather than exploits them for the benefit of the 1 percent.

And again, this process has to empower workers. Mass movements are a great thing. We need people marching in the street against corporate exploitation. We need outrage leading to consumers demanding concrete change. I hope that after reading this book you are going to get involved in the struggles of your community to bring justice to the world's workers, connect environmentalism with the lives of everyday people, and demand a global fair trade system.

But giving workers the power to demand the changes they need to live dignified lives is the only way to ensure the actions we as activists take are permanent. Reformers' attention drifts over time; one decade they focus on workers, the next on something else. When progressives' attention wandered from economic justice and fair trade as the primary issue of concern after 9/11, it was for a good reason. The torture of American prisoners at Guantánamo Bay, the U.S. invasion of Iraq, the torture of prisoners at Abu Ghraib, the decline of civil liberties in the wake of the Patriot Act—all of these things were horrible and deserved our attention. Today, there are a lot of other issues that need our attention, too. Organizing against America's racist criminal justice system, for instance, is something that needs to happen. Right now, economic inequality has captured the attention of activists around the country and world. We must act on this now before our attention gets distracted by something else, as indeed it will. Thus, only by ensuring that power is placed in the hands of those who have experienced the depredations of global capitalism every day can we move toward a system of permanent justice that survives this moment of activism.

This is not going to solve all the problems of inequality in the United States or around the world. Much more is needed here. A global wealth tax that forces the rich to pay their fair share would help, as would raising property taxes on wealthy properties, corporate taxes for companies located in the United States, and capital gains and other taxes. The government needs to directly employ citizens to rebuild the American infrastructure and stimulate the economy. A massive investment in clean energy technology would create jobs and direct the nation toward a greener future that might mitigate climate change. Student loan debt forgiveness, public transit expansion, and urban housing programs would do much to create a more just economy. But taking away many of the incentives for capital mobility while also empowering workers overseas would help keep more jobs at home while making the jobs that are outsourced dignified and safe. This should be a central strategy for globalized justice in a globalized world.

We aren't going to tame corporations tomorrow. But as concerned citizens, we need to move away from thinking about activism only in terms of the next election cycle, expecting politicians to solve our problems. Without a long-term strategy, the problem is not going away. Americans have overcome even longer odds than we face today. The labor movement was a mess in the 1920s, under attack from antiradical communist hunters, corporations seeking to push back from gains organized labor had made in the previous decade, and a hostile Republican Party that controlled national and state politics. Ten years later, millions of Americans had signed up for unions and the government had instituted vast new programs to help Americans get back to work and create economic security for the future.

Similarly, in the 1950s, people concerned with conservation were in despair. The nation was sprawling across the landscape with new suburbs. Dams, energy projects, and mines ate up pristine habitat and landscape. Protecting workers and nature was a secondary concern to militarizing against a potential war with the Soviet Union and expanding corporate profits. This period is widely considered a low point in our environmental history. Yet fifteen years later, millions of Americans were celebrating Earth Day and the Johnson administration had passed groundbreaking environmental legislation creating a wilderness system and clean air and water laws. The United States had entered a long period of environmental transformation.

This can happen again. And it can happen faster than we think. No one expected Occupy Wall Street to change the conversation about economic inequality, yet that happened almost overnight in 2011. Even if that movement could not be sustained, the next one might. The only way we can make the change we want is to demand that change. That change is not going to come from electing a better politician as president. All politicians are reeds blowing in the breeze. If we don't provide a stronger wind than the corporations, the politicians will sway toward promoting business-friendly policies. Globalization will not be repealed. The era of protectionism is dead. But if the economy is to be globalized, so must labor standards. Corporations have escaped legal restraint and they have reset the play button on a century of labor rights. Leveling the playing field has to be a priority to protect all the workers of the world.

Hopefully, after reading this book, you will be inspired to make change. You have seen how people in this country fought to tame corporate behavior and how people around the world are continuing that fight today. I am a historian, but I have no idea what will happen in the future. No one can predict it. No one could tell that a woman named Rosa Parks refusing to move to the back of a bus in Montgomery, Alabama, would launch the civil rights movement into its most successful period. No one knew that resistance to police repression of gays at the Stonewall Inn in New York City would create the modern gay rights movement. No one could have guessed that the first protesters at what became Occupy Wall Street would change the national conversation on income inequality. All I can say is that the only way to create change is to fight for the change you want to see. Political change is caused by the combination of mass movements and legal transformations. It will take both to end the scourge of capital mobility and bring dignified work to the world's working class. I want to close the book then by suggesting five concrete steps you can take to move this process along, creating history as you act.

1. **Gain Knowledge.** Sweeping back the curtain of concealment that corporations have placed between you and your
products is key for anyone to act for change. Reading this
book is part of this process, but you can pay attention to
newspapers, websites, Twitter feeds, and other forms of
news. Watch for stories on labor unions, working conditions, food, climate change, etc. Read some of the books
listed in the footnotes at the back of this book. Start piec-
ing together the problems you see. Build connections between different movements and problems. What links
them? Why don't people act on these issues? It's because
they don't know about them. The corporate power of concealment is strong. Peel it back and let people know about
what you find.

2. **Influence Your Community.** Most of us are part of organizations. If you are a college student, demand that not
only are the eggs and meat in your cafeteria organic, but
that they are produced under a system of fair labor. How
are the working conditions at the farm? What happens to
the waste? Demand that your college knows this information and publicizes it. Push them to use suppliers that will
provide that information. It is the same with apparel suppliers and the working conditions of janitors and food service workers. You can create campus organizations to work
on these issues. Together with other colleges and universities and high schools and churches and consumers' organization, you can build toward the mass movement necessary
to enact global workplace and environmental standards.

3. **Go into the Streets.** You don't have to be part of a big organization to act. Go outside a store and hand out flyers about
the horrors of a sweatshop producing clothes for Gap. You
and your friends can create street theater around the issue
of workers dying on the job, grabbing people's attention in
front of the stores that sell sweatshop-made clothing. You
can march with unions, with environmentalists, with the
immigration activists who are demanding legal status for

the people doing much of the hardest and most dangerous work in this nation. Protest! To quote the great IWW organizer Joe Hill, "Don't mourn. Organize." Mourning the dead in Bangladesh is OK, but make sure that more don't die by embarrassing Gap and Walmart where it hurts—in front of their stores.

4. **Make Demands of Politicians.** Ultimately, we have to craft laws to tame corporate behavior. Right now, our politicians mostly don't care about these issues. They want corporate donations and are afraid of criticizing corporate leaders. We have to force them to take positions on neoliberal globalization—how it is destroying the American middle class—and on American corporate responsibility for dead workers and degraded ecosystems around the world. They won't expect to be asked questions about these issues, but once we start asking the questions, it provides cover for progressive politicians to make speeches, craft legislation, and buck the corporations they fear. This isn't easy, but it is doable and necessary. Think about how fast gay marriage has progressed. Twenty years ago, it was almost unmentionable. Today, we are on the verge of it being legal nationwide. This is because brave activists started organizing, calling out politicians, and creating the space for change. It is a model of political organizing. We can do the same thing for the moral issue of corporate concealment of tragedy.

5. **Work for Change.** There are many organizations working for justice. Some are focused on national issues, others on international ones. Some focus on workers, others on women's rights, still others on the environment. You can both join and shape these movements, serving their traditional goals while also being the bridge between movements that is necessary for alliance building. For example, if you are an environmentalist and you want to work for a green organization, help move that organization to ally with workers' movements to ensure sustainability for the people who

have to live with the pollution produced by corporations at home and abroad. Join the labor movement and help organize workers while also attempting to connect that work with international labor and environmental movements. Become a member of organizations that work on international justice issues. Be the change you want to see.

Not everyone is in a position to do all of these things, but almost everyone is in a position to do at least one of them. If we demand change and create a mass movement identifying the plague of capital mobility as a central problem in our society, we can force change. For the sake of the world's workers, the future of the United States, and the ecological balance of the Earth, we must succeed.

NOTES

INTRODUCTION: THE SCOURGE OF CAPITAL MOBILITY

1. William Greider, *One World, Ready or Not: The Manic Logic of Global Capitalism* (New York: Simon & Schuster, 1997), 24. Date of quote from an e-mail exchange with author.

2. On the Triangle Fire, see Richard A. Greenwald, *The Triangle Fire, the Protocols of Peace, and Industrial Democracy in Progressive Era New York* (Philadelphia: Temple University Press, 2005); John F. McClymer, *The Triangle Strike and Fire* (Orlando, FL: Harcourt Brace College Publishers, 1998); David von Drehle, *Triangle: The Fire That Changed America* (New York: Grove Press, 2003); and Jo Ann E. Argersinger, *The Triangle Fire: A Brief History with Documents* (Boston: Bedford/St. Martin's, 2009).

3. On working conditions and death in the workplace during these years, see Andrew Mason Prouty, *More Deadly Than War! Pacific Coast Logging, 1827–1981* (New York; Garland, 1985); Thomas G. Andrews, *Killing for Coal: America's Deadliest Labor War* (Cambridge, MA: Harvard University Press, 2008); Christopher C. Sellers, *Hazards of the Job: From Industrial Disease to Environmental Health Science* (Chapel Hill: University of North Carolina Press, 1997); Alan Derickson, *Black Lung: Anatomy of a Public Health Disaster* (Ithaca, NY: Cornell University Press, 1998); David Rosner and Gerald Markowitz, *Deadly Dust: Silicosis and the Politics of Occupational Disease in Twentieth-Century America* (Princeton, NJ: Princeton University Press, 1991); Christian Warren, *Brush with Death: A Social History of Lead Poisoning* (Baltimore: Johns Hopkins University Press, 2000); and Claudia Clark, *Radium Girls: Women and Industrial Health Reform, 1910–1935* (Chapel Hill: University of North Carolina Press, 1997).

4. Frances Perkins speech at Cornell University, September 30, 1964, www
.ilr.cornell.edu/trianglefire/primary/lectures/FrancesPerkinsLecture.html.

5. Kristin Downey, *The Woman Behind the New Deal: The Life of Frances Perkins, FDR's Secretary of Labor and His Moral Conscience* (New York: Nan A. Talese, 2009); Frances Perkins, *The Roosevelt I Knew* (New York: Viking Press, 1946); Bill Severn, *Frances Perkins: A Member of the Cabinet* (New York: Hawthorn Books, 1976).

6. Nan Enstad, *Ladies of Labor, Girls of Adventure: Working Women, Popular Culture, and Labor Politics at the Turn of the Twentieth Century* (New York: Columbia University Press, 1999), 84–160; Maxine Schwartz Seller, "The Uprising of the Twenty Thousand: Sex, Class, and Ethnicity in the Shirtwaist Makers' Strike of 1909," in "*Struggle a Hard Battle*": *Essays on Working-Class Immigrants*, ed. Dirk Hoerder (DeKalb: Northern Illinois Press, 1986), 254–79.

7. Nancy Quam-Wickham, "Cities Sacrificed on the Altar of Oil: Popular Opposition to Oil Development in 1920s Los Angeles," *Environmental History* 3, no. 2 (April 1998): 189–209.

8. Harvey Molotch and Marilyn Lester, "Accidental News: The Great Oil Spill as Local Occurrence and National Event," *Journal of Sociology* 81, no. 2 (September 1975): 235–60.

9. David Stradling and Richard Stradling, "Perceptions of the Burning River: Deindustrialization and Cleveland's Cuyahoga River," *Environmental History* 13, no. 3 (July 2008): 515–35.

10. "The Cities: The Price of Optimism," *Time*, August 1, 1969, 41.

11. Gordon Young, "Pollution, Threat to Man's Only Home," *National Geographic*, December 1970: 737–80.

12. Stradling and Stradling, "Perceptions of the Burning River."

13. "Price of Optimism," 41; Carl B. Stokes, *Promises of Power: A Political Autobiography* (New York: Simon & Schuster, 1973), 119–20.

14. "Legislation: Policing the Polluters," *Time*, August 1, 1969, 42.

15. See Adam Rome, *The Genius of Earth Day: How a 1970 Teach-In Unexpectedly Made the First Green Generation* (New York: Hill and Wang, 2013); Robert Gottlieb, *Forcing the Spring: The Transformation of the American Environmental Movement*, rev. ed. (1993; repr., Washington, DC: Island Press, 2005); Kirkpatrick Sale, *The Green Revolution: The American Environmental Movement, 1962–1992* (New York: Hill and Wang, 1993); and Philip Shabecoff, *A Fierce Green Fire: The American Environmental Movement*, rev. ed. (1993; repr., Washington, DC: Island Press, 2003).

16. Jim Yardley, "Garment Trade Wields Power in Bangladesh," *New York Times*, July 24, 2013.

17. Clare O'Connor, "'Extreme Pricing' at What Cost? Retailer Joe Fresh Sends Reps to Bangladesh as Death Toll Rises," *Forbes*, April 30, 2013, www.forbes.com/sites/clareoconnor/2013/04/30/extreme-pricing-at-what-cost-retailer-joe-fresh-sends-reps-to-bangladesh-as-death-toll-rises/; Clare O'Connor, "These Retailers Involved in Bangladesh Factory Disaster Have Yet to Compensate Victims," *Forbes*, April 26, 2014, www.forbes.com/sites

/clareoconnor/2014/04/26/these-retailers-involved-in-bangladesh-factory
-disaster-have-yet-to-compensate-victims/.

18. Pamela Engel, "Here Are Some of the Biggest Brands That Make Clothes in Bangladesh," *Business Insider*, May 13, 2013, www.businessinsider.com/big -brands-in-bangladesh-factories-2013-5; Victor Luckerson, "Bangladesh Factory Collapse: Is There Blood on Your Shirt?" *Time*, May 2, 2013, business.time .com/2013/05/02/bangladesh-factory-collapse-is-there-blood-on-your-shirt/.

19. Jason Burke, "Bangladesh Factory Collapse Leaves Trail of Shattered Lives," *The Guardian*, June 6, 2013, www.guardian.co.uk/world/2013/jun/06 /bangladesh-factory-building-collapse-community.

20. Mark Memmott, "Bangladesh Survivor Thought She Would Never See Daylight," *The Two-Way* (blog), National Public Radio, May 10, 2013, www.npr.org/blogs/thetwo-way/2013/05/10/182810766/reports-survivor -rescued-17-days-after-bangladesh-building-collapse.

21. Jim Yardley, "After Bangladesh Factory Collapse, Bleak Struggle for Survivors," *New York Times*, December 18, 2013.

22. "Bangladeshi Workers Set Fire to Factories," *The Australian*, September 23, 2013.

23. Andrew Herod, "Placing Labor," in *Labor Rising: The Past and Future of Working People in America*, ed. Daniel Katz and Richard A. Greenwald (New York: The New Press, 2012), 85.

24. David Naguib Pellow, *Resisting Global Toxics: Transnational Movements for Environmental Justice* (Cambridge, MA: MIT Press, 2007), 9–10; "Summers Memo," en.wikipedia.org/wiki/Summers_memo.

25. Joseph E. Stiglitz, *Globalization and Its Discontents* (New York: W.W. Norton, 2002), 9.

26. The literature on globalization's history is immense, but a couple of key works are Alfred W. Crosby, *Ecological Imperialism: The Biological Expansion of Europe, 900–1900* (New York: Cambridge University Press, 1986); Janet L. Abu-Lughod, *Before European Hegemony: The World System, A.D. 1250–1350* (New York: Oxford University Press, 1989); and Peter N. Stearns, *Globalization in World History* (New York: Routledge, 2010).

27. "Climate Change and Financial Instability Seen as Top Global Threats," Pew Research Global Attitudes Project, June 24, 2013, www.pew global.org/2013/06/24/climate-change-and-financial-instability-seen-as -top-global-threats/.

28. Charles Noble, *Liberalism at Work: The Rise and Fall of OSHA* (Philadelphia: Temple University Press, 1986), 125.

29. "Environment," Gallup, www.gallup.com/poll/1615/environment.aspx.

30. Josh Lederman, "Obama Administration Set to Unveil New Limits on Power Plants in Response to Climate Change," *MassLive*, May 7, 2014, www.masslive.com/news/index.ssf/2014/05/obama_administration_set _to_un.html.

31. Steven Greenhouse, "Share of the Work Force in a Union Drops to a 97-Year Low, 11.3%," *New York Times*, January 23, 2013; Bureau of Labor

Statistics, "Union Members Summary," January 24, 2014, www.bls.gov/news.release/union2.nr0.htm.

32. Diane Ravitch, *Reign of Error: The Hoax of the Privatization Movement and the Danger to America's Public Schools* (New York: Alfred A. Knopf, 2013).

33. Mike Elk, "Why Is Earth Day So Much More Popular than Workers Memorial Day," *Working in These Times* (blog), *In These Times*, April 29, 2011, inthesetimes.com/working/entry/7254/; Lee Fang, "Austerity, Deregulation and the Texas Fertilizer Plant Explosion," *The Nation*, April 18, 2013, www.thenation.com/blog/173931/austerity-deregulation-and-texas-fertilizer-plant-explosion.

1: STANDING UP TO CORPORATE DOMINATION: A BRIEF HISTORY

The notes in this chapter are not intended to be comprehensive literature discussions on the subjects but rather are intended to provide a reading list for those interested in further reading.

1. E.P. Thompson, *The Making of the English Working Class* (New York: Pantheon, 1963); Paul Mason, *Live Working or Die Fighting: How the Working Class Went Global* (Chicago: Haymarket Books, 2007), 1–27.

2. Chad Montrie, *Making a Living: Work and Environment in the United States* (Chapel Hill: University of North Carolina Press, 2008), 13–34; Thomas Dublin, *Transforming Women's Work: New England Lives in the Industrial Revolution* (Ithaca, NY: Cornell University Press, 1994); Thomas Dublin, *Women at Work: The Transformation of Work and Community in Lowell, Massachusetts, 1826–1860*, 2nd ed. (New York: Columbia University Press, 1993).

3. Harriet Hanson Robinson, "The Lowell Mill Girls Go on Strike, 1836," *History Matters*, historymatters.gmu.edu/d/5714.

4. Dublin, *Women at Work*; Mary H. Blewett, *Men, Women, and Work: Class, Gender, and Protest in the New England Shoe Industry, 1780–1910* (Urbana: University of Illinois Press, 1990).

5. On slavery, see Walter Johnson, *River of Dark Dreams: Slavery and Empire in the Cotton Kingdom* (Cambridge, MA: Harvard University Press, 2013); Eugene D. Genovese, *Roll, Jordan, Roll: The World the Slaves Made* (New York: Pantheon Books, 1974); Ira Berlin, *Many Thousands Gone: The First Two Centuries of Slavery in North America* (Cambridge, MA: Harvard University Press, 1998); and Walter Johnson, *Soul by Soul: Life Inside the Antebellum Slave Market* (Cambridge, MA: Harvard University Press, 1999).

6. Eric Foner, *The Fiery Trial: Abraham Lincoln and American Slavery* (New York: W.W. Norton, 2011); Chandra Manning, *What This Cruel War Was Over: Soldiers, Slavery, and the Civil War* (New York: Vintage, 2008); John C. Waugh, *Reelecting Lincoln: The Battle for the 1864 Presidency* (New York: Crown, 1997); James McPherson, *Battle Cry of Freedom: The Civil War*

Era (New York: Oxford University Press, 1988); Martin H. Blatt and David Roediger, eds., *The Meaning of Slavery in the North* (New York: Garland, 1998).

7. Eric Foner, *Reconstruction: America's Unfinished Revolution, 1863–1877* (New York: Harper & Row, 1988); Tera W. Hunter, *To 'Joy My Freedom: Southern Black Women's Lives and Labors After the Civil War* (Cambridge, MA: Harvard University Press, 1997); Heather Cox Richardson, *The Death of Reconstruction: Race, Labor, and Politics in the Post–Civil War North, 1865–1901* (Cambridge, MA: Harvard University Press, 2001).

8. Alan Trachtenberg, *The Incorporation of America: Culture and Society in the Gilded Age* (New York: Hill and Wang, 1982); Robert C. Bannister, *Social Darwinism: Science and Myth in Anglo-American Social Thought* (Philadelphia: Temple University Press, 1979); Alfred D. Chandler Jr., *The Visible Hand: The Managerial Revolution in American Business* (Cambridge, MA: Harvard University Press, 1977); Rebecca Edwards, *New Spirits: America in the Gilded Age, 1875–1905* (New York: Oxford University Press, 2006).

9. Paul Krause, *The Battle for Homestead, 1880–1892: Politics, Culture, and Steel* (Pittsburgh: University of Pittsburgh Press, 1992); Paul Kahan, *The Homestead Strike: Labor, Violence, and American Industry* (New York: Routledge, 2014).

10. Richard White, *"It's Your Misfortune and None of My Own": A New History of the American West* (Norman: University of Oklahoma Press, 1991); Patricia Nelson Limerick, *The Legacy of Conquest: The Unbroken Past of the American West* (New York: W.W. Norton, 1987).

11. Elizabeth Jameson, *All That Glitters: Class, Conflict, and Community in Cripple Creek* (Urbana: University of Illinois Press, 1998); Erik Loomis, "The Battle for the Body: Work and Environment in the Pacific Northwest Lumber Industry, 1800–1940," PhD diss., University of New Mexico, 2008; Andrew Mason Prouty, *More Deadly than War! Pacific Coast Logging, 1827–1981* (New York: Garland, 1985); Mark Fiege, *The Republic of Nature: An Environmental History of the United States* (Seattle: University of Washington Press, 2012).

12. Mine Safety and Health Administration, "Coal Fatalities for 1900 Through 2013," www.msha.gov/stats/centurystats/coalstats.asp.

13. Chris Hamby, Brian Ross, and Matthew Mosk, "Johns Hopkins Medical Unit Rarely Finds Black Lung, Helping Coal Industry Defeat Miners' Claims," Center for Public Integrity, October 30, 2013, www.publicintegrity.org/2013/10/30/13637/johns-hopkins-medical-unit-rarely-finds-black-lung-helping-coal-industry-defeat.

14. Alan Derickson, *Black Lung: Anatomy of a Public Health Disaster* (Ithaca, NY: Cornell University Press, 1998); David Rosner and Gerald Markowitz, *Deadly Dust: Silicosis and the Politics of Occupational Disease in Twentieth-Century America* (Princeton, NJ: Princeton University Press, 1991); Christian Warren, *Brush with Death: A Social History of Lead Poisoning* (Baltimore: Johns Hopkins University Press, 2000); Claudia Clark, *Radium Girls: Women and Industrial Health Reform, 1910–1935* (Chapel Hill: University of

North Carolina Press, 1997); Christopher C. Sellers, *Hazards of the Job: From Industrial Disease to Environmental Health Science* (Chapel Hill: University of North Carolina Press, 1997).

15. Richard White, *Railroaded: The Transcontinentals and the Making of Modern America* (New York: W.W. Norton, 2011); Sven Beckert, *The Monied Metropolis: New York City and the Consolidation of the American Bourgeoisie, 1850–1896* (New York: Cambridge University Press, 2001); Alfred D. Chandler Jr., *The Visible Hand: The Managerial Revolution in American Business* (Cambridge, MA: Harvard University Press, 1977).

16. Mark Grossman, *Political Corruption in America: An Encyclopedia of Scandal, Power, and Greed* (Santa Barbara, CA: ABC-CLIO, 2003), 56–57.

17. Thomas G. Andrews, *Killing for Coal: America's Deadliest Labor War* (Cambridge, MA: Harvard University Press, 2008); David Ray Papke, *The Pullman Case: The Clash of Labor and Capital in Industrial America* (Lawrence: University Press of Kansas, 1999); David O. Stowell, ed., *The Great Strikes of 1877* (Urbana: University of Illinois Press, 2008); David O. Stowell, *Streets, Railroads, and the Great Strike of 1877* (Chicago: University of Chicago Press, 1999); Rosanne Currarino, *The Labor Question in America: Economic Democracy in the Gilded Age* (Urbana: University of Illinois Press, 2011); Paul Michael Taillon, *Good, Reliable, White Men: Railroad Brotherhoods, 1877–1917* (Urbana: University of Illinois Press, 2009); Susan Eleanor Hirsch, *After the Strike: A Century of Labor Struggle at Pullman* (Urbana: University of Illinois Press, 2003); Nick Salvatore, *Eugene V. Debs: Citizen and Socialist* (Urbana: University of Illinois Press, 2007).

18. Leon Fink, *Workingmen's Democracy: The Knights of Labor and American Politics* (Urbana: University of Illinois Press, 1983); James R. Green, *Death in the Haymarket: A Story of Chicago, the First Labor Movement, and the Bombing that Divided Gilded Age America* (New York: Pantheon Books, 2006); Roy Rosenzweig, *Eight Hours for What We Will: Workers and Leisure in an Industrial City, 1870–1920* (New York: Cambridge University Press, 1983); Michael Kazin, *Barons of Labor: The San Francisco Building Trades and Union Power in the Progressive Era* (Urbana: University of Illinois Press, 1989); Carlos A. Schwantes, *Coxey's Army: An American Odyssey* (Lincoln: University of Nebraska Press, 1985).

19. Melvyn Dubofsky, *We Shall Be All: A History of the Industrial Workers of the World* (Chicago: Quadrangle Books, 1969); Eric Rauchway, *Murdering McKinley: The Making of Theodore Roosevelt's America* (New York: Hill and Wang, 2003); Bruce Watson, *Bread and Roses: Mills, Migrants, and the Struggle for the American Dream* (New York: Penguin, 2006); Howard Kimeldorf, *Battling for American Labor: Wobblies, Craft Workers, and the Making of the Union Movement* (Berkeley: University of California Press, 1999).

20. Charles Postel, *The Populist Vision* (New York: Oxford University Press, 2007); Robert H. Wiebe, *The Search for Order, 1877–1920* (New York: Hill and Wang, 1967); Daniel T. Rodgers, *Atlantic Crossings: Social Politics in a Progressive Age* (Cambridge, MA: Harvard University Press, 1998); Law-

rence Goodwyn, *The Populist Moment: A Short History of the Agrarian Revolt in America* (New York: Oxford University Press, 1978); Shelton Stromquist, *Reinventing "the People": The Progressive Movement, the Class Problem, and the Origins of Modern Liberalism* (Urbana: University of Illinois Press, 2006); Matthew Hild, *Greenbackers, Knights of Labor, and Populists: Farmer-Labor Insurgency in the Late-Nineteenth-Century South* (Athens: University of Georgia Press, 2007).

21. Samuel P. Hays, *Conservation and the Gospel of Efficiency: The Progressive Conservation Movement, 1890–1920* (Cambridge, MA: Harvard University Press, 1959); William G. Robbins, *American Forestry: A History of National, State, and Private Cooperation* (Lincoln: University of Nebraska Press, 1985); Harold K. Steen, *The U.S. Forest Service: A History* (Seattle: University of Washington Press, 1976); Char Miller, *Gifford Pinchot and the Making of Modern Environmentalism* (Washington, DC: Island Press, 2001).

22. Joseph A. McCartin, *Labor's Great War: The Struggle for Industrial Democracy and the Origins of Modern American Labor Relations, 1912–1921* (Chapel Hill: University of North Carolina Press, 1997); David M. Kennedy, *Over Here: The First World War and American Society* (New York: Oxford University Press, 1980); Ernest Freeberg, *Democracy's Prisoner: Eugene V. Debs, the Great War, and the Right to Dissent* (Cambridge, MA: Harvard University Press, 2010); Robert Whitaker, *On the Laps of Gods: The Red Summer of 1919 and the Struggle for Justice That Remade a Nation* (New York: Crown, 2008).

23. Mae M. Ngai, *Impossible Subjects: Illegal Aliens and the Making of Modern America* (Princeton, NJ: Princeton University Press, 2004); Matthew Frye Jacobson, *Whiteness of a Different Color: European Immigrants and the Alchemy of Race* (Cambridge, MA: Harvard University Press, 1999); Roland Marchand, *Advertising the American Dream: Making Way for Modernity, 1920–1940* (Berkeley: University of California Press, 1985); Irving Bernstein, *The Lean Years: A History of the American Worker, 1920–1933* (Boston: Houghton Mifflin, 1969).

24. Randi Storch, *Red Chicago: American Communism at Its Grassroots, 1928–1935* (Urbana: University of Illinois Press, 2007); Michael A. Bernstein, *The Great Depression: Delayed Recovery and Economic Change in America, 1929–1939* (New York: Cambridge University Press, 1987); Alan Brinkley, *Voices of Protest: Huey Long, Father Coughlin, and the Great Depression* (New York: Vintage, 1983); Rosemary Feurer, *Radical Unionism in the Midwest, 1900–1950* (Urbana: University of Illinois Press, 2006).

25. Ira Katznelson, *Fear Itself: The New Deal and the Origins of Our Time* (New York: Liveright, 2013); Neil M. Maher, *Nature's New Deal: The Civilian Conservation Corps and the Roots of the American Environmental Movement* (New York: Oxford University Press, 2008); Roy Lubove, *The Struggle for Social Security, 1900–1935* (Cambridge, MA: Harvard University Press, 1968); Jennifer Klein, *For All These Rights: Business, Labor, and the Shaping of America's Public-Private Welfare State* (Princeton, NJ: Princeton University

Press, 2003); David M. Kennedy, *Freedom from Fear: The American People in Depression and War, 1929–1945* (New York: Oxford University Press, 2001); William E. Leuchtenberg, *Franklin D. Roosevelt and the New Deal* (New York: Harper & Row, 1963).

26. Bruce Nelson, *Workers on the Waterfront: Seamen, Longshoremen, and Unionism in the 1930s* (Urbana: University of Illinois Press, 1988); Janet Irons, *Testing the New Deal: The General Textile Strike of 1934 in the American South* (Urbana: University of Illinois Press, 2000); G.C. Waldrep III, *Southern Workers and the Search for Community: Spartanburg County, South Carolina* (Urbana: University of Illinois Press, 2000); David F. Selvin, *A Terrible Anger: The 1934 Waterfront and General Strikes in San Francisco* (Detroit: Wayne State University Press, 1996).

27. Robert H. Zieger, *The CIO, 1935–1955* (Chapel Hill: University of North Carolina Press, 1995); Lizabeth Cohen, *Making a New Deal: Industrial Workers in Chicago, 1919–1939* (New York: Cambridge University Press, 1990); Irving Bernstein, *The Turbulent Years: A History of the American Worker, 1933–1941* (Boston: Houghton Mifflin, 1969).

28. George Lipsitz, *Rainbow at Midnight: Labor and Culture in the 1940s* (Urbana: University of Illinois Press, 1994); Ruth Milkman, *Gender at Work: The Dynamics of Job Segregation by Sex During World War II* (Urbana: University of Illinois Press, 1987); Nelson Lichtenstein, *Labor's War at Home: The CIO in World War II* (New York: Cambridge University Press, 1982).

29. Dana Frank, *Buy American: The Untold Story of Economic Nationalism* (Boston: Beacon Press, 1999), 102–28.

30. Chris Rhomberg, *No There There: Race, Class, and Political Community in Oakland* (Berkeley: University of California Press, 2004); James J. Lorence, *The Suppression of Salt of the Earth: How Hollywood, Big Labor, and Politicians Blacklisted a Movie in Cold War America* (Albuquerque: University of New Mexico Press, 1999); Judith Stepan-Norris and Maurice Zeitlin, *Left Out: Reds and America's Industrial Unions* (New York: Cambridge University Press, 2003).

31. Jack Metzgar, *Striking Steel: Solidarity Remembered* (Philadelphia: Temple University Press, 2000); Nancy MacLean, *Freedom Is Not Enough: The Opening of the American Workplace* (Cambridge, MA: Harvard University Press, 2006); Kathleen M. Barry, *Femininity in Flight: A History of Flight Attendants* (Durham, NC: Duke University Press, 2007).

32. Elizabeth A. Fones-Wolf, *Selling Free Enterprise: The Business Assault on Labor and Liberalism, 1945–60* (Urbana: University of Illinois Press, 1994).

33. Aviva Chomsky, *Linked Labor Histories: New England, Colombia, and the Making of a Global Working Class* (Durham, NC: Duke University Press, 1998); Jefferson Cowie, *Capital Moves: RCA's 70-Year Quest for Cheap Labor* (New York: The New Press, 1999); James M. Rubenstein, *The Changing US Auto Industry: A Geographical Analysis* (London: Routledge, 1992), 119, 240–41.

34. Robert Rodgers Korstad, *Civil Rights Unionism: Tobacco Workers and*

the Struggle for Democracy in the Mid-Twentieth-Century (Chapel Hill: University of North Carolina Press, 2003); Barbara S. Griffith, *The Crisis of American Labor: Operation Dixie and the Defeat of the CIO* (Philadelphia: Temple University Press, 1988); Jacquelyn Dowd Hall et al., *Like a Family: The Making of a Southern Cotton Mill World* (Chapel Hill: University of North Carolina Press, 1987).

35. James A. Hodges, "J.P. Stevens and the Union: Struggle for the South," in *Race, Class, and Community in Southern Labor History*, ed. Gary M. Fink and Merl E. Reed (Tuscaloosa: University of Alabama Press, 1994), 53–63.

36. Chomsky, *Linked Labor Histories*, 106–16.

37. Ronald L. Mize and Alicia C.S. Swords, *Consuming Mexican Labor: From the Bracero Program to NAFTA* (Toronto: University of Toronto Press, 2010); Deborah Cohen, *Braceros: Migrant Citizens and Transnational Subjects in the Postwar United States and Mexico* (Chapel Hill: University of North Carolina Press, 2011).

38. Richard H. Robbins, *Global Problems and the Culture of Capitalism* (Boston: Allyn and Bacon, 2002), 47; David Bacon, *Illegal People: How Globalization Creates Migration and Criminalizes Immigrants* (Boston: Beacon Press, 2008), 57; Kathleen C. Schwartzman, *The Chicken Trail: Following Workers, Migrants, and Corporations Across the Americas* (Ithaca, NY: ILR Press, 2013), 45–47; Frank, *Buy American*, 131; John R. MacArthur, *The Selling of "Free Trade": NAFTA, Washington, and the Subversion of American Democracy* (Berkeley: University of California Press, 2000), 133.

39. Frank, *Buy American*; Good Jobs First, "Foreign Auto Plants," www .goodjobsfirst.org/corporate-subsidy-watch/foreign-auto-plants.

40. Kim Phillips-Fein, *Invisible Hands: The Making of the Conservative Movement from the New Deal to Reagan* (New York: W.W. Norton, 2009); Noam Chomsky, *Profit over People: Neoliberalism and the Global Order* (New York: Seven Stories Press, 1999); Luis Suarez-Villa, *Globalization and Technocapitalism* (Burlington, VT: Ashgate, 2012); Joseph A. McCartin, *Collision Course: Ronald Reagan, the Air Traffic Controllers, and the Strike That Changed America* (New York: Oxford University Press, 2011); Jonathan D. Rosenblum, *Copper Crucible: How the Arizona Miners' Strike of 1983 Recast Labor-Management Relations in America* (Ithaca, NY: Cornell University Press, 1995); Barbara Kingsolver, *Holding the Line: Women in the Great Arizona Mine Strike of 1983* (Ithaca, NY: Cornell University Press, 1989); Douglas Jehl, "As Cities Move to Privatize Water, Atlanta Steps Back," *New York Times*, February 10, 2003.

41. Naomi Klein, *The Shock Doctrine: The Rise of Disaster Capitalism* (New York: Metropolitan Books, 2007).

42. Quoted in Michael Woodin and Caroline Lucas, *Green Alternatives to Globalisation: A Manifesto* (London: Pluto Press, 2004), 11.

43. Norman Caulfield, *NAFTA and Labor in North America* (Urbana: University of Illinois Press, 2010); Robert E. Scott, "Heading South: U.S.-Mexico Trade and Job Displacement After NAFTA," Economic Policy Institute,

May 3, 2011, epi.3cdn.net/fdade52b876e04793b_7fm6ivz2y.pdf; Lori Wallach, "NAFTA at 20: One Million U.S. Jobs Lost, Higher Income Inequality," *Huffington Post*, January 6, 2014, www.huffingtonpost.com/lori-wallach/nafta-at -20-one-million-u_b_4550207.html; Mark Vorpahl, "The North American Free Trade Agreement (NAFTA) Resulted in Increasing Unemployment in the U.S.," *Global Research*, Centre for Research on Globalization, August 3, 2010, www.globalresearch.ca/the-north-american-free-trade-agreement-nafta -resulted-in-increasing-unemployment-in-the-u-s/20444; Ken Kollman, *Outside Lobbying: Public Opinion and Interest Group Strategies* (Princeton, NJ: Princeton University Press, 1998), 143–44.

44. Kate Bronfenbrenner, "The Effects of Plant Closing or the Threat of Plant Closing on the Right of Workers to Organize" (Ithaca, NY: Cornell University ILR School, 1996). digitalcommons.ilr.cornell.edu/cgi/viewcontent .cgi?article=1000&context=intl.

45. James Shoch, "Organized Labor Versus Globalization: NAFTA, Fast Track, and PNTR with China," in *Rekindling the Movement: Labor's Quest for Relevance in the Twenty-First Century*, ed. Lowell Turner, Harry C. Katz, and Richard W. Hurd (Ithaca, NY: ILR Press, 2001), 281n14; James A. Piazza, *Going Global: Unions and Globalization in the United States, Sweden, and Germany* (Lanham, MD: Lexington Books, 2001), 1–2.

46. Bureau of Labor Statistics, "Union Members—2013," news release, January 24, 2014, www.bls.gov/news.release/pdf/union2.pdf.

47. Bacon, *Illegal People*, 59.

48. Bethany Moreton, *To Serve God and Wal-Mart: The Making of Christian Free Enterprise* (Cambridge, MA: Harvard University Press, 2009); Nelson Lichtenstein, *The Retail Revolution: How Wal-Mart Created a Brave New World of Business* (New York: Henry Holt, 2009).

49. Bill Raden and Gary Cohn, "The Dirty Truth Behind Fast Food Lettuce," *Huffington Post*, May 28, 2014, www.huffingtonpost.com/2014/05/28 /taylor-farms-exploited-labor_n_5406238.html.

50. Tom Juravich, *At the Altar of the Bottom Line: The Degradation of Work in the 21st Century* (Amherst: University of Massachusetts Press, 2009); David K. Shipler, *The Working Poor: Invisible in America* (New York: Vintage, 2005); Barbara Ehrenreich, *Nickel and Dimed: On (Not) Getting By in America* (New York: Metropolitan Books, 2001); Vikas Bajaj, "A New Capital of Call Centers," *New York Times*, November 25, 2011.

51. Drew DeSilver, "U.S. Income Inequality, on Rise for Decades, Is Now Highest Since 1928," Pew Research Center, December 5, 2013, www .pewresearch.org/fact-tank/2013/12/05/u-s-income-inequality-on-rise -for-decades-is-now-highest-since-1928/; Derek Thompson, "A Giant Statistical Round-Up of the Income Inequality Crisis in 16 Charts," *The Atlantic*, December 12, 2012, www.theatlantic.com/business/archive/2012/12 /a-giant-statistical-round-up-of-the-income-inequality-crisis-in-16-charts /266074; Han Tang, "China's Young Workers Fight Back at Foxconn," *Labor*

Notes, August 13, 2013, www.labornotes.org/2013/08/china%E2%80%99s -young-workers-fight-back-foxconn.

52. Aun Pheap and Zsombor Peter, "GMAC Defends Use of Force Against Striking Workers," *Cambodia Daily*, January 6, 2014, www.cambodiadaily .com/news/gmac-defends-use-of-force-against-striking-workers-50136/; Michelle Tolson, "One Week Later: Coming to Terms with Cambodia's Brutal Protest Crackdown," *Asian Correspondent*, January 10, 2014, asiancorrespon dent.com/118064/cambodia-garment-worker-crackdown/; Jennifer Wells, "Pressure Grows for Reforms of Cambodia Garment Industry," *Toronto Star*, January 12, 2014; Sonorng Khe and Joshua Lipes, "Factory Owners Boycott Wage Talks for Cambodian Garment Workers," *Radio Free Asia*, April 24, 2014, www.rfa.org/english/news/cambodia/talks-04242014182701.html.

53. Frances Fox Piven and Richard A. Cloward, "Power Repertoires and Globalization," *Politics and Society* 28, no. 3 (September 2000): 413.

2: WORKPLACE CATASTROPHES

1. Brian Mayer, *Blue-Green Coalitions: Fighting for Safe Workplaces and Healthy Communities* (Ithaca, NY: Cornell University Press, 2009), 31.

2. Robert Gordon, "Shell No! OCAW and the Labor-Environmental Alliance," *Environmental History* 3, no. 4 (October 1998): 460–87; Les Leopold, *The Man Who Hated Work and Loved Labor: The Life and Times of Tony Mazzocchi* (White River Junction, VT: Chelsea Green Publishing, 2007).

3. Jonathan Levy, *Freaks of Fortune: The Emerging World of Capitalism and Risk in America* (Cambridge, MA: Harvard University Press, 2012), 7–20.

4. Erik Loomis, "This Day in Labor History: November 13, 1909," *Lawyers, Guns & Money* (blog), November 13, 2013, www.lawyersgunsmoneyblog .com/2013/11/this-day-in-labor-history-november-13-1909; Thomas White and Louis Murphy, "Eight Days in a Burning Mine," *The World*, October 1911; State of Illinois Bureau of Labor Statistics, *Report on the Cherry Mine Disaster* (Springfield: Illinois State Journal Co., State Printers, 1910).

5. Jamie Lincoln Kitman, "The Secret History of Lead," *The Nation*, March 2, 2000.

6. Christopher C. Sellers, *Hazards of the Job: From Industrial Disease to Environmental Health Science* (Chapel Hill: University of North Carolina Press, 1997), 15.

7. Robert Gottlieb, *Forcing the Spring: The Transformation of the American Environmental Movement*, rev. ed. (1993; repr., Washington, DC: Island Press, 2005), 83–120.

8. Sellers, *Hazards of the Job*.

9. Donald W. Rogers, *Making Capitalism Safe: Work Safety and Health Regulation in America, 1880–1940* (Urbana: University of Illinois Press, 2009).

10. Claudia Clark, *Radium Girls: Women and Industrial Health Reform 1910–1935* (Chapel Hill: University of North Carolina Press, 1997).

11. On merchant capitalism, see Nelson Lichtenstein, "Supply-Chain

Tourist: Or How Wal-Mart Has Transformed the Contemporary Labor Question," in *Labor Rising: The Past and Future of Working People in America*, ed. Daniel Katz and Richard A. Greenwald (New York: The New Press, 2012), 267–77.

12. Frederick H. Abernathy, John T. Dunlop, Janice H. Hammond, and David Weil, *A Stitch in Time: Lean Retailing and the Transformation of Manufacturing—Lessons from the Apparel and Textile Industries* (New York: Oxford University Press, 1999), 30.

13. Gottlieb, *Forcing the Spring*, 107.

14. Bruce Watson, *Bread and Roses: Mills, Migrants, and the Struggle for the American Dream* (New York: Penguin, 2006).

15. Beth English, *A Common Thread: Labor, Politics, and Capital Mobility in the Textile Industry* (Athens: University of Georgia Press, 2006), 49.

16. Charles Levenstein, Dianne Plantamura, and William Mass, "Labor and Byssinosis, 1941–1969," in *Dying for Work: Workers' Safety and Health in Twentieth-Century America*, ed. David Rosner and Gerald Markowitz (Bloomington: University of Indiana Press, 1987), 208–23.

17. Beverly J. Silver, *Forces of Labor: Workers' Movements and Globalization Since 1870* (New York: Cambridge University Press, 2003), 86–88; Jane L. Collins, *Threads: Gender, Labor, and Power in the Global Apparel Industry* (Chicago: University of Chicago Press, 2003), 68–77.

18. Andrew Hurley, *Environmental Inequalities: Class, Race, and Industrial Pollution in Gary, Indiana, 1945–1980* (Chapel Hill: University of North Carolina Press, 1995).

19. Frank Bardacke, *Trampling Out the Vintage: Cesar Chavez and the Two Souls of the United Farm Workers* (New York: Verso, 2012); Matthew Garcia, *From the Jaws of Victory: The Triumph and Tragedy of Cesar Chavez and the Farm Worker Movement* (Berkeley: University of California Press, 2012).

20. Charles Noble, *Liberalism at Work: The Rise and Fall of OSHA* (Philadelphia: Temple University Press, 1986).

21. Daniel M. Fox and Judith F. Stone, "Black Lung: Miners' Militancy and Medical Uncertainty, 1968–1972," in *Sickness and Health in America: Readings in the History of Medicine and Public Health*, rev. 3rd ed., ed. Judith Walzer Leavitt and Ronald L. Numbers (Madison: University of Wisconsin Press, 1997), 32–44.

22. Noble, *Liberalism at Work*, 51.

23. Hurley, *Environmental Inequalities*, 77–110.

24. Phaedra C. Pezzullo, "What Gets Buried in a Small Town: Toxic E-Waste and Democratic Frictions in the Crossroads of the United States," in *Histories of the Dustheap: Waste, Material Cultures, Social Justice*, ed. Stephanie Foote and Elizabeth Mazzolini (Cambridge, MA: MIT Press, 2012), 119–45.

25. Richard Kazis and Richard L. Grossman, *Fear at Work: Job Blackmail, Labor and the Environment* (New York: Pilgrim Press, 1982), 8–12, 19–21.

26. Steve Fox, *Toxic Work: Women Workers at GTE Lenkurt* (Philadelphia: Temple University Press, 1991).

27. Benjamin C. Waterhouse, *Lobbying America: The Politics of Business from Nixon to NAFTA* (Princeton, NJ: Princeton University Press, 2013).

28. David Weil, *The Fissured Workplace: Why Work Became So Bad for So Many and What Can Be Done to Improve It* (Cambridge, MA: Harvard University Press, 2014), 216.

29. Daniel Faber, *Capitalizing on Environmental Injustice: The Polluter-Industrial Complex in the Age of Globalization* (Lanham, MD: Rowman & Littlefield, 2008), 36.

30. Kenneth M. York, *Applied Human Resource Management: Strategic Issues and Experiential Exercises* (Thousand Oaks, CA: Sage Publications, 2009), 247–48.

31. Melissa W. Wright, *Disposable Women and Other Myths of Global Capitalism* (New York: Routledge, 2006); Anne Elizabeth Moore, "Here's Why It Matters When a Human Rights Crusader Builds Her Advocacy on Lies," *Salon*, May 28, 2014, www.salon.com/2014/05/28/heres_why_it_matters_when _a_human_rights_crusader_builds_her_advocacy_on_lies/.

32. Kathryn Kopinak, *Desert Capitalism: Maquiladoras in North America's Western Industrial Corridor* (Tucson: University of Arizona Press, 1996), 9.

33. Collins, *Threads*, 27–61.

34. Richard H. Robbins, *Global Problems and the Culture of Capitalism* (Boston: Allyn and Bacon, 2002), 47.

35. María Patricia Fernández-Kelly, *For We Are Sold, I and My People: Women and Industry in Mexico's Frontier* (Albany: State University of New York Press, 1983), 47–69, 71.

36. Jefferson Cowie, *Capital Moves: RCA's 70-Year Quest for Cheap Labor* (New York: The New Press, 1999), 119.

37. Roksana Bahramitash, *Liberation from Liberalization: Gender and Globalization in Southeast Asia* (London: Zed Books, 2005), 47.

38. Norma Iglesias Prieto, *Beautiful Flowers of the Maquiladora: Life Histories of Women Workers in Tijuana* (Austin: University of Texas Press, 1997), 21.

39. Colectiva Feminista Binacional, Servicio Desarrollo y Paz, A.C. (SEDE-PAC), and Comité de Obreras y Obreros en Lucha, "Sexual Harassment: A Maquila Reality," laborrights.org/sites/default/files/publications-and-resour ces/Mexico2006.pdf; Judith Sunderland, *From the Household to the Factory: Sex Discrimination in the Guatemalan Labor Force* (New York: Human Rights Watch, 2002); Fernández-Kelly, *For We Are Sold*, 122.

40. Cowie, *Capital Moves*, 54.

41. Sunderland, *From the Household to the Factory*.

42. Lance Compa, "Free Trade, Fair Trade, and the Battle for Labor Rights," in *Rekindling the Movement: Labor's Quest for Relevance in the Twenty-First Century*, ed. Lowell Turner, Harry C. Katz, and Richard W. Hurd (Ithaca, NY: ILR Press, 2001), 324–26.

43. Charles Kernaghan, *Gap and Old Navy in Bangladesh: Cheating the Poorest Workers in the World* (Pittsburgh: Institute for Global Labour and Human Rights, 2013), www.globallabourrights.org/reports/gap-and-old-navy-in-bangladesh-cheating-the-poorest-workers-in-the-world; "Nike to Pay Indonesian Workers $1 Million," *Voice of America*, January 11, 2012, www.voanews.com/content/nike-to-pay-indonesian-workers-1-million--137173608/150598.html.

44. Ian Urbina, "U.S. Flouts Its Own Advice in Procuring Overseas Clothing," *New York Times*, December 22, 2013.

45. IHLO,SACOM, Clothes Campaign, and War on Want, "Breathless for Blue Jeans: Health Hazards in China's Denim Factories," sacom.hk/wp-content/uploads/2013/07/WOW-DISTRESSED-PRF6.pdf; Michelle Chen, "Your 'Distressed' Jeans Are Wearing Out Workers' Lungs," *In These Times*, July 22, 2013, inthesetimes.com/working/entry/15324/your_distressed_jeans_are_wearing_out_workers_lungs/. On the Hawk's Nest incident, see Martin Cherniack, *The Hawk's Nest Incident: America's Worst Industrial Disaster* (New Haven, CT: Yale University Press, 1986).

46. Terry J. Allen, "Clothing to Die For," *In These Times*, January 31, 2013, inthesetimes.com/article/14443/clothing_to_die_for; quote from Ralph Armbruster-Sandoval, *Globalization and Cross-Border Labor Solidarity: The Anti-Sweatshop Movement and the Struggle for Social Justice* (New York: Routledge, 2005), 36.

47. Mark S. Anner, *Solidarity Transformed: Labor Responses to Globalization and Crisis in Latin America* (Ithaca, NY: ILR Press, 2011), 24–26.

48. "Painted Into a Corner: Factory Worker Left with Nowhere to Go After Contracting Anaemia," *China Labour Bulletin*, March 25, 2014, www.clb.org.hk/en/content/painted-corner-factory-worker-left-nowhere-go-after-contracting-anaemia.

49. Richard Pearshouse, *Toxic Tanneries: The Health Repercussions of Bangladesh's Hazaribagh Leather* (New York: Human Rights Watch, 2012), quote from 52; John Maurice, "Tannery Pollution Threatens Health of Half-Million Bangladesh Residents," *Bulletin of the World Health Organization* 79, no. 1 (January 2001): 78–79; Alex Renton, "Bangladesh's Toxic Tanneries Turning a Profit at an Intolerable Human Price," *The Guardian*, December 13, 2012, www.theguardian.com/global-development/2012/dec/13/bangladesh-toxic-tanneries-intolerable-human-price.

50. Fiona Haines, *Globalization and Regulatory Character: Regulatory Reform After the Kader Toy Factory Fire* (Burlington, VT: Ashgate Press, 2005); William Greider, *One World, Ready or Not: The Manic Logic of Global Capitalism* (New York: Simon & Schuster, 1997), 337–40.

51. Carol Divjak, "Appalling Conditions Continue in China's Toy Factories," *World Socialist Web Site*, March 25, 2006, www.wsws.org/en/articles/2006/03/toys-m25.html; Eric S. Lipton and David Barboza, "As More Toys Are Recalled, Trail Ends in China," *New York Times*, June 19, 2007.

52. Jane Spencer and Juliet Ye, "Toxic Factories Take Toll on China's Labor Force," *Wall Street Journal*, January 15, 2008.

53. Liza Featherstone and United Students Against Sweatshops (USAS), *Students Against Sweatshops* (New York: Verso, 2002), 80–83.

54. Worker Rights Consortium, *Stealing from the Poor: Wage Theft in the Haitian Apparel Industry*, October 15, 2013, quote from 41, www.workers rights.org/Freports/WRC%20Haiti%20Minimum%20Wage%20Report %2010%2015%2013.pdf, 35.

55. Featherstone and USAS, *Students Against Sweatshops*, 75–79.

56. Anner, *Solidarity Transformed*, 69–70.

57. Michelle Chen, "This Is How You Make Garment Factories Safer," *The Nation*, March 28, 2014, www.thenation.com/blog/179059/how-you-make -garment-factories-safer#.

58. Steven Greenhouse, "U.S. Retailers See Big Risk in Safety Plan for Factories in Bangladesh," *New York Times*, May 22, 2013.

3: OUTSOURCING POLLUTION

1. "Death over Donora: Smoky, Lethal Fog Kills 19 People in a Little Pennsylvania Mill Town," *Life*, November 15, 1948, 107–10; Lynne Page Snyder, "'The Death-Dealing Smog over Donora, Pennsylvania': Industrial Air Pollution, Public Health Policy, and the Politics of Expertise, 1948–1949," *Environmental History Review* 18, no.1 (Spring 1994): 117–39.

2. Ward Morehouse, "The Ethics of Industrial Disasters in a Transnational World: The Elusive Quest for Justice and Accountability in Bhopal," *Alternatives: Global, Local, Political* 18, no. 4 (Fall 1993): 475–504; Sanjoy Hazarika, "In Hospitals of Bhopal, the Suffering Goes On," *New York Times*, December 5, 1984; Moira Sutcliffe, "An Eyewitness in Bhopal," *British Medical Journal* 290, no. 6485 (June 22, 1985): 1883–84.

3. Ibid. See also V. Ramana Dhara et al., "Personal Exposure and Long-Term Health Effects in Survivors of the Union Carbide Disaster at Bhopal," *Environmental Health Perspectives* 110, no. 5 (May 2002): 487–500; P. Cullinan, S. Acquilla, and V. Ramana Dhara, "Respiratory Morbidity 10 Years After the Union Carbide Gas Leak at Bhopal: A Cross Sectional Survey," *British Medical Journal* 314, no. 7077 (February 1, 1997): 338–42; Dinesh C. Sharma, "Bhopal's Contamination Legacy Ongoing," *Frontiers in Ecology and the Environment* 1, no. 10 (December 2003): 515. On the West Virginia release, see Benjamin A. Goldman, *The Truth About Where You Live: An Atlas for Action on Toxins and Mortality* (New York: Times Books, 1991), 171–72.

4. William N. Rom, *Environmental Policy and Public Health: Air Pollution, Global Climate Change, and Wilderness* (San Francisco: Jossey-Bass, 2012).

5. Martin V. Melosi, *Effluent America: Cities, Industry, Energy, and the Environment* (Pittsburgh: University of Pittsburgh Press, 2001), 23–67, 211–24.

6. Robert Gottlieb, *Forcing the Spring: The Transformation of the American*

Environmental Movement, rev. ed. (1993; repr., Washington, DC: Island Press, 2005), 97–106.

7. Scott Hamilton Dewey, *Don't Breathe the Air: Air Pollution and U.S. Environmental Politics, 1945–1970* (College Station: Texas A&M Press, 2000), 23; Gottlieb, *Forcing the Spring*, 90–91. On smoke pollution in the nineteenth and early twentieth centuries, see Joel A. Tarr and Carl Zimring, "The Struggle for Smoke Control in St. Louis: Achievement and Emulation," in *Common Fields: An Environmental History of St. Louis*, ed. Andrew Hurley (St. Louis: Missouri Historical Society Press, 1997), 199–220.

8. Adam Rome, *The Bulldozer in the Countryside: Suburban Sprawl and the Rise of American Environmentalism* (New York: Cambridge University Press, 2001), 87–118. On the rise of concern about pollution after World War II, see Samuel P. Hays, *A History of Environmental Politics Since 1945* (Pittsburgh: University of Pittsburgh Press, 2000), 52–65; Dewey, *Don't Breathe the Air*, 175–225

9. Quote from Dewey, *Don't Breathe the Air*, 233.

10. Rachel Carson, *Silent Spring* (Boston: Houghton Mifflin, 1962); Mark Hamilton Lytle, *The Gentle Subversive: Rachel Carson, Silent Spring, and the Rise of the Environmental Movement* (New York: Oxford University Press, 2007); Linda Lear, *Rachel Carson: Witness for Nature* (Boston: Houghton Mifflin, 2009). On the rise of DDT during the war, see Edmund Russell, *War and Nature: Fighting Humans and Insects with Chemicals from World War I to Silent Spring* (New York: Cambridge University Press, 2001); Ted Steinberg, *Down to Earth: Nature's Role in American History* (New York: Oxford University Press, 2002), 246–47.

11. Amy Swerdlow, *Women Strike for Peace: Traditional Motherhood and Radical Politics in the 1960s* (Chicago: University of Chicago Press, 1993). See also Robbie Lieberman, *The Strangest Dream: Communism, Anticommunism, and the U.S. Peace Movement, 1945–1963* (New York: Syracuse University Press, 2000), 159–78.

12. Gottlieb, *Forcing the Spring*, 154–56; Adam Rome, *The Genius of Earth Day: How a 1970 Teach-In Unexpectedly Made the First Green Generation* (New York: Hill and Wang, 2013).

13. Gottlieb, *Forcing the Spring*, 179.

14. On Love Canal, see Lois Marie Gibbs, *Love Canal and the Birth of the Environmental Health Movement* (Washington, DC: Island Press, 2011); Elizabeth D. Blum, *Love Canal Revisited: Race, Class, and Gender in Environmental Activism* (Lawrence: University Press of Kansas, 2008).

15. Richard Kazis and Richard L. Grossman, *Fear at Work: Job Blackmail, Labor and the Environment* (New York: Pilgrim Press, 1982), 131.

16. Richard Grossman, "Environmentalists and the Labor Movement," *Socialist Review* 15, nos. 4 and 5 (July–October 1985): 63.

17. Brian Mayer, *Blue-Green Coalitions: Fighting for Safe Workplaces and Healthy Communities* (Ithaca, NY: Cornell University Press, 2009).

18. Brian K. Obach, *Labor and the Environmental Movement: The Quest for Common Ground* (Cambridge, MA: MIT Press, 2004), 1–7.

19. Robert D. Bullard, *Dumping in Dixie: Race, Class, and Environmental Quality* (Boulder, CO: Westview Press, 1990), 59–63; Luke W. Cole and Sheila R. Foster, *From the Ground Up: Environmental Racism and the Rise of the Environmental Justice Movement* (New York: New York University Press, 2001), 4.

20. Bullard, *Dumping in Dixie*; Cole and Foster, *From the Ground Up*; Robert D. Bullard, ed., *Unequal Protection: Environmental Justice and Communities of Color* (San Francisco: Sierra Club Books, 1994); Associated Press, "700 Million Settlement in Alabama PCB Lawsuit," *New York Times*, August 21, 2003.

21. Melissa Checker, *Polluted Promises: Environmental Racism and the Search for Justice in a Southern Town* (New York: New York University Press, 2005); Robert D. Bullard, "Neighborhoods 'Zoned' for Garbage," in *The Quest for Environmental Justice: Human Rights and the Politics of Pollution*, ed. Robert D. Bullard (San Francisco: Sierra Club Books, 2006), 43–61; Steve Lerner, *Diamond: A Struggle for Environmental Justice in Louisiana's Chemical Corridor* (Cambridge, MA: MIT Press, 2006); Ibrahim Hirsi, "Huge Gap in Pollution Exposure by Race Surprises U of M Researchers," *MinnPost*, April 16, 2014, www.minnpost.com/community-sketchbook/2014/04/huge-gap-pollution-exposure-race-surprises-u-m-researchers; Daniel Faber, *Capitalizing on Environmental Injustice: The Polluter-Industrial Complex in the Age of Globalization* (Lanham, MD: Rowman & Littlefield, 2008), 26–27.

22. Quote from Amy Larkin, *Environmental Debt: The Hidden Costs of a Changing Global Economy* (New York: Palgrave Macmillan, 2013), 21.

23. Kazis and Grossman, *Fear at Work*, 3–6.

24. Ibid., 36.

25. Obach, *Labor and the Environmental Movement*, 57–61.

26. Faber, *Capitalizing on Environmental Injustice*, 53.

27. Jennifer Clapp, *Toxic Exports: The Transfer of Hazardous Wastes from Rich to Poor Countries* (Ithaca, NY: Cornell University Press, 2001), 115.

28. Mary E. Kelly, "Free Trade and the Politics of Toxic Waste," *North American Congress on Latin America Report on the Americas* 26, no. 2 (September 1992): 4–7.

29. Sierra Club, *NAFTA's Impact on Mexico*, www.sierraclub.org/trade/downloads/nafta-and-mexico.pdf.

30. Peter Newell, *Globalization and the Environment: Capitalism, Ecology and Power* (Cambridge, UK: Polity Press, 2012), 80–81; Kevin P. Gallagher, "NAFTA and the Environment: Lessons from Mexico and Beyond," in *The Future of North American Trade Policy: Lessons from NAFTA*, ed. Kevin P. Gallagher, Enrique Dussel Peters, and Timothy A. Wise (Boston: Frederick S. Pardee Center for the Study of the Longer-Range Future, Boston University, 2009), 61–62.

31. William J. Kelly, "U.S. Trade Deals from the 90's Set Up China as a

Pollution Haven," *InsideClimate News*, March 6, 2014, insideclimatenews.org /print/30435.

32. "Rich Nations Outsourcing Pollution to China, Says UN Report," *South China Morning Post*, January 21, 2014, www.scmp.com/news/china /article/1409983/rich-nations-outsourcing-pollution-china-says-un-report.

33. Nat Rudarakanchana, "Cheap Foreign Steel Drives Heavy U.S. Imports in January," *International Business Times*, January 27, 2014.

34. Linda Greer, "The Ugly Side of Globalization in the *New York Times* This Week," *NRDC Switchboard* (blog), January 27, 2012, switchboard.nrdc .org/blogs/lgreer/the_ugly_side_of_globalization.html.

35. Ma Jun et al., *Sustainable Apparel's Critical Blind Spot* (Friends of Nature, the Institute of Public & Environmental Affairs, Envirofriends, and Nanjing Green Stone, 2012), www.ipe.org.cn/Upload/Report-Textiles-Phase -II-EN.pdf.

36. On Chinese protests against pollution, see for example Brian Spegele, "Behind Chinese Protests, Growing Dismay at Pollution," *Wall Street Journal*, May 17, 2013; Gloria S. Riviera, "Pollution in China: The Business of Bad Air," *World Affairs*, May–June 2013.

37. World Health Organization, *Burden of Disease from Air Pollution for 2012*, March 24, 2014, www.who.int/phe/health_topics/outdoorair/databases /FINAL_HAP_AAP_BoD_24March2014.pdf?ua=1.

38. Jintai Lin et al., "China's International Trade and Air Pollution in the United States," *Proceedings of the National Academy of Sciences of the United States of America* 111, no. 5 (February 4, 2014): 1736–41; William Wan, "Study: Pollution from Chinese Factories Is Harming Air Quality on U.S. West Coast," *Washington Post*, January 21, 2014.

39. Rachel Louise Snyder, *Fugitive Denim: A Moving Story of People and Pants in the Borderless World of Global Trade* (New York: W.W. Norton, 2008), 130–32.

40. Jo Tuckman, "Distressed Denim Trend Costs Mexican Farmers the Earth," *The Guardian*, August 17, 2007, www.theguardian.com/environment /2007/aug/17/waste.pollution.

41. Jim Yardley, "Bangladesh Pollution, Told in Colors and Smells," *New York Times*, July 14, 2013.

42. Richard Pearshouse, *Toxic Tanneries: The Health Repercussions of Bangladesh's Hazaribagh Leather* (New York: Human Rights Watch, 2012).

43. Craig E. Colten, "An Incomplete Solution: Oil and Water in Louisiana," *Journal of American History* 99, no. 1 (June 2012): 91–99. See Bullard, *Dumping in Dixie*, for this use of the term "sacrifice zones."

44. Linda Greer, "Top Clothing Brands Linked to Water Pollution Scandal in China," *China Dialogue* (blog), October 9, 2012, www.china dialogue.net/blog/5203-Top-clothing-brands-linked-to-water-pollution -scandal-in-China/en.

45. Katie Jennings, "Deadly Pet Treats Are Still Showing Up in the US Af-

ter Years of FDA Investigation," *Business Insider,* May 22, 2014, www.business insider.com/deadly-chinese-dog-treats-2014-5.

46. Ma et al., *Sustainable Apparel's Critical Blind Spot.*

47. Emily Achtenberg, "A Mining Ban in El Salvador?" *NACLA Report on the Americas* 44, no. 5 (September–October 2011): 3–4.

48. Roger Bybee, "Free Trade Deal in Action: Milwaukee Firm Seeks $100 Million from El Salvador Govt.," *In These Times,* November 3, 2011, inthese times.com/working/entry/12214/milwaukee_firm_digs_for_cafta_gold_by _undermining_global_democracy/.

49. On recycling, see Samantha MacBride, *Recycling Reconsidered: The Present Failure and Future Promise of Environmental Action in the United States* (Cambridge, MA: MIT Press, 2011). For a broader look at the waste system and its failures, see Heather Rogers, *Gone Tomorrow: The Hidden Life of Garbage* (New York: The New Press, 2005).

50. "Pope: Recycling Good for Environment, for Workers," Associated Press, December 20, 2013, bigstory.ap.org/article/pope-recycling-good -environment-workers.

51. MacBride, *Recycling Reconsidered,* 180.

52. Andrew Revkin, "Old Batteries Crossing Borders Leave a Toxic Lead Trail," *Dot Earth* (blog), *New York Times,* May 24, 2013, dotearth.blogs .nytimes.com/2013/05/24/old-batteries-crossing-borders-leave-a-toxic -lead-trail/; Carolina Bank-Muñoz, *Transnational Tortillas: Race, Gender, and Shop-Floor Politics in Mexico and the United States* (Ithaca, NY: ILR Press, 2008), 154–55; Environmental Health Coalition, "Metales y Derviados Toxic Site," www.environmentalhealth.org/index.php/en/what-we-do /border-environmental-justice/metales-y-derivados-toxic-site.

53. Ted Steinberg, *Down to Earth: Nature's Role in American History,* 3rd ed. (New York: Oxford University Press, 2012), 236–38.

54. Feng Wang et al., "E-Waste in China: A Country Report," United Nations University Institute for Sustainability and Peace, April 5, 2013, isp.unu .edu/publications/scycle/files/ewaste-in-china.pdf; Daniel Powell, "Assessing and Improving China's E-Waste Problem," *Our World,* April 8, 2013, our world.unu.edu/en/assessing-and-improving-the-e-waste-problem-in-china; Ivan Watson, "China: The Electronic Wastebasket of the World," *On China* (blog), CNN.com, May 30, 2013, www.cnn.com/2013/05/30/world/asia/china -electronic-waste-e-waste/; David Naguib Pellow, *Resisting Global Toxics: Transnational Movements for Environmental Justice* (Cambridge, MA: MIT Press, 2007).

55. Elizabeth Grossman, *High Tech Trash: Digital Devices, Hidden Toxics, and Human Health* (Washington, DC: Island Press, 2006), 2, 182–210.

56. Pellow, *Resisting Global Toxics,* 185–224.

57. Clapp, *Toxic Exports*; Jerry Schwartz, "Odyssey of Ash: Trash Won't Go Away," *Seattle Times,* September 17, 2000.

58. Giovanna Di Chiro, "Beyond Ecoliberal 'Common Futures': Environmental Justice, Toxic Touring, and a Transcommunal Politics of Place," in

Race, Nature, and the Politics of Difference, ed. Donald S. Moore, Jake Kosek, and Anand Pandian (Durham, NC: Duke University Press, 2003), 204–32.

59. International Brotherhood of Boilermakers, "U.S. Exports Jobs, Imports Pollution," www.boilermakers.org/news/commentary/V53N1/US-expo rts-jobs-imports-pollution.

4: CONCEALED FOOD, BROKEN WORKERS

1. Eric Schlosser, *Fast Food Nation: The Dark Side of the All-American Meal* (New York: HarperCollins, 2002), 169–92; David Bacon, *Illegal People: How Globalization Creates Migration and Criminalizes Immigrants* (Boston: Beacon Press, 2008), 12–21; Deborah Fink, *Cutting Into the Meatpacking Line: Workers and Change in the Rural Midwest* (Chapel Hill: University of North Carolina Press, 1998), 39–71, 134–37; "Massive Raid at Kosher Meat Plant in Iowa," *Immigration News Briefs* (blog), June 2, 2008, immigrationnewsbriefs .blogspot.com/2008/06/inb-6208-massive-raid-at-kosher-meat.html.

2. David Bacon, *The Right to Stay Home: How US Policy Drives Mexican Migration* (Boston: Beacon Press, 2013), 1–40.

3. John Upton, "Maryland Gov. O'Malley Protects Poultry Industry Instead of Chesapeake Bay," *Grist*, February 11, 2014, grist.org/news/maryland -gov-omalley-protects-poultry-industry-instead-of-chesapeake-bay/.

4. Steve Striffler, *Chicken: The Dangerous Transformation of America's Favorite Food* (New Haven, CT: Yale University Press, 2005), 5.

5. Timothy Pachirat, *Every Twelve Seconds: Industrialized Slaughter and the Politics of Sight* (New Haven, CT: Yale University Press, 2011), 3.

6. Jeffrey M. Pilcher, *Food in World History* (New York: Routledge, 2006); Arturo Warman, *Corn and Capitalism: How a Botanical Bastard Grew to Global Dominance* (Chapel Hill: University of North Carolina Press, 2003).

7. The literature on these issues is far too large to provide a comprehensive list here. The classic explanation of the Columbian Exchange is Alfred W. Crosby, *The Columbian Exchange: Biological and Cultural Consequences of 1492* (Westport, CT: Greenwood, 1972). See also Alfred W. Crosby, *Ecological Imperialism: The Biological Expansion of Europe, 900–1900* (New York: Cambridge University Press, 1986); John W. Verlano and Douglas H. Ubelaker, eds., *Disease and Demography in the Americas* (Washington, DC: Smithsonian Institution Press, 1992). On the spread of food and its impacts, see James C. McCann, *Maize and Grace: Africa's Encounter with a New World Crop, 1500–2000* (Cambridge, MA: Harvard University Press, 2005); Sidney W. Mintz, *Sweetness and Power: The Place of Sugar in Modern History* (New York: Viking, 1985). On the environmental impact of Europeans and their animals on the New World, see William Cronon, *Changes in the Land: Indians, Colonists, and the Ecology of New England* (New York: Hill and Wang, 1983); Elinor G.K. Melville, *A Plague of Sheep: Environmental Consequences of the Conquest of Mexico* (New York: Cambridge University Press, 1994); Warren Dean, *With Broadax and Firebrand: The Destruction of the Brazilian Atlantic*

Forest (Berkeley: University of California Press, 1995). On the spread of disease through technology and transportation, see Randy Shilts, *And the Band Played On: Politics, People, and the AIDS Epidemic* (New York: St. Martin's, 1987); J.R. McNeill, *Mosquito Empires: Ecology and War in the Greater Caribbean, 1620–1914* (New York: Cambridge University Press, 2010).

8. Lydia DePillis, "Quinoa Should Be Taking Over the World. This Is Why It Isn't," *Wonkblog* (blog), *Washington Post*, July 11, 2013, www.washingtonpost.com/blogs/wonkblog/wp/2013/07/11/quinoa-should-be-taking-over-the-world-this-is-why-it-isnt/. On how Western products have transformed indigenous food traditions, see Jeffrey Pilcher, *Que Vivan Los Tamales! Food and the Making of Mexican Identity* (Albuquerque: University of New Mexico Press, 1998). On the effects of Western food on the health of indigenous people, see Deborah Gewertz and Frederick Errington, *Cheap Meat: Flap Food Nations in the Pacific Islands* (Berkeley: University of California Press, 2010); R.G. Hughes and M.A. Lawrence, "Globalization, Food and Health in Pacific Island Countries," *Asia Pacific Journal of Clinical Nutrition* 14, no. 4 (2005): 298–306.

9. Sierra Club, *NAFTA's Impact on Mexico*, www.sierraclub.org/trade /downloads/nafta-and-mexico.pdf.

10. Walden Bello, *The Food Wars* (London: Verso, 2009), 49; Kathleen C. Schwartzman, *The Chicken Trail: Following Workers, Migrants, and Corporations Across the Americas*, (Ithaca, NY: ILR Press, 2013), 130–55. See also, Bank-Muñoz, *Transnational Tortillas*.

11. Bacon, *The Right to Stay Home*, 60.

12. Susana G. Baumann, "Agricultural Subsidies Impact on Mexican Farmers," *Voxxi*, January 11, 2013, voxxi.com/2013/01/11/agricultural -subsidies-mexican-farmers/.

13. James Smith, *Biofuels and the Globalisation of Risk: The Biggest Change in North-South Relations Since Colonialism?* (London: Zed Books, 2010); Bello, *Food Wars*, 1.

14. Margaret Wurth, *Tobacco's Hidden Children: Hazardous Child Labor in United States Tobacco Farming* (New York: Human Rights Watch, 2014).

15. Linda Nash, *Inescapable Ecologies: A History of Environment, Disease, and Knowledge* (Berkeley: University of California Press, 2006), 161–208, quote from 163; David Naguib Pellow, *Resisting Global Toxics: Transnational Movements for Environmental Justice* (Cambridge, MA: MIT Press, 2007), 153; Sasha Khokha, "Teen Farmworker's Heat Death Sparks Outcry," National Public Radio, June 6, 2008, www.npr.org/templates/story/story .php?storyId=91240378.

16. Frank Bardacke, *Trampling Out the Vintage: Cesar Chavez and the Two Souls of the United Farm Workers* (New York: Verso, 2012); Matthew Garcia, *From the Jaws of Victory: The Triumph and Tragedy of Cesar Chavez and the Farm Worker Movement* (Berkeley: University of California Press, 2012).

17. Steven Greenhouse, "In Florida Tomato Fields, a Penny Buys Progress," *New York Times*, April 24, 2014.

18. Kate Davies, *The Rise of the U.S. Environmental Health Movement* (Lanham, MD: Rowman & Littlefield, 2013), 74–80.

19. Angus Wright, *The Death of Ramón González: The Modern Agricultural Dilemma*, rev. ed. (Austin: University of Texas Press, 2005), 3; Pellow, *Resisting Global Toxics*, 146–74; Claire Meeghan, "Pesticide Poisoning: Confronting the Hidden Menace," *Poverty Matters* (blog), *The Guardian*, August 2, 2013, www.theguardian.com/global-development/poverty-matters/2013/aug/02 /pesticide-poisoning-hidden-menace-ghana; Josef G. Thundiyil et al., "Acute Pesticide Poisoning: A Proposed Classification Tool," *Bulletin of the World Health Organization*, www.who.int/bulletin/volumes/86/3/07-041814/en/; J.M. Bertolote et al., "Deaths from Pesticide Poisoning: A Global Response," *British Journal of Psychiatry* 189 (2006): 201–3.

20. For a good overview of the impact of the Green Revolution on Mexico, see Joseph Cotter, *Troubled Harvest: Agronomy and Revolution in Mexico, 1880–2002* (Westport, CT: Praeger, 2002), 233–320.

21. Vandana Shiva, *The Violence of the Green Revolution: Third World Agriculture, Ecology and Politics* (London: Third World Network, 1991); R. Scott Frey, "The International Traffic in Pesticides," *Technological Forecasting and Social Change* 50 (1995): 151–69; Tony Weis, *The Global Food Economy: The Battle for the Future of Farming* (London: Zed Books, 2007), 107–10.

22. Theodore Saloutos, *The American Farmer and the New Deal* (Ames: Iowa State University Press, 1982); David Eugene Conrad, *The Forgotten Farmers: The Story of Sharecroppers in the New Deal* (Urbana: University of Illinois Press, 1965).

23. Bello, *Food Wars*, 35; Sarah Elton, *Consumed: Food for a Finite Planet* (Chicago: University of Chicago Press, 2013), 34–38; Raj Patel, *Stuffed and Starved: The Hidden Battle for the World Food System* (New York: Melville House, 2007), 22–27.

24. Kelsey Gee, "U.S. Meatpackers Fight New Country-of-Origin Labels," *Wall Street Journal*, November 18, 2013.

25. Paul Solotaroff, "In the Belly of the Beast," *Rolling Stone*, December 10, 2013.

26. Weis, *Global Food Economy*, 34.

27. Tom Philpott, "Mysterious Poop Foam Causes Explosions on Hog Farms," *Mother Jones*, May 15, 2013, www.motherjones.com/tom -philpott/2013/05/menace-manure-foam-still-haunting-huge-hog-farms.

28. Brendon Bosworth, "Altered Amphibians," *High Country News*, November 12, 2012.

29. Lindsay Abrams, "Idaho Passes Industry-Backed 'Ag-Gag' Bill," *Salon*, February 28, 2014, www.salon.com/2014/02/28/idaho_passes_industry _backed_ag_gag_bill/; Peter Moskowitz, "Idaho Gov. Signs 'Ag Gag' Bill into Law," *Al Jazeera America*, February 28, 2014, america.aljazeera.com /articles/2014/2/28/idaho-gov-signs-aggagbillintolaw.html.

30. William Cronon, *Nature's Metropolis: Chicago and the Great West* (New York: W.W. Norton, 1991), 207–59.

31. Upton Sinclair, *The Jungle* (New York: Modern Library, 2002); James Harvey Young, *Pure Food: Securing the Federal Food and Drugs Act of 1906* (Princeton, NJ: Princeton University Press, 1989).

32. On the UPWA, see Rick Halpern, *Down on the Killing Floor: Black and White Workers in Chicago's Packinghouses, 1904–54* (Champaign: University of Illinois Press, 1997); Roger Horowitz, *"Negro and White, Unite and Fight!"*: *A Social History of Industrial Unionism in Meatpacking, 1930–90* (Champaign: University of Illinois Press, 1997). See also Charles Craypo, "Meatpacking: Industry Restructuring and Union Decline," in *Contemporary Collective Bargaining in the Private Sector*, ed. Paula B. Voos (Madison: Industrial Relations Research Association, 1994), 63–94.

33. Shane Hamilton, *Trucking Country: The Road to America's Wal-Mart Economy* (Princeton, NJ: Princeton University Press, 2008).

34. Schlosser, *Fast Food Nation*, 153–55.

35. Hamilton, *Trucking Country*, 156.

36. Schwartzman, *Chicken Trail*, 62–66, 87–94.

37. Lance Compa, *Blood, Sweat, and Fear: Workers' Rights in U.S. Meat and Poultry Plants* (New York: Human Rights Watch, 2004).

38. Steven Greenhouse, "Wal-Mart Suspends Supplier of Seafood," *New York Times*, June 29, 2012; Worker Rights Consortium, "Worker Rights Consortium Assessment C.J.'s Seafood/Wal-Mart Stores, Inc. Findings and Recommendations," June 20, 2012, workersrights.org/freports/WRC%20 Assessment%20re%20CJ%27s%20Seafood,%206-20-12.pdf; Cecilia Garza, "Meet the Crawfish-Peeling Guestworkers Who Inspired Walmart Walkouts," *Yes!*, October 11, 2012, www.yesmagazine.org/people-power/meet-the-craw fish-peeling-guestworkers-who-inspired-walmart-walkouts. On guestworker exploitation, see Cindy Hahamovitch, "Protecting Immigrant Farm Workers," *Miami Herald*, March 13, 2013. On the history of guestworkers and their exploitation in the United States' food industry, see Cindy Hahamovitch, *No Man's Land: Jamaican Guestworkers in America and the Global History of Deportable Labor* (Princeton, NJ: Princeton University Press, 2011).

39. John Sifton, "Walmart's Human Trafficking Problem," *Human Rights Watch*, September 17, 2012, www.hrw.org/news/2012/09/17/walmarts -human-trafficking-problem.

40. EJF, *Sold to the Sea: Human Trafficking in Thailand's Fishing Industry* (London: Environmental Justice Fund, 2013), ejfoundation.org/sites/default /files/public/Sold_to_the_Sea_report_lo-res-v2.pdf; Gwynn Guilford, "If Your Mackerel Came from Thailand, an Enslaved Migrant Probably Caught It," *Quartz*, May 31, 2013, qz.com/89452/if-your-mackerel-came-from-thai land-an-enslaved-migrant-probably-caught-it/; Phil Robertson, *From the Tiger to the Crocodile: Abuse of Migrant Workers in Thailand* (New York: Human Rights Watch, 2010).

41. Steve Payne, "Kellogg's Delivers Memphis a Slap in the Face," *Labor Notes*, January 20, 2014, labornotes.org/2014/01/kelloggs-delivers-memphis -slap-face; The Bakery, Confectionery, Tobacco Workers, and Grain Millers

International Union, "Federal Judge Orders Kellogg to End Memphis Lockout; Immediately Return Workers to Jobs," July 31, 2014, www.bctgm.org/2014/07/federal-judge-orders-kellogg-to-end-memphis-lockout-immediately-return-workers-to-jobs/.

42. Mónica Ortiz Uribe, "Investigation into Factory Explosion in Juárez Ongoing," *Fronteras*, November 12, 2013, www.fronterasdesk.org/content/9223/investigation-factory-explosion-ju%C3%A1rez-ongoing; Angela Kocherga, "Juarez Candy Factory Had Troubled Safety Record Before Explosion," KVIA, November 1, 2013, www.kvia.com/news/juarez-candy-factory-had-troubled-safety-record-before-explosion/-/391068/22757636/-/1c5uo4z/-/index.html.

43. On Jolly Rancher, see "Jolly Rancher Plant Closes," *Denver Business Journal*, October 18, 2002, www.bizjournals.com/denver/stories/2002/10/14/daily42.html, and Pam Bennett, "Jolly Rancher Leaves the U.S.," *Daily Kos*, February 22, 2009, www.dailykos.com/story/2009/02/22/700672/-Jolly-Rancher-Leaves-the-U-S. On Hershey outsourcing more broadly, see Steve Chawkins, "Town Sees Nothing Sweet in Chocolate Plant Closing," *Los Angeles Times*, May 31, 2007. On the guest worker case, see Dave Jamieson, "Hershey Student Guest Workers Win $200,000 in Back Pay After Claims of Abusive Conditions," *Huffington Post*, November 14, 2012, www.huffingtonpost.com/2012/11/14/hershey-student-guest-workers_n_2131914.html, and Stephanie Luce, "Hershey Still Silent After Student Guestworkers Strike," *Labor Notes*, September 20, 2011, labornotes.org/2011/09/hershey-still-silent-after-student-guestworkers-strike.

44. Saru Jayaraman, *Behind the Kitchen Door* (Ithaca, NY: Cornell University Press, 2013).

45. Josh Harkinson, "Are Starbucks and Whole Foods Union Busters?," *Mother Jones*, April 6, 2009, www.motherjones.com/politics/2009/04/are-starbucks-and-whole-foods-union-busting; John Mackey, "The Whole Foods Alternative to ObamaCare," *Wall Street Journal*, August 11, 2009, online.wsj.com/news/articles/SB10001424052970204251404574342170072865070; Nick Paumgarten, "Food Fighter: Does Whole Foods' C.E.O. Know What's Best for You?," *New Yorker*, January 4, 2010; Neetzan Zimmerman, "Whole Foods Workers Suspended for Violating 'English Only' Policy," *Gawker*, June 7, 2013, gawker.com/whole-foods-workers-suspended-for-violating-english-onl-511867493.

46. John Upton, "Meat Industry Doesn't Want to Tell You Where Your Meat Comes From," *Grist*, July 10, 2013, grist.org/news/meat-industry-doesnt-want-to-tell-you-where-your-meat-comes-from/; "Mandatory Country-of-Origin Meat Labeling Now in Effect," *Food Safety News*, November 26, 2013, www.foodsafetynews.com/2013/11/mandatory-country-of-origin-labeling-on-meat-goes-into-full-effect/.

47. Thomas Barrabi, "OSI Group: A Look at the US-Based Company Behind China's Meat Scandal," *International Business Times*, July 23, 2014, www.ibtimes.com/osi-group-look-us-based-company-behind-chinas-meat-scandal-1636976; Laurie Burkitt, "McDonald's Sticks with Chinese Meat Supplier," *Wall Street Journal*, July 24, 2014; "China Shuts US Meat Factory

OSI Supplying McDonald's, KFC on Quality Issues," *Economic Times,* July 21, 2014, economictimes.indiatimes.com/news/international/business/china -shuts-us-meat-factory-osi-supplying-mcdonalds-kfc-on-quality-issues /articleshow/38788658.cms.

48. Oxfam, *Milking the CAP: How Europe's Dairy Regime Is Devastating Livelihoods in the Developing World,* Oxfam Briefing Paper No. 34 (Oxford, UK: Oxfam, 2002).

49. Caroline Wright, "Fairtrade Food: Connecting Producers and Consumers," in *The Globalization of Food,* ed. David Inglis and Debra Gimlin (New York: Berg, 2009), 139–57.

50. Mark Bittman, "Not All Industrial Food Is Evil," *Opinionator* (blog), *New York Times,* August 17, 2013, opinionator.blogs.nytimes.com/2013/08/17 /not-all-industrial-food-is-evil/.

5: THE CLIMATE IS FOR SALE

1. Nicole Fabricant and Kathryn Hicks, "Bolivia vs. the Billionaires: Limitations of the 'Climate Justice Movement' in International Negotiations," *NACLA Report on the Americas* 46, no. 1 (Spring 2013): 27–31.

2. Brian Black, *Petrolia: The Landscape of America's First Oil Boom* (Baltimore: Johns Hopkins University Press, 2000). An excellent overall history of American energy use is David E. Nye, *Consuming Power: A Social History of American Energies* (Cambridge, MA; MIT Press, 1998).

3. Brian Black, *Crude Reality: Petroleum in World History* (Lanham, MD: Rowman & Littlefield, 2012), 73–77; Kathleen Brady, *Ida Tarbell: Portrait of a Muckraker* (Pittsburgh: University of Pittsburgh Press, 1989); Steve Weinberg, *Taking on the Trust: How Ida Tarbell Brought Down John D. Rockefeller and Standard Oil* (New York: W.W. Norton, 2009); Thomas G. Andrews, *Killing for Coal: America's Deadliest Labor War* (Cambridge, MA: Harvard University Press, 2008).

4. On postwar environmentalism, see Samuel P. Hays, *A History of Environmental Politics Since 1945* (Pittsburgh: University of Pittsburgh Press, 2000). On the growing middle classes recreating in the forest, see William Philpott, *Vacationland: Tourism and Environment in the Colorado High Country* (Seattle: University of Washington Press, 2013). On early American oil exploration overseas, see Matthew F. Jacobs, *Imagining the Middle East: The Building of an American Foreign Policy, 1918–1967* (Chapel Hill: University of North Carolina Press, 2011).

5. Douglas Little, *American Orientalism: The United States and the Middle East Since 1945,* 3rd ed. (Chapel Hill: University of North Carolina Press, 2008); Stephen Kinzer, *All the Shah's Men: An American Coup and the Roots of Middle East Terror* (Hoboken, NJ: John Wiley & Sons, 2011); Steven Hurst, *The United States and Iraq Since 1979: Hegemony, Oil and War* (Edinburgh, Scotland: Edinburgh University Press, 2009).

6. Kenneth T. Jackson, *Crabgrass Frontier: The Suburbanization of the*

United States (New York: Columbia University Press, 1985); Adam Rome, *The Bulldozer in the Countryside: Suburban Sprawl and the Rise of American Environmentalism* (New York: Cambridge University Press, 2001); Thomas J. Sugrue, *The Origins of the Urban Crisis: Race and Inequality in Postwar Detroit* (Princeton, NJ: Princeton University Press, 1996); Jane Jacobs, *The Death and Life of Great American Cities* (New York: Random House, 1961).

7. Edward D. Berkowitz, *Something Happened: A Political and Cultural Overview of the Seventies* (New York: Columbia University Press, 2006), 62–64; 127–28; Bruce J. Schulman, *The Seventies: The Great Shift in American Culture, Society, and Politics* (New York: Free Press, 2001); Karen R. Merrill, *The Oil Crisis of 1973–1974: A Brief History with Documents* (New York: Bedford St. Martin's, 2007); Franklin Tugwell, *The Energy Crisis and the American Political Economy: Politics and Markets in the Management of Natural Resources* (Stanford, CA: Stanford University Press, 1988); Keith Bradsher, *High and Mighty: The Dangerous Rise of the SUV* (New York: PublicAffairs, 2003).

8. Ashley Ahearn, "25 Years Later, Scientists Still Spot Traces of Oil from Exxon Valdez Spill," *PBS Newshour*, March 24, 2014, www.pbs.org/newshour /updates/25-years-later-scientists-remember-exxon-valdez-spill/#the -rundown; Steve Coll, *Private Empire: ExxonMobil and American Power* (New York: Penguin Press, 2012).

9. Tomás Mac Sheoin and Stephen Zavestoski, "Corporate Catastrophes from UC Bhopal to BP Deepwater Horizon: Continuities in Causation, Corporate Negligence, and Crisis Management," in *Black Beaches and Bayous: The BP Deepwater Horizon Oil Spill Disaster*, ed. Lisa A. Eargle and Ashraf Esmail (Lanham, MD: University Press of America, 2012), 53–93.

10. Agustino Fontevecchia, "BP Fighting a Two Front War as Macondo Continues to Bite and Production Drops," *Forbes*, February 5, 2013, www .forbes.com/sites/afontevecchia/2013/02/05/bp-fighting-a-two-front-war-as -macondo-continues-to-bite-and-production-drops/; Steven Mufson, "BP Regains Ability to Bid on Leases for U.S. Land, Water," *Washington Post*, March 13, 2014; Louis Sahagun, "Toxins Released by Oil Spills Send Fish Hearts into Cardiac Arrest," *Los Angeles Times*, February 23, 2014, www.latimes.com /science/sciencenow/la-sci-sn-tuna-hearts-oil-spill-toxins-20140213,0 ,5212912.story#ixzz2tbQVLgxI.

11. Louisiana Bucket Brigade, *Mission: Zero Accidents: Why Cooperation to Reduce Accidents at Louisiana Refineries Is Needed Now* (New Orleans: Louisiana Bucket Brigade, 2013), www.scribd.com/doc/183372910/Mission -Zero-Accidents. More broadly on environmental justice in Louisiana and the Chemical Corridor, see Robert D. Bullard, *Dumping in Dixie: Race, Class, and Environmental Quality* (Boulder, CO: Westview Press, 1990); Steve Lerner, *Diamond: A Struggle for Environmental Justice in Louisiana's Chemical Corridor* (Cambridge, MA: MIT Press, 2006); and Barbara L. Allen, *Uneasy Alchemy: Citizens and Experts in Louisiana's Chemical Corridor Disputes* (Cambridge, MA: MIT Press, 2003).

12. Erik Loomis, "US Workers Were Once Massacred Fighting for the Pro-

tections Being Rolled Back Today," *Long View* (blog), *Moyers & Company*, April 23, 2014, billmoyers.com/2014/04/23/us-workers-were-once-massacred -fighting-for-the-protections-being-rolled-back-today.

13. Claudia Rowe, "Coal Mining on Navajo Nation in Arizona Takes Heavy Toll," *Huffington Post*, June 6, 2013, www.huffingtonpost.com/2013/06/06 /coal-mining-navajo-nation_n_3397118.html; Kathy Helm, "18,000 Navajo Homes Still Lack Electrical Access," *News from Indian Country*, June 2008, www.indiancountrynews.com/news/9-news-from-through-out-indian -country/3833-18000-navajo-homes-still-lack-electrical-access.

14. Michelle Meyer Lueck and Lori Peek, "The Crude Awakening: Gulf Coast Residents Reflect on the BP Oil Spill and the 2010 Hurricane Season," in *Black Beaches and Bayous: The BP Deepwater Horizon Oil Spill Disaster*, ed. Lisa A. Eargle and Ashraf Esmail (Lanham, MD: University Press of America, 2012), 159–80.

15. Craig Pittman, "Gulf Oil Spill's Effects Still Has Seafood Industry Nervous," *Tampa Bay Times*, April 13, 2013.

16. Mike Tidwell, *Bayou Farewell: The Rich Life and Tragic Death of Louisiana's Cajun Coast* (New York: Vintage, 2003).

17. Bronwen Manby, *The Price of Oil: Corporate Responsibility and Human Rights Violations in Nigeria's Oil Producing Communities* (New York: Human Rights Watch, 1999); Patrick Kane and Sarah Shoraka, "Oil Uprising: Two Decades After Ken Saro-Wiwa's Death, the Ogoni Struggle is Reigniting," *Red Pepper*, March 2014, www.redpepper.org.uk/oil-uprising-two-decades-after -ken-saro-wiwas-death-the-ogoni-struggle-is-reigniting/.

18. Black, *Crude Reality*, 175.

19. Michael Watts, "A Tale of Two Gulfs: Life, Death, and Dispossession Along Two Oil Frontiers," *American Quarterly* 64, no. 3 (September 2012): 437–67; "Govt to Look Into Niger Delta Pollution," afrol News, April 15, 2002, afrol.com/News2002/nig021_warri_pollution.htm; Augustine Ikelegbe, ed., *Oil, Environment, and Resource Conflicts in Nigeria* (Berlin: LIT Verlag Munster, 2013); Sam Olukoya, "Environmental Justice from the Niger Delta to the World Conference Against Racism," *CorpWatch*, August 30, 2001, www .corpwatch.org/article.php?id=18.

20. Paul Lewis, "Blood and Oil: A Special Report," *New York Times*, February 13, 1996.

21. Paul Sabin, "Searching for Middle Ground: Native Communities and Oil Extraction in the Northern and Central Ecuadorian Amazon, 1967–1993," *Environmental History* 3, no. 2 (April 1998): 144–68; William Langewiesche, "Jungle Law," *Vanity Fair*, May 2007.

22. Nate Raymond, "Chevron Seeks $32 Million in Legal Fees in Ecuador Case," Reuters, March 19, 2014, www.reuters.com/article/2014/03/19 /us-chevron-ecuador-idUSBREA2I1PS20140319.

23. Steven Mufson, "Improving U.S. Oil Production Reaches Milestone in October, Agency Says," *Washington Post*, November 13, 2013.

24. Bureau of Labor Statistics, "Employment in the Oil and Gas Well Drilling Industry," April 2010, www.bls.gov/cew/oil_gas_drilling.htm.

25. Steven Hsieh, "What's Causing the Huge Spike in Earthquakes in Oklahoma?," *The Nation*, February 19, 2014, www.thenation.com/blog/178449 /whats-causing-huge-spike-earthquakes-oklahoma; Steven Mufson, "Can the Shale Gas Boom Save Ohio?," *Washington Post*, March 3, 2012; Suzanne Goldenberg, "A Texan Tragedy: Ample Oil, No Water," *The Guardian*, April 11, 2013, www.theguardian.com/environment/2013/aug/11/texas-tragedy-ample -oil-no-water; Neil Irwin, "Are Fracking Proponents Wrestling Enough with the Environmental Risks?" *Wonkblog* (blog), *Washington Post*, August 14, 2013, www.washingtonpost.com/blogs/wonkblog/wp/2013/08/14/are-frack ing-proponents-wrestling-enough-with-the-environmental-risks/.

26. Marjorie Childress, "NM Legislator from Oil and Gas Industry Opposes Fracking Chemical Disclosure, Says There's No Water Pollution," *El Grito de Nuevo México*, February 1, 2013, www.elgritonm.org/2013/02/01 /nm-legislator-from-oil-and-gas-industry-opposes-fracking-chemical -disclosure-says-theres-no-water-pollution/; Julie Carr Smyth, "After Quakes, Ohio Plans Tough Gas-Drilling Rules," *Denver Post*, March 9, 2012; Erik Loomis, "Fracking in New York: The Real Cost," *Global Comment*, July 18, 2011, globalcomment.com/fracking-in-new-york-the-real-cost/; Lauren Steiner, "Cuomo in Hollywood!" New Yorkers Against Fracking, nyagainstfracking .org/cuomo-in-hollywood/; Molly Redden, "North Carolina GOP Pushes Unprecedented Bill to Jail Anyone Who Discloses Fracking Chemicals," *Mother Jones*, May 19, 2014, www.motherjones.com/blue-marble/2014/05 /north-carolina-felony-fracking-chemicals-disclosure.

27. Among those speaking out in Canada is the singer Neil Young. Ben Rayner, "Neil Young Blasts Stephen Harper's Tories Before Kicking Off 'Honour the Treaties' Tour," *The Star*, January 12, 2014.

28. Carly Pildis, "Mayflower Oil Spill: Exxon Doesn't Want You to Know People Are Getting Very, Very Sick," *PolicyMic*, May 31, 2013, www.policymic .com/articles/45577/mayflower-oil-spill-exxon-doesn-t-want-you-to-know -people-are-getting-very-very-sick.

29. National Transportation Safety Board, "Preliminary Report Railroad DCA14MR004," www.ntsb.gov/doclib/reports/2014/Casselton_ND_Prelimi nary.pdf.

30. Diane Sweet, "Texas Town Evacuated After Massive Pipeline Explosion," *Crooks and Liars*, November 14, 2013, crooksandliars.com/diane-sweet /texas-town-evacuated-after-massive.

31. John Upton, "Pipeline Builder Says Oil Spills Can Be Good for the Economy," *Grist*, May 5, 2014, grist.org/news/pipeline-builder-says -oil-spills-can-be-good-for-the-economy/.

32. James Wells, "Outsourcing Carbon Pollution—Not So Fast!" *Daily Kos*, July 31, 2013, www.dailykos.com/story/2013/07/31/1228047/-Outsourcing -Carbon-Pollution-Not-So-Fast.

33. Matthew Daly, "Senators Call for Action on Oil Train Derailments,"

Associated Press, January 9, 2014, bigstory.ap.org/article/senators-call-action-oil-train-derailments.

34. See Peter Newell, *Globalization and the Environment: Capitalism, Ecology and Power* (Cambridge, UK: Polity Press, 2012), 67.

35. Vandana Shiva, "Outsourcing Pollution and Energy-Intensive Production," in *The Energy Reader: Overdevelopment and the Delusion of Endless Growth*, ed. Tom Butler, Daniel Lerch, and George Wuerthner (Healdsburg, CA: Watershed Media, 2012), 256–63.

36. Christopher L. Weber and H. Scott Matthews, "Embodied Environmental Emissions in U.S. International Trade, 1997–2004," *Environmental Science and Technology* 41, no. 14 (July 15, 2007): 4875–81; Emily Beament, "UK Pollution 'Outsourced Overseas,'" *The Independent*, April 18, 2012.

37. David V. Carruthers, "Where Local Meets Global: Environmental Justice on the US-Mexico Border," in *Environmental Justice in Latin America: Problems, Promise, and Practice*, ed. David V. Carruthers (Cambridge, MA: MIT Press, 2008), 137–60; Daniel Faber, *Capitalizing on Environmental Injustice: The Polluter-Industrial Complex in the Age of Globalization* (Lanham, MD: Rowman & Littlefield, 2008), 190–91; J.P. Ross, "U.S.-Mexico Border Region to Pay the Price for California's Power," *CorpWatch*, May 27, 2002, www.corpwatch.org/article.php?id=2588.

38. Mark Carey, *In the Shadows of Melting Glaciers: Climate Change and Andean Society* (New York: Oxford University Press, 2010); Rory Carroll and Andres Schipani, "Bolivia: Water People of the Andes Face Extinction," *The Guardian*, April 23, 2009, www.theguardian.com/world/2009/apr/24/andes-tribe-threat-bolivia-climate-change.

39. George Black, "Your Clothes Were Made by a Bangladeshi Climate Refugee," *Mother Jones*, July 30, 2013, www.motherjones.com/environment/2013/07/bangladesh-garment-workers-climate-change; Gardiner Harris, "Borrowed Time on Disappearing Land," *New York Times*, March 28, 2014. On the Rio Convention, see Irving M. Mintzer and J. Amber Leonard, eds., *Negotiating Climate Change: The Inside Story of the Rio Convention* (New York: Cambridge University Press, 1994).

40. Robin McKie, "Miami, the Great World City, Is Drowning While the Powers That Be Look Away," *The Guardian*, July 11, 2014, www.theguardian.com/world/2014/jul/11/miami-drowning-climate-change-deniers-sea-levels-rising; Coral Davenport, "Miami Finds Itself Ankle-Deep in Climate Change Debate," *New York Times*, May 7, 2014.

41. Andrew Freedman, "How Global Warming Made Hurricane Sandy Worse," *Climate Central*, November 1, 2012, www.climatecentral.org/news/how-global-warming-made-hurricane-sandy-worse-15190; Terrence Henry, "3 Ways Climate Change Made Hurricane Sandy Worse," *State Impact*, October 30, 2012, stateimpact.npr.org/texas/2012/10/30/three-ways-climate-change-made-hurricane-sandy-worse/.

42. "Science Links Drought to Human-Caused Climate Change," NASA Energy and Water Cycle Study News, news.cisc.gmu.edu/doc/CA_drought

_research.pdf; Joe Romm, "Leading Scientists Explain How Climate Change Is Worsening California's Epic Drought," *Think Progress*, January 31, 2014, thinkprogress.org/climate/2014/01/31/3223791/climate-change-california -drought/; John Upton, "America's Largest Reservoir Is Hitting New Re-cord Lows Every Day," *Grist*, July 14, 2014, grist.org/news/americas-largest -reservoir-is-hitting-new-record-lows-every-day/; Virginia H. Dale et al., "Climate Change and Forest Disturbances," *BioScience* 51, no. 9 (September 2001): 723–34. For context on the water system of the West, see Donald Wor-ster, *Rivers of Empire: Water, Aridity, and the Growth of the American West* (New York: Pantheon Books, 1985), and Marc Reisner, *Cadillac Desert: The American West and Its Disappearing Water* (New York: Viking, 1986).

43. Katy Steinmetz, "Falling Stars: Starfish Dying from 'Disintegrat-ing' Disease," *Time*, November 5, 2013, science.time.com/2013/11/05/falling -stars-starfish-dying-from-disintegrating-disease/.

44. Ted Steinberg, *Acts of God: The Unnatural History of Natural Disaster in America* (New York: Oxford University Press, 2000); Matthew Perzanowski et al., "Early-Life Cockroach Allergen and Polycyclic Aromatic Hydrocarbon Exposures Predict Cockroach Sensitization Among Inner-City Children," *Journal of Allergy and Clinical Immunology* 131, no. 3 (March 2013): 886–93; Sarah Bridges, "Global Warming and the Asthma Epidemic," *Plenty*, March 17, 2008, www.mnn.com/earth-matters/climate-weather/stories/global-warm ing-and-the-asthma-epidemic.

45. Brandon DeMelle, "ExxonMobil Gave $1.5 Million to Climate Denier Groups Last Year, Breaking Its Pledge to Stop Funding Denial Machine," *Desmogblog* (blog), July 19, 2010, www.desmogblog.com/exxonmobil-gave -15m-climate-denier-groups-last-year-breaking-its-pledge-stop-funding -denial-machine.

46. "Global Warming's Denier Elite," *Rolling Stone*, September 12, 2013.

47. Danny Boyd, "Soaring Oil Production Spurs Infrastructure Growth Across Booming Bakken Play," *American Oil and Gas Reporter*, July 26, 2014.

48. Natasha Geiling, "Why Doesn't Anyone Know How to Talk About Global Warming?" Smithsonian.com, May 1, 2014, www.smithsonianmag .com/science-nature/talking-about-climate-change-how-weve-failed-and -how-we-can-fix-it-180951070/?no-ist.

49. "Climate Change and Financial Instability Seen as Top Global Threats," Pew Research Global Attitudes Project, June 24, 2013, www .pewglobal.org/2013/06/24/climate-change-and-financial-instability -seen-as-top-global-threats/.

50. Michelle Innis, "Environmentalists Denounce Repeal of Australia's Carbon Tax," *New York Times*, July 17, 2014.

51. John Upton, "Congress Successfully Took the Wind Out of Wind Energy's Sails Last Year," *Grist*, March 27, 2014, grist.org/news /congress-successfully-took-the-wind-out-of-wind-energys-sails-last-year/.

52. Juliet Eilperin, "Mass. Wind Farm That Obama Administration Might Support Meets Strong Resistance," *Washington Post*, February 8, 2010.

6: THE WAY FORWARD

1. Clearwater, "Anatomy of a Toxic Spill: The Hudson River PCB Story," www.clearwater.org/pcbs/slideshow/slide1.html. On the history of PCBs, see Phaedra C. Pezzullo, "What Gets Buried in a Small Town: Toxic E-Waste and Democratic Frictions in the Crossroads of the United States," in *Histories of the Dustheap: Waste, Cultures, Social Justice*, ed. Stephanie Foote and Elizabeth Mazzolini (Cambridge, MA: MIT Press, 2012), 119–45.

2. Jon Flanders, "GE Set to Close Plant on Superfund Site, Strand Workers," *Labor Notes*, October 8, 2013, www.labornotes.org/2013/10/ge-set-close-plant-superfund-site-strand-workers.

3. David Farber, *The Age of Great Dreams: America in the 1960s* (New York: Hill and Wang, 1994); Todd Gitlin, *The Sixties: Years of Hope, Days of Rage* (New York: Bantam Books, 1987); Sara Evans, *Personal Politics: The Roots of Women's Liberation in the Civil Rights Movement and the New Left* (New York: Vintage, 1979); Kevin M. Kruse, *White Flight: Atlanta and the Making of Modern Conservatism* (Princeton, NJ: Princeton University Press, 2005); Matthew D. Lassiter, *The Silent Majority: Suburban Politics in the Sunbelt South* (Princeton, NJ: Princeton University Press, 2006).

4. Samuel P. Hays, *Beauty, Health, and Permanence: Environmental Politics in the United States, 1955–1985* (New York: Cambridge University Press, 1987).

5. J. Brooks Flippen, *Nixon and the Environment* (Albuquerque: University of New Mexico Press, 2000).

6. Robert E. Gallman, "Trends in the Size Distribution of Wealth in the Nineteenth Century: Some Speculations," in *Six Papers on the Size Distribution of Wealth and Income*, ed. Lee Soltow (Cambridge, MA: National Bureau of Economic Research, 1969), www.nber.org/chapters/c4339.pdf; Philip Vermeulen, "How Fat Is the Top Tail of the Wealth Distribution?," working paper, European Central Bank Working Paper Series No. 1692, July 2014, www.ecb.europa.eu/pub/pdf/scpwps/ecbwp1692.pdf.

7. Amity Shlaes, "Repeal the Minimum Wage," *National Review Online*, May 21, 2014, www.nationalreview.com/article/378433/repeal-minimum-wage-amity-shlaes; Nicolas Lemann, "The Controller," *New Yorker*, May 12, 2003; John Aloysius Farrell, "Beck's Bad History: Roosevelt Was No Socialist," *Thomas Jefferson Street* (blog), *U.S. News & World Report*, February 25, 2010, www.usnews.com/opinion/blogs/john-farrell/2010/02/25/becks-bad-history-roosevelt-was-no-socialist.

8. "Richest One Percent Take Home Record Share of US Income in 2012," *Al Jazeera America*, September 10, 2013, america.aljazeera.com/articles/2013/9/10/top-1-percent-takehomerecordshareof2012usincome.html.

9. Estelle Sommeiller and Mark Price, "The Increasingly Unequal States of America: Income Inequality by State, 1917 to 2011," Economic Policy Institute, February 19, 2014, www.epi.org/publication/unequal-states/.

10. Ned Resnikoff, "CEO Pay Still Skyrocketing," MSNBC.com, October 22, 2013, www.msnbc.com/all/ceo-pay-still-skyrocketing.

11. Alexander E.M. Hess, Vince Calio, and Thomas C. Frohlich, "Countries with the Widest Gap Between Rich and Poor," *24/7 Wall St*, May 20, 2014, 247wallst.com/special-report/2014/05/20/countries-with-the-widest-gap -between-rich-and-poor/.

12. Igor Bobic, "Fed Chair Not Sure Whether to Call U.S. an Oligarchy or Democracy," *Huffington Post*, May 9, 2014, www.huffingtonpost .com/2014/05/09/janet-yellen-oligarchy_n_5296399.html.

13. "U.S. Firms Beat Corporate Taxes by Moving Their Headquarters Abroad," *National Public Radio*, July 17, 2014, www.npr.org /2014/07/17/332205140/u-s-firms-beat-corporate-taxes-by-moving -their-head|quarters-abroad; National Taxpayers Union, "History of Federal Individual Income Bottom and Top Tax Rates," www.ntu.org/tax-basics /history-of-federal-individual-1.html.

14. Economic Policy Institute, "As Union Membership Declines, Inequality Rises," www.epi.org/news/union-membership-declines-inequality-rises/; Leslie Patton, "McDonald's $8.25 Man and $8.75 Million CEO Shows Pay Gap," Bloomberg.com, December 12, 2012, www.bloomberg.com/news/2012 -12-12/mcdonald-s-8-25-man-and-8-75-million-ceo-shows-pay-gap.html.

15. W.J. Hennigan, "Boeing Profit Falls 12.7% but It Tops Analyst Forecasts," *Los Angeles Times*, April 23, 2014.

16. Danny Westneat, "Anguish Many of Us Understand," *Seattle Times*, November 9, 2013; Chaz Bolte, "Boeing's Wage-Slashing Move to SC Backfires as Company Can't Meet 787 Production Demand," *We Party Patriots*, August 23, 2013, wepartypatriots.com/wp/2013/08/23/boeings-wage-slashing-move-to-sc-backfires-as-company-cant-meet-787-production-demand/; John Logan, "Will Boeing's Union-Busting Fly," *The Guardian*, May 20, 2011, www .theguardian.com/commentisfree/cifamerica/2011/may/20/us-unions -boeing.

17. Daniel Faber, *Capitalizing on Environmental Injustice: The Polluter-Industrial Complex in the Age of Globalization* (Lanham, MD: Rowman & Littlefield, 2008), 22.

18. Annie Lowrey, "Benefits Ending for One Million Unemployed," *New York Times*, December 27, 2013.

19. Craig Becker, "A Court Just Gutted Your Right to Sue Your Boss," *Politico*, January 5, 2014, www.politico.com/magazine/story/2014/01/a-court-just -gutted-your-right-to-sue-your-boss-101756.html#.UtQo7_bjAuc.

20. Mike Hall, "U.S. Rated Alarmingly High in Global Survey of Worst Places for Workers' Rights," *AFL-CIO Now* (blog), May 22, 2014, www.aflcio .org/Blog/Global-Action/U.S.-Rated-Alarmingly-High-in-Global-Survey-of -Worst-Places-for-Workers-Rights; International Trade Union Confederation, *ITUC Global Rights Index: The World's Worst Countries for Workers* (Brussels: International Trade Union Confederation, 2014), www.ituc-csi.org/IMG/pdf /survey_ra_2014_eng_v2.pdf.

21. Lise Olsen, "Oil Field Deaths Rose Sharply from 2008 to 2012," *Houston Chronicle*, April 27, 2014; Tomás Mac Sheoin and Stephen Zavestoski,

"Corporate Catastrophes from UC Bhopal to BP Deepwater Horizon: Continuities in Causation, Corporate Negligence, and Crisis Management," in *Black Beaches and Bayous: The BP Deepwater Horizon Oil Spill Disaster*, ed. Lisa A. Eargle and Ashraf Esmail (Lanham, MD: University Press of America, 2012), 53–93.

22. Megan Woolhouse and Michael Grabell, "Hummus Maker Warned of 'Extreme Safety Risk' Before Temp Worker's Death," *ProPublica*, May 21, 2014, www.propublica.org/article/hummus-maker-warned-of-extreme-safety-risk-before-temp-workers-death.

23. Steven Verburg, "'Bulletproof' Arizona Security Team Raises Hackles at Gogebic Mine Site," *Wisconsin State Journal*, July 9, 2013.

24. Communication Workers of America, "The Trans-Pacific Partnership Will Reward Vietnam for the Systematic Violation of Human Rights," cwafiles.org/national/issues/PolicyIssues/Trade/TPP_Fact_Sheets_11_19_and_on/CWA-TPP-Vietnam-FINAL-12.4.13.pdf.

25. Harold Meyerson, "Free Trade and the Loss of U.S. Jobs," *Washington Post*, January 14, 2014.

26. Steven Greenhouse, "U.S. Retailers See Big Risk in Safety Plan for Factories in Bangladesh," *New York Times*, May 22, 2013.

27. Jake Blumgart, "Even After One of Worst Worker Atrocities in Human History, Gap & Walmart Won't Get Serious About Preventing Another," *AlterNet*, July 1, 2013, www.alternet.org/gap-walmart-wont-help-workers-bangladesh.

28. "Woman Holds Store to Account Over Sweatshop Tragedy," *Wiltshire Times*, May 4, 2014.

29. Ari Rabin-Havt, "Dumbledore's Army Marches on Warner Bros.," *The Nation*, September 17, 2013.

30. Pramila Jayapal, "'We Wanted to Let Them Know Who Is Making Their Clothes': A Q&A with Kalpona Akter," *The Nation*, May 2, 2013 .

31. Jennifer Gordon, *Suburban Sweatshops: The Fight for Immigrant Rights* (Cambridge, MA: Harvard University Press, 2005); Janice Fine, *Worker Centers: Organizing Communities at the Edge of the Dream* (Ithaca, NY: Cornell University Press, 2006).

32. "Fast Food Workers Gather in Chicago, Prepare to Escalate Wage Demands," *Al Jazeera America*, July 25, 2014, america.aljazeera.com/articles/2014/7/25/fast-food-workersgatherinchicagopreparetoescalatewagedemands.html; Bruce Horovitz, "Thousands of Fast-Food Workers Strike: Arrests Made," *USA Today*, September 4, 2014.

33. Peter Dreier, "Will Occupy Wall Street Be Co-Opted," *Huffington Post*, October 11, 2011, www.huffingtonpost.com/peter-dreier/occupy-wall-street_b_1005708.html.

34. Lorraine Woellert, "Mr. Moneybags Acts Out Union Lessons on U.S. Inequality: Economy," Bloomberg.com, May 21, 2014, www.bloomberg.com/news/2014-05-21/mr-moneybags-teaches-union-s-lessons-on-curing-u-s-inequality.html.

35. Geert Van Goethem and Robert Anthony Waters Jr., eds., *American*

Labor's Global Ambassadors: The International History of the AFL-CIO During the Cold War (New York: Palgrave Macmillan, 2013); Frank Koscielski, *Divided Loyalties: American Unions and the Vietnam War* (New York: Garland, 1999); Kim Scipes, *AFL-CIO's Secret War Against Developing Country Workers: Solidarity or Sabotage?* (Lanham, MD: Lexington Books, 2010).

36. M. Victoria Murillo and Andrew Schrank, "With a Little Help from My Friends: Partisan Politics, Transnational Alliances, and Labor Rights in Latin America," *Comparative Political Studies* 38, no. 8 (October 2005): 971–99.

37. Solidarity Center and Social Activities for Environment, *The Plight of Shrimp-Processing Workers of Southwestern Bangladesh* (Washington, DC: Solidarity Center, 2012), www.solidaritycenter.org/Files/pubs_bangladesh _shrimpreport2012.pdf; Solidarity Center, *Tunisian Women: Sustaining the Fight for Equal Rights* (Washington, DC: Solidarity Center, 2013),www.soli daritycenter.org/Files/Tunisia.English%20Final.bug.pdf; Solidarity Center, *Ledriz: Unions Create Democratic Space in Zimbabwe* (Washington, DC: Solidarity Center, 2013), www.solidaritycenter.org/Files/Zimbabwe.English%20 Final.bug.pdf.

38. Gay W. Seidman, *Beyond the Boycott: Labor Rights, Human Rights, and Transnational Activism* (New York: Russell Sage Foundation, 2007).

39. European Commission, "Timber Regulation," ec.europa.eu/environment/forests/timber_regulation.htm; European Commission, "Do You Deal in Wood?" ec.europa.eu/environment/eutr2013/index_en.htm; Tim Bartley, "Forum: Can Global Brands Create Just Supply Chains," *Boston Review*, May 21, 2013, www.bostonreview.net/forum/can-global-brands-create -just-supply-chains/buy-slow-goods.

40. Leon Fink, "The Hour When the Ship Comes In," in *Labor Rising: The Past and Future of Working People in America*, ed. Daniel Katz and Richard A. Greenwald (New York: The New Press, 2012), 154–64; Leon Fink, *Sweatshops at Sea: Merchant Seamen in the World's First Globalized Industry, from 1812 to the Present* (Chapel Hill: University of North Carolina Press, 2011), quote from 96.

41. George Tsogas, *Labor Regulation in a Global Economy* (Armonk, NY: M.E. Sharpe, 2001), 86–93; Frank Langfitt, "U.S. Teacher: I Did 7 Months of Forced Labor in a Chinese Jail," *Parallels* (blog), National Public Radio, May 29, 2014, www.npr.org/blogs/parallels/2014/05/29/314597050/u-s-teacher-i -did-seven-months-of-forced-labor-in-a-chinese-jail; Gary Feuerberg, "China's Prison Labor System Criticized in 2008 U.S.-China Commission Annual Report," *Epoch Times*, November 27, 2008, www.theepochtimes.com/n2 /united-states/china-prison-labor-us-china-commission-report-7788.html; Leonard Greene, "Saks Shoe Shopper Finds Plea from China Factory 'Slave,'" *New York Post*, April 30, 2014; Victoria Cavaliere, "Oregon Woman Finds Letter in Sealed Toy Box, Purportedly from Chinese Worker in a Labor Camp Pleading for Help," *New York Daily News*, December 27, 2012.

42. Ian Urbina, "Using Jailed Migrants as a Pool of Cheap Labor," *New York Times*, May 24, 2014.

43. Lance Compa, "Free Trade, Fair Trade, and the Battle for Labor Rights," in *Rekindling the Movement: Labor's Quest for Relevance in the Twenty-First Century*, ed. Lowell Turner, Harry C. Katz, and Richard W. Hurd (Ithaca, NY: ILR Press, 2001), 322–24.

44. Rachel Louise Snyder, *Fugitive Denim: A Moving Story of People and Pants in the Borderless World of Global Trade* (New York: W.W. Norton, 2008), 23–25.

45. Robert Kuttner, "Fashioning Justice for Bangladesh," *American Prospect*, August 13, 2013, prospect.org/article/fashioning-justice-bangladesh; Snyder, *Fugitive Denim*, 180–208.

46. Seidman, *Beyond the Boycott*, 72–101.

47. Fink, *Sweatshops at Sea*, 113–14. The key case was *Lauritzen v. Larsen*, 1953.

48. David Naguib Pellow, *Resisting Global Toxics: Transnational Movements for Environmental Justice* (Cambridge, MA: MIT Press, 2007), 216–18.

49. Fink, *Sweatshops at Sea*, 182–83.

50. Peter Newell, *Globalization and the Environment: Capitalism, Ecology and Power* (Cambridge, UK: Polity Press, 2012), 105; Kali Borkoski, "*Kiobel v. Royal Dutch Petroleum*: What's at Stake, and for Whom?," *SCOTUSblog* (blog), September 30, 2012, www.scotusblog.com/2012/09/kiobel-v-royal-dutch-petroleum-whats-at-stake-and-for-whom/; Kristin Linsley Myles and James Rutten, "*Kiobel* Commentary: Answers . . . and More Questions," *SCOTUSBlog* (blog), April 18, 2013, www.scotusblog.com/2013/04/commentary-kiobel-answers-and-more-questions/.

51. For example, see Kenichi Ohmae, *The End of the Nation State: The Rise of Regional Economies* (New York: Free Press, 1995), and Susan Strange, *The Retreat of the State: The Diffusion of Power in the World Economy* (New York: Cambridge University Press, 1996).

52. On the rise of the Republican Party, see Eric Foner, *Free Soil, Free Labor, Free Men: The Ideology of the Republican Party Before the Civil War* (New York: Oxford University Press, 1970).

53. Andy Giegerich, "Portland Jettisons Walmart Investments from City Portfolio," *Portland Business Journal*, May 16, 2014, www.bizjournals.com/portland/morning_call/2014/05/portland-jettisons-walmart-investments-from-city.html; Michelle Chen, "How Local Governments Are Using Their Purchasing Power to End Sweatshop Labor," *The Nation*, May 30, 2014, www.thenation.com/blog/180055/how-local-governments-are-using-their-purchasing-power-end-sweatshop-labor.

54. Matthew Yglesias, "Different Places Have Different Safety Rules and That's OK," *Moneybox* (blog), *Slate*, April 24, 2013, www.slate.com/blogs/moneybox/2013/04/24/international_factory_safety.html.

55. Human Rights Watch, *Not Yet a Workers' Paradise: Vietnam's Suppression of the Independent Workers' Movement* (New York: Human Rights Watch, 2009).

56. Quote from Ralph Armbruster-Sandoval, *Globalization and Cross-*

Border Labor Solidarity: The Anti-Sweatshop Movement and the Struggle for Social Justice (New York: Routledge, 2005), 11.

57. Kuttner, "Fashioning Justice for Bangladesh"; Rob Cooper, "Inside Apple's Chinese 'Sweatshop' Factory Where Workers Are Paid Just £1.12 per Hour to Produce iPhones and iPads for the West," *Daily Mail*, January 25, 2013,.

58. Richard M. Locke, *The Promise and Limits of Private Power: Promoting Labor Standards in a Global Economy* (New York: Cambridge University Press, 2013); Richard M. Locke, "Forum: Can Global Brands Create Just Supply Chains," *Boston Review*, May 21, 2013, www.bostonreview.net/forum /can-global-brands-create-just-supply-chains-richard-locke.

59. Steven Greenhouse, "Labor Ruling on McDonald's Has Business Worried," *New York Times*, July 30, 2014.

60. Eberhard Schmidt, "Sustainability and Unions: International Trade Union Action to Implement Sustainability Norms at Corporate Level," in *Trade Union Responses to Globalization: A Review by the Global Union Research Network*, ed. Verena Schmidt (Geneva: International Labour Office, 2007), 17–18; Marion F. Hellmann, "Social Partnership at the Global Level: Building and Wood Workers' International Experiences with International Framework Agreements," in Schmidt, *Trade Union Responses to Globalization*, 23–34.

61. Catherine Rampell, "Upset About Burger King's Tax Inversion? Blame Congress," *Washington Post*, September 4, 2014.

INDEX

ABOUT THE AUTHOR

Erik Loomis is an assistant professor of history at the University of Rhode Island. He blogs at *Lawyers, Guns, and Money* on labor and environmental issues past and present. His ongoing series "This Day in Labor History" won the Cliopatria Award for History Blogging. His work has also appeared in *AlterNet, Truthout,* and *Salon.* His book *Empire of Timber: Labor Unions and the Pacific Northwest Forests in the Twentieth Century* is forthcoming from Cambridge University Press. He lives in Providence, Rhode Island.

PUBLISHING IN THE PUBLIC INTEREST

Thank you for reading this book published by The New Press. The New Press is a nonprofit, public interest publisher. New Press books and authors play a crucial role in sparking conversations about the key political and social issues of our day.

We hope you enjoyed this book and that you will stay in touch with The New Press. Here are a few ways to stay up to date with our books, events, and the issues we cover:

- Sign up at www.thenewpress.com/subscribe to receive updates on New Press authors and issues and to be notified about local events
- Like us on Facebook: www.facebook.com/newpressbooks
- Follow us on Twitter: www.twitter.com/thenewpress

Please consider buying New Press books for yourself; for friends and family; or to donate to schools, libraries, community centers, prison libraries, and other organizations involved with the issues our authors write about.

The New Press is a 501(c)(3) nonprofit organization. You can also support our work with a tax-deductible gift by visiting www.thenewpress.com/donate.